The
Indigo
Children

TEN YEARS LATER

The Indigo Children

TEN YEARS LATER

WHAT'S HAPPENING WITH THE INDIGO TEENAGERS!

Lee Carroll and Jan Tober

HAY HOUSE

HAY HOUSE, INC.
Carlsbad, California • New York City
London • Sydney • Johannesburg
Vancouver • Hong Kong • New Delhi

Published and distributed in the United States by: Hay House, Inc.: www.hayhouse.
com • *Published and distributed in Australia by:* Hay House Australia Pty. Ltd.:
www.hayhouse.com.au • *Published and distributed in the United Kingdom by:*
Hay House UK, Ltd.: www.hayhouse.co.uk • *Published and distributed in the
Republic of South Africa by:* Hay House SA (Pty), Ltd.: www.hayhouse.co.za •
Distributed in Canada by: Raincoast: www.raincoast.com • *Published in India
by:* Hay House Publishers India: www.hayhouse.co.in

Editorial supervision: Jill Kramer • *Design:* Tricia Breidenthal

Library of Congress Cataloging-in-Publication Data

Carroll, Lee.
  The indigo children ten years later : what's happening with the indigo teenagers!
/ Lee Carroll and Jan Tober.
    p. cm.
  Includes bibliographical references.
  ISBN 978-1-4019-2317-4 (tradepaper : alk. paper) 1. Exceptional teenagers. 2.
Gifted teenagers. 3. New Age movement. 4. Parapsychology. 5. Indigo children.
I. Tober, Jan (Jan M.) II. Title.
  HQ796.C355 2008
  155.45--dc22

                                                              2008026723

ISBN: 978-1-4019-2317-4

12 11 10 09   4 3 2 1
1st edition, January 2009

Printed in the United States of America

Contents

Never doubt that a small group of thoughtful, committed citizens can change the world. Indeed, it's the only thing that ever has.

— MARGARET MEAD

Foreword

There is a revolution going on. As many parents, teachers, caregivers, and holistic practitioners are aware, today's children are quite different from the generations that preceded them.

If we had any doubts before we launched the original quarterly print edition of *Children of the New Earth* magazine in April 2003, the reaction we have since received from around the world has confirmed this belief. From the U.S. and Canada to Spain, Holland, Italy, Germany, Great Britain, Turkey, China, Australia, New Zealand, Israel, and South Africa, letters have been pouring in to our offices welcoming the fact that, finally, someone is acknowledging that today's children represent an evolution of the human species.

Without exception, the message we've been hearing for the past three years is one of overwhelming relief that at long last, information about the extraordinary changes that are now becoming evident in our children is finally being aired before the general public.

And it's about time . . . for when 1 in fewer than 500 children is being diagnosed with autism or some form of autistic symptoms, 5 percent or more of American children are receiving special education for learning disabilities, and two million children (yes, two million—and that's just in the U.S. alone!) are being forced to take the drug Ritalin for so-called behavioral-related problems, it is most certainly time for society to wake up and accept that something extraordinary is happening with our children.

On the one hand, as many caregivers are reporting, we're seeing more and more evidence of children being born with what appears to be a highly developed range of extrasensory perceptions and capabilities.

On the other hand, as many health and medical professionals will attest, we're witnessing alarming increases in the incidences of certain physical ailments and disorders, such as celiac disease, asthma, autism, digestive problems, food intolerances, and allergies.

Regardless of whether we view these changes as positive evidence of a quantum leap in the physical, mental, and spiritual evolution of our species, or the negative consequences of society's wanton pollution of our atmosphere, crops and other natural resources, the message is unequivocal: It's time for science to investigate the changing consciousness of today's children. It's time for medicine to start looking at the physical, chemical, and/ or biological anomalies that are increasingly being reported. And it's time that we, as parents, grandparents, caretakers, and caregivers stop all unnecessary medication of children and start reevaluating the way we nurture, nourish, and educate them.

On our own, we may not feel we can do much to effect change. In reality, we have a lot more power than we think we do.

There's a saying that if we want to see change, we must *be* change. This is one of the reasons that we at *Children of the New Earth* decided to expand our content and increase our frequency of publication by moving from a quarterly print publication to a monthly online magazine. We felt we could better serve the children and provide more access to this information for a wider audience.

There's an awful lot that we, as individuals and as a collective, can do. Every time we exercise our right to follow our inner guidance and say *no*—whether it be to a practice, a drug, a system, a method, an authority, or an unnatural or unhealthy way of doing things that does not truly serve the best and highest interests of our children—we're taking a step toward creating change.

There is a revolution going on. It's being led by our children. You know it; we know it. Many healers, therapists, psychologists, physicians, and teachers are now recognizing it. For the sake of our children and the future of humanity, it's time we started opening our eyes and truly looking, listening, and heeding what our children are showing us. Instead of drugging our kids out of their creativity and into conformity, it's time we started paying attention to the lessons they have to teach us.

Children of the New Earth online magazine is dedicated to honoring children everywhere, to providing them with a voice, to fighting for their rights, to protecting them from unscrupulous and ultimately harmful practices, to learning the lessons they can teach us, to celebrating their differences, and to challenging society's established way of doing things in order to better serve their needs. This book will also be a vital reference work as we all work together for this cause.

For nothing is more important than our children, who *are* our future.

Sandie Sedgbeer,
Managing Editor,
Children of the New Earth magazine
www.childrenofthenewearth.com

• • • • •

Introduction

by Lee Carroll

An unusual thing happened in 1999. Jan Tober and I had just authored one of the fastest-selling books in a small niche market. The book was *The Indigo Children,* and it was the first to open the door into the investigation of a wild premise: that humanity was seeing a consciousness shift, and that it was observable within our children, the forerunners.

Counting sales in all 24 languages in which it was printed, the Indigo book sold over a half-million copies and started a very controversial movement composed of those who believed in the Indigo phenomenon, and those who didn't. The ones who lined up on the believer side were parents, day-care workers, teachers and college professors, and alternative-therapy professionals. The nonbeliever side was almost entirely made up of administrators, medical doctors, scientists, and those who really didn't wish to "go there" with such unusual ideas, at least not without one of their own in the lead.

I've written 13 other books, and Jan has participated in 3 of them, including this one. As you read these words, I'm the one who's doing the reporting. Jan represents the research, and many of the authors who agreed to be featured in this book are a result of her efforts in obtaining their articles.

Ten years ago, the original Indigo Children book was one that was out of the purview of our expertise and knowledge. Jan and I saw the phenomenon clearly and were the first to put it out there, but we didn't have the training or worldly experience to write about it succinctly. So we asked others to get involved—including pioneers working with gifted children and also the woman who first "saw" and named the entire concept.

This book isn't just about teenage Indigo Children. It's about *all* Indigo Children ten years later. We now have to deal with older Indigos, and at the same time we're learning a great deal about the children, too. A decade after the fact, there's new information for the very young, and freshly developed information for the Indigos who are now teenagers. Our contributors address both issues.

There are really two reasons why this book you're holding needed to be written. Naturally, after ten years, some of these children are now young adults. Parents in particular, along with many teachers, have begged for information on how to deal with teenagers showing very different behavior than anything in current parenting books. The first Indigo book was a primer for the entire issue, and didn't really address preteens and teens. Dealing with Indigo infants and 10-year-olds is much different from doing so with youngsters ages 12 and up, and we know this.

Many wondered, *Is there something else we should know about the Indigos? Is there more information now about the phenomenon than there was seven years ago?* The answer is yes to both questions. So in *this* book, we bring you a strong group of educators, child-related professionals, health workers, and business executives who deal with this very issue day in and day out. Again, we mainly want to help parents and kids, but there are also some very fine suggestions from teaching pros who are faced with the Indigo situation. So for the first time, we have some ideas for teachers as well.

The second purpose of this book is to reemphasize what this Indigo phenomenon is about—and what it isn't. Unfortunately, over the last few years, the whole subject has exploded into "Indigo misinformation." The mainstream media has deliberately steered valuable discussion off course so that the topic will eventually be dismissed as the rantings of a lunatic fringe. The result is that thousands of kids will be ignored instead of helped, and professionals won't look twice at the very real possibility that our children are actually evolving before our eyes, and that they deserve to benefit from a different approach to parenting and teaching.

If you've read any articles on the subject or have seen the television specials about this "Indigo explosion," you might think that Indigo Children are *special, gifted, superpsychic kids from space with dark blue auras who are going to save the world.* This particular message is wrong on *all* counts. It isn't what we presented, nor is it what we teach. The press has had a field day with the misconceptions, though, and it's a shame that those who promote national Indigo efforts have thrown publicity money at an uncaring media only to have this happen. One of our contributing authors experienced a situation where a major news network deliberately tricked her into participating in an "Indigo interview," only to spin it into an occult special!

Indigos in the News

In the past year, CNN, ABC, *USA Today,* and *The New York Times* have had their fun with the subject of Indigo Children, and many other news outlets have done the same. Almost exclusively, they tell of psychic kids with dark blue auras, putting the phenomenon squarely into what they wish you to believe is New Age weirdness. This makes it very easy to poke fun at the subject. Here's a sample of some of the press:

- *The New York Times:* "Are They Here To Save the World?" January 12, 2006

- ABC News video: "Are These Children Psychic?" November 21, 2005

- CNN video special: "Psychic Children?" November 15, 2005

- *USA Today:* "Indigo Kids: Does the Science Fly?"
  May 31, 2005

In December 2003, the movie *Indigo* was released. It starred Neale Donald Walsch, the author of the *Conversations with God* series, who did a fine job in the lead role. (After all, he had been an actor before being an author who talked to God.) This sweet fictional story was about a psychic little girl. The film was shown mostly in churches and community centers across the nation, taking advantage of those in our niche market, out of the mainstream, who knew of the Indigo subject due to our books. It was never released nationally in the way normal films are.

The storyline never specifically revealed that the protagonist was an Indigo Child, but the marketing and the title were obviously meant to take advantage of the growing awareness of Indigo kids. Most people who saw the film really liked it, and it should be commended for being well directed and well acted. However, the mold was set, and the media coverage that followed continued to play upon the sensational aspects of these new children rather than serious factual attributes.

In all fairness, the film was designed to make money (as most are) and never pretended to be any kind of educational aid for Indigo Children. There's nothing wrong with that. Look at the movie version of *The Da Vinci Code:* it wasn't meant to do anything but be a fictional thriller and make money. However, it was seen by many as having the "possibility of promoting an idea," so it was banned in some places, and there were occasional protests where it was shown. This is the well-known power of filmmaking and good storytelling. Similarly, whether it was right or wrong, the public got a movie called *Indigo* that really had nothing to do with Indigo Children.

The documentary *Indigo Evolution* was released next. Although Jan and I introduced the world to the term *Indigo Children,* the subject really doesn't belong to us, nor should it. Anyone can take this information and do anything they wish with it. Jan and I were honored that a documentary was produced on the subject, even though we weren't a part of it. This film attempted to tell the Indigo story and help inform the public about these kids. Unfortunately, it also stirred the pot of public misinformation due to its mainstream marketing strategy.

Its publicity dollars were spent alerting the media via press kits, a Website, and other publicity packages, which seemed to be sent everywhere and put the inevitable media circus into play. This was probably not the intent of the participants of this documentary, who included well-respected authors and teachers, some of whom are our friends. But turning a light on the subject in this way and throwing the information into the public arena means that the media will stomp all over you and what you might be trying to do. The result was the unfortunate press we've been seeing.

There are those who believe that "any press" is good. In this case, we don't agree. We're not selling soap here or just trying to get attention. We're really trying to get a message across to the public to honor a big change that's taking place within human consciousness and attitudes, beginning with our own children. However, the American media has biased the public toward this entire subject in a way that might take years to correct—at the expense of the kids.

Here's some advice for anyone who wishes to make films or write books about these new children: make the product first class—get your facts right—and then place it where it belongs, with teachers and parents everywhere. Don't throw it to the wolves of the mainstream media, who will devour you and your subject in the name of news entertainment. Concentrate on a niche market, and let well-placed publicity do its job in the education, self-help, and holistic-health industries. Word will get around fast if you have something valuable, and you won't ever have to explain yourself to a group of uncaring pseudojournalists who are charged with finding topics to make fun of in order to sell more cars or Viagra during the commercial breaks from your story.

Where Are We Coming From?

Let's begin by setting the record straight on several accounts. In order to do so, Jan and I will again bring you the tale of Nancy Tappe, who was featured in *The Indigo Children*. It's time we gave you the whole story and filled in some of the blank spaces.

Before we begin, however, we need to face the fact that some readers are waiting for us to steer this whole thing right into the New Age. We can't, since it didn't start there, won't end there, and isn't about such a philosophy at all. It's about humanity and how it's potentially changing . . . and that includes everybody on all continents.

There are those who know our background and the subject of our other books (channelling), who will immediately dismiss anything we have to say as part of that seemingly weird topic. Well, believe it or not, we can walk and chew gum at the same time, and this Indigo subject is more grounded than many may think. It isn't part of our "other life." Most of those who know us also realize that we tend to combine our philosophical thoughts with grounded science. That's the case in this book.

The Beginning of It All

Let us tell you about a woman who has a disorder called *synesthesia*, which disturbs the way the brain perceives everyday things. It's kind of a mix-up of functions, where it appears that perceptions are often cross wired in the brain.

Nancy Tappe has this disorder. She tells of sitting down to eat in her early days of trying to deal with this condition, and instead of tasting the potatoes on her plate, she "tasted triangles"! This is tough for those of us with normal senses to even imagine, but the condition mixes up basic sensory perception: shapes with taste, for instance. A person with this condition might also smell or hear a color.

If you wish to know more, the Internet is the place to go. If you do a search for the word *synesthesia,* you'll get lots of good information. Here are some descriptions to get you started:

— **"Synesthesia and the Synesthetic Experience"**: "Synesthesia is an involuntary joining in which the real information of one sense is accompanied by a perception in another sense. In addition to being involuntary, this additional perception is regarded by the synesthete as real, often outside the body, instead of imagined in the mind's eye. It also has some other interesting features that clearly separate it from artistic fancy or purple prose. Its reality and vividness are what make synesthesia so interesting in its violation of conventional perception. Synesthesia is also fascinating because logically it should not be a product of the human brain, where the evolutionary trend has been for increasing separation of function anatomically." R. Cytowic, "Synesthesia: A Union of the Senses," Springer-Verlag, NY (p.1); **http://web.mit.edu/ synesthesia/www**

— **"Hearing Colors, Tasting Shapes"**: "People with synesthesia —whose senses blend together—are providing valuable clues to understanding the organization and functions of the human brain." Vilayanur S. Ramachandran and Edward M. Hubbard

— *Scientific American:* "When Matthew Blakeslee shapes hamburger patties with his hands, he experiences a vivid bitter taste in his mouth. Esmerelda Jones (a pseudonym) sees blue when she listens to the note C sharp played on the piano; other notes evoke different hues—so much so that the piano keys are actually color-coded, making it easier for her to remember and play musical scales. And when Jeff Coleman looks at printed black numbers, he sees them in color, each a different hue. Blakeslee, Jones and Coleman are among a handful of otherwise normal people who have synesthesia. They experience the ordinary world in extraordinary ways and seem to inhabit a mysterious no-man's-land between fantasy and reality. For them the senses—touch, taste, hearing, vision and smell—get mixed up instead of remaining separate." *Scientific American:* May 2003, **http://www.sciam.com**

— **Mixed Signals:** "Does your favorite book smell like textured circles? . . . Do you dislike the personality of your bedroom's doorframe? Do you see white when you stub your toe? Does the odor of road tar taste salty? Does Sting's voice look like golden spheres?

"If so, you are almost certainly a synesthete." Mixed Signals, **http://www.mixsig.net/**

Energy Fields

Early in life, Nancy Tappe began experiencing one of the biggest anomalies of her disorder: she started seeing colors around people! These weren't spiritual auras, which are a subject of the New Age, but instead probably have to do with basic human energy. Right here, we lose readers. When we talk about energy around human beings, we get blank stares from men and women of science. They often walk away smirking, having made up their minds about "who we really are" as authors.

If you are one of those people, we're sorry to lose you, since we feel this work is about kids and not weirdness. For the rest of you, thanks for having enough of an open mind to listen to the science here. Indeed, we're going to bring you proof of human energy being studied by the mainstream.

We'll describe Nancy's experiences in more detail soon, but first we want to explain this subject further. We aren't speaking of fairy dust or angels, but of real energy around living human beings. There have been many studies about this, but few, if any, have really explained it. It's very much like the current studies of interdimensionality: the "shadows" of the subject show themselves, but they can't be nailed down to anything we're used to seeing in 3-D . . . which is the way we usually perceive the world.

Instead of mentioning human energy, some research projects are labeled "human-consciousness studies." These are trying to measure the actual conscious energy around a person or a group of people by observing this energy actually changing matter. The work is often done with random-particle generators, and the premise is that if you can get natural randomness to pattern itself in coordination with human emotional disturbance in a controlled situation, you can prove that human consciousness changes matter. Well, it does, which has given scientists some puzzles to solve in order to figure out what process this might actually be part of.

So again, scientists have seen this energy, but they still don't know what it actually is. Recent studies on the placebo effect show that our minds can do some amazing things within our own chemistry, and this should be looked at more carefully by the health-care industry. Measurements of the placebo effect are revealing that people who *expect* a pain pill to work are actually receiving the same mechanics of pain relief that the actual drug would offer. MRI brain studies are now clearly showing pain sites exhibiting physical effects, such as blood flow, representing the same changes caused by the actual drug (*Time* magazine, March 1, 2004, "Picturing the Placebo Effect").

Could human consciousness be that powerful?

Beginning in 1998, Princeton University funded an ongoing study to try to measure overall human consciousness on the planet. Originally headed up by Dr. Roger Nelson, "The Global Consciousness Project" or GCP (**http://noosphere.princeton .edu**) showed compelling evidence of consciousness shifts coordinating with world events. Using more than 30 Random Event Generators placed all over the globe and continually "reporting" to a server at Princeton, the researchers graphed some startling results, those surrounding the death of Princess Diana and the events of 9/11 being two of the most potent. You can read more about this at **http://noosphere.princeton.edu/terror.html**. You can also see a scientific review of this project here: **www.indigochild.com/ GCP**.

What this means is that there must be some kind of energy field around humans that's collectively biasing these random generators. Is it a field? Is it in 3-D, or is it interdimensional?

Russian quantum biologist Dr. Vladimir Poponin has discovered that human DNA has a field around it. He's the senior research scientist at the Institute of Biochemical Physics of the Russian Academy of Sciences, and he's currently working with the Institute of HeartMath in the U.S. in a collaborative research project. In highly controlled experiments at an American university, he showed that when human DNA was placed into a controlled, contained environment, it continually made randomly spaced laser light photons into the symmetry of a sine wave. This happened each time the photons were exposed to the DNA. It wasn't subtle, and it was repeatable over and over. The next surprise was that these photons stayed in the pattern even when the DNA was removed from the chamber!

Dr. Poponin reported that not only does human DNA have a field of some kind, but that it must be so potent that whatever photons it puts into patterns stay that way, even when the DNA field is removed. He also indicated that this might be interdimensional energy. He named the phenomenon "The DNA Phantom Effect." (**www.twm.co.nz/DNAPhantom.htm**)

I don't want to lose anyone here due to the science talk, but basically the idea of an energy field around humans is no longer fantasy. Science is finding that (1) it's there, (2) it's potent enough to cause nature to shift into mathematical symmetry, and (3) it's probably an interdimensional field. Superstring theory supports these ideas as being more viable than ever, since it proposes that there are many dimensions within every atom, and that much of what we "don't see" in regular life is in a quantum state (interdimensionally connected to everything else).

Nancy's Experience:
The Creator of the Term "Indigo Children"

We now understand that Nancy Tappe perceives something outside of normal human perception, and her awareness is verified by science as a real brain disorder and a credible experience.

Although she looks at the world with her eyes, the odd color perception exists within her brain. Could she be *seeing* interdimensional energy? A magnetic field? The jury is out, but at least now there's science on our side, saying that it's a very real possibility since such fields exist. What did Nancy first see all those years ago? That's the fun part. You might say, "She saw her future!"

Nancy began to realize that the colors around people weren't random at all. They seemed to correlate with personalities. *Could it be,* she theorized, *that the colors might be indicators of consciousness, or perhaps a combination of consciousness and behavioral traits?* She watched and observed for many years. Indeed, her *sight* seemed to tell a story about how each specific color had a corresponding human behavior.

Nancy slowly began her research. There were only a handful colors, but they correlated with traits she observed over and over. They seemed to be indicators of thought processes, reactions, and how people lived their day-to-day lives. Soon, she began leading courses on these personality traits, training others in her "system." This led to many kinds of teachings, one of which concentrated on "your own color," to help you know "who you are." (Introspection often reveals secrets to help us become better balanced.) Other classes helped people experience improved emotional balance and figure out who they might best partner with romantically and in business (what colors do best with other colors in the system). They learned some of the pitfalls of specific types of human nature. This was clearly part of the color-perception system that Nancy had developed.

About 25 years ago, I actually took one of her courses at the encouragement of Jan Tober . . . who dragged me there, as I recall. It was a gas! (That means "fun" for those of the younger generation reading this.) We all had great laughs and revelations as Nancy stood before us and "pegged" exactly how we thought; how we reacted to others; and what made us sad, mad, and happy. She'd even researched how we might walk . . . and she was right! She was able to "see" each of our colors as we arrived and knew who we were and what we might do. She was right again!

Then Nancy wrote a book: *Understanding Your Life Thru Color.* Sadly, it's now out of print; it represented the only true publication of her profound system. It's interesting that along the way, her information was absorbed and published by others, who didn't give her credit. This situation seems to be the "badge" of many authors who have profound information but don't have mainstream support. If you're a writer and never get your information . . . er . . . emulated . . . then you know it isn't worth much! Alas, this is the way of human nature, but many people still benefited from this wonderful knowledge, no matter who was or wasn't quoted as the source.

Enter the Indigo

Some years ago, Nancy began seeing a new color around human beings. You might think, *So what?* But you have to put yourself in her place and understand that her entire life she'd only seen the same few hues. These drifted a bit, and she saw them combine to produce different kinds of personality traits, but she'd never actually seen a *new* color around anyone. It was like suddenly looking up and seeing that the sky was green with polka dots. You've seen many sunsets in your life, but never one like that! It would get your attention, much the way this new human color got hers.

Nancy began her observation research on this new color as only a person with synethesia can, and she concluded that this new *indigo blue* was only appearing around children. Therefore, it seemed to represent a new kind of person being born on the planet. Her brain disorder had not only provided her with valuable knowledge, but also a way to make a nice living by helping many people. Now it was giving her a hint of something very unusual and profound . . . a potential change within the evolution of human beings in the way of a new consciousness.

She categorized the few types of Indigo behavior she was seeing, and we presented it in the first book, *The Indigo Children.* We aren't going to do so again here, but we wish to state something obvious, something that needs to be clarified: in subsequent years, there have been no "new" human colors seen by Nancy. Therefore, no matter what anyone decides to call these kids, they're all Indigos by the definition of the one who originally gave us this term, the one who saw the colors that made the whole subject possible.

All kinds of different names are out there now. Jan and I don't care what the definitions are, and we have no objection to Iron kids, Malachite kids, Paper kids, Star kids, or whatever. We believe these new labels represent perceived categories of "children of new consciousness." They're now being identified and categorized all over the globe by those who can sense human energy, but who don't necessarily have Nancy's specific brain disorder.

The fact remains that the actual source of this special sight (Nancy) is still with us, and she's firm in her statement that there are *no new colors*. She also makes it clear that these children aren't super-psychic kids with dark blue auras! The color has nothing to do with auras or being psychic. Some of these individuals are teenagers who are strapping on bombs and blowing up public places. You see, the subject here is far more profound than the sensational absurdity being propagated by some. It's all about the children of our planet, what really might be happening, why they do things, and what *we* can do to help them survive all this. In other words, not all of these kids are whom you expect them to be. That's what we'll focus on. There are many sides to this phenomenon.

Even within the pages of this book, Jan and I openly welcome those who have named these children other things and who have separated themselves from the "Indigo" label. Truly, it doesn't make any difference what the children are called, as long as the public is being informed about a new kind of consciousness that's in the kids now becoming young adults.

For example, you'll see Crystal Children referenced several times by certain contributing authors. According to Nancy, this is a profound category of the children of new consciousness, but they're still very much Indigo according to the definition stemming from her synesthesia.

As you'll see in the interview that follows, Nancy herself "sees" 12 categories within the Indigos. There are probably lots more, named by those who have taken the time to research their behavior. Again, Jan and I welcome all of this diversity. Many books with many kinds of titles have been written about these new children. Almost all of them have been wonderful; beneficial to all involved in the projects; and very helpful to parents, teachers, and the children themselves. We congratulate all the authors who have taken risks and published this information . . . some in the mainstream and some not. If you wish to see some of these books, they're on our Indigo Child Website: **www.indigochild.com**. We promote those who are trying to help these children of new consciousness, and we've included excerpts from a few of their books within this one.

Use your discretion. Do you realize what we're really trying to do here? We're endeavoring to help the children of our human society. This book isn't about religion or politics. This is a completely new premise: that human evolution might actually be changing before our eyes. Yet many find this offensive, political, and yes, even religious. Can this truly be such an upsetting idea? Can you afford to dismiss it out of hand because it's just too spooky or too much of a "hot potato"?

Updates on Human Consciousness

Several years ago, an obscure book review caught my eye. It was for *Fifth Wave Leadership,* by sociologist Morris R. Shechtman, reviewed on the business page of the *Fresno Bee* on Sunday, May 11, 2003. Fresno is in California and is known for being very hot. (Sorry, Fresno.) What made the article so compelling was that sociologists study the ways humans shape society. You might also say that they study the human-consciousness shift. Suddenly, however, they've begun stating that there's a new kind of thinking going on. The article told of only four waves of societal change since the beginning of time, and we're now seeing a fifth one!

— A new compass to lead you? "Social scientists have isolated four breakthroughs or 'waves' in societal change: hunter/gatherers became farmers. Farmers were transformed by the Industrial Revolution into factory workers; then the Industrial Revolution gave way to the informational age; and the information culture has progressed to a fast-paced global communication-intensive society. We are now in a Fifth Wave, where our futures are no longer predicated on what happens out there, they are predicated on what happens in ourselves." *The Fresno Bee;* May 11, 2003; book reviews.

Jan and I bring you this information since it gives us license to speak about what has heretofore been seen as impossible. Now science and sociology are beginning to line up on our side. There's the possibility that we're seeing the changing of actual human nature, and it's being noticed first in those born with these new attributes. Due to what Nancy saw, we continue to identify humans who have these attributes as *Indigo Children.*

The Great Divide:
The Medical Community vs. Real Experience

It might seem odd that the most vocal opponents of this whole idea are the very frontline professionals who you'd think would champion it. They interact with kids continually—they're pediatricians. Time after time, Jan and I have seen articles and television interviews regarding Indigos from these fine M.D.'s who exclusively work with children. In every case, they're taking the premise to task and asking people not to get carried away with a new fad. They wink, as if to say, "Come on, guys, get real. Kids are kids."

Meanwhile, a new occurrence presses upon the pediatrics community: ADD and ADHD rage on almost as if they were communicable diseases, increasing at an exponential rate and causing these very same professionals to drug their patients as a solution.

When asked about this, most of them explain it away: they say that ADD and ADHD were *always there,* but that researchers are only now defining and being able to deal with the disorders. So early in my research on Indigos, I challenged the *always-there* philosophy by going to the trenches and asking day-care workers with more than 20 years' experience if they'd been aware of these problems *always being there,* or if perhaps they were seeing something new. If the doctors wouldn't talk about it because it was out of the scope of their training or willingness to accept a new premise, I wanted to hear about real-life experience from those who continued to see it firsthand.

That's when Jan and I got excited enough to write the first book. It seemed that everywhere we turned, we got an earful from those who actually *worked daily with kids.* They all told us the same thing: the kids were changing! Their personalities were shifting, and so were the ways the adults had to deal with them. Discipline had gone out the window. (Unless, that is, the grown-ups understood what the kids now wanted and could change their tack.)

The relationships between children had also changed. The way they shared their toys shifted, as had (gasp!) the way they were caring for each other. Adults who spent hours upon hours with other people's kids said they were starting to see compassion at a very early age that they'd never observed before. That's new and wasn't *always there.* It remained unidentified until we wrote about it.

What follows from that research is one of the finest lineups of authors we've ever been able to present. We have college professors, trained Ph.D.'s who deal with kids, health-care workers, intellectuals, and business leaders, all ready to give you a very real look at this phenomenon. Some will offer advice on what to do if you're a parent or teacher, and some will just let you in on some experiences that show what's taking place.

In the first Indigo book, Jan and I stated that we hoped the reality of this Indigo phenomena would be seen someday by professionals who work with children. Back then, we had all kinds of tales from parents . . . but we needed those in academia to finally speak up. They have, and this book is the result (hence, Chapter 1, "From the Educators" is the longest chapter).

You may notice that we also have an international flavor this time, for if there's a change in consciousness occurring within humanity, it will occur all over the world and be seen in the children of all countries. It has, and we bring you some of those authors and stories as well.

From the One Who Saw It First . . .

Let's hear from Nancy Tappe herself, in a short interview conducted by Jan Tober specifically for this book.

Interview with Nancy Ann Tappe
by Jan Tober

J: I'd like to ask you about the Crystal and Golden Children. Do you see these as new colors?

N: I don't know anything about the Crystal and Golden Children.

J: Do you know that there are people out there who see these colors?

N: I only see Indigo. Early on, I sensed that there would be two colors, but so far I've only seen the one.

J: And that's Indigo?

N: Yes, Indigo.

J: So, as far as we know, there's only the Indigo?

N: Yes, only the Indigo, but there are 12 personalities within the Indigo dynamic. Within that color, there are four categories of Indigo; and then within each category, there are three additional personality types.

J: We'd like to know what you feel intuitively about what the Indigo experience will mean to humanity in the future.

N: They're going to change the course of our world. You see, we all grew up under the idea of "Don't ask; don't tell." We got away with things, and if no one said anything, then it must be right. We grew up trusting our rulers and the authorities. These Indigos don't do that. They're straight talkers, and they want straight answers. So they're going to change the value system in the world; and the Indigos are international, so it's also going to promote globalization. We already see it today. We see children traveling very nicely either alone or with parents, which we never saw 30 years ago.

J: Nancy, we'd like to know what percentage of Indigos are under ten years old.

N: Ninety-seven percent of the children under age 10 are Indigos, and 60 percent of the children older than 15 are as well.

J: How old is the oldest Indigo you've experienced?

N: The oldest in years is 38 or 39; but I have seen one 41-year-old woman in Switzerland, and she almost died as a baby. You see, they've been coming in for about 45 years, but those who did so earliest came in sporadically. During the first five years, they often died in infancy. Many of the first Indigos didn't make it. What some of them did to survive was to take on other life colors and add an Indigo overlay instead.[1]

J: So do a lot of people who feel or say that they're Indigos probably have an Indigo overlay?

N: Yes, that, or else they're "wannabes." Human nature is always wanting to be more than we are. And since we see Indigos as more "evolved," it's enticing to want to have that as your life color. I don't say this to be derogatory in any way. It's just human nature. I want to be rich, and I'm not. We all have our "want to be" issues.

J: Now, seven years later, what's your advice for parents of Indigo teenagers?

N: Talk to them. Treat them like they have a brain in their head, even if it may seem as though they don't. Ask them where, how, and when.

There has been a study done with teenagers that looked at how you talk to them and how they respond. The study found that if you talk to them as people rather than from a position of authority—parent, teacher, or the like—if you chat with them, you'll find that they're really quite bright. They'll show you that they're quite intelligent. But the minute you talk down to them or speak questioningly to them, they may act shallow or speak of the forbidden-fruit topics, such as "I love to do all wild things"; or they start putting out the abstract "youth jargon" [that you aren't supposed to understand].

This morning, I was watching an interview with Shaun White from Carlsbad [California], who won a gold medal for snow-boarding. He was talking, and the interviewer was saying that he noticed Shaun was crying. Shaun said, "My mom was crying; my dad was crying; and I was crying, too." He was very open, and he's an Indigo. I think that he's 23.

What we're going to see is a lot of proficiency in them. When they do something, they do it well, whether it's in a productive way or a nonproductive way.

J: That leads us into the next question. I know you were recently a guest of the people showing the Indigo documentary film. What did you think of it?

N: I liked it much better than I did the first one.

J: You're speaking of the film called *Indigo,* with Neale Donald Walsch?

N: Yes, it didn't portray the Indigos. It showed an extremely precocious child who happened to be psychic. Children just don't go around calling adults "interdimensionally deficient"; those words are not even part of their language. It's something that was just written in the movie script.

J: I think when people saw the first Indigo movie, they felt frustration and wanted to know more about the Indigos. That's why the documentary was made.

N: Yes, and I think that it was much better because the creators didn't pretend to make the children act any particular way. They let the kids speak for themselves. I thought that was extremely good. There were a lot of gaps in it, however.

J: What were those gaps?

N: Not fully putting it on the line. There was no introduction to it.

J: I quote from the panel discussion that you and I and several others, including the filmmaker, participated in. You said, "It only showed one side. It didn't show the dark side; it only showed the light side."

N: Yes, everything has a light and dark side. We have to realize that we live in a world today where things are different from what they were in the past. Before, people got married, raised their family, and stayed together even if they didn't love each other. They took responsibility for those things and stayed with it. Today, families may include three or four different partners, and that adds more influences to the dynamic. We also have to look at the psychological ramifications in the home versus the esoteric process that goes on there. Both happen in every home whether the family believes in this work or not.

J: So if the Indigos have had a more difficult home life . . .

N: . . . then their process is limited in its ambition.

J: Perhaps even the way that they process?

N: Yes, it affects the way that they process and/or how they express themselves in the world. They can be very dangerous, and we've seen that already.

J: Can you explain?

N: At Columbine High School, you had children killing children; and now you have a 14-year-old shooting his parents [in the news at the time of the interview]. I can't think of all of them, but there are many instances of that dynamic. We have 13-year-olds running away from home. We see predators left and right because the children are out there without parental guidance. We have adults who don't know how to parent because they weren't parented themselves. That, of course, comes from the postwar era when parents have been busy working, trying to make themselves successful. This isn't the Indigos' program, and they really have to deal with it, so they're very angry about it.

J: So when we ask parents to treat their children with respect or to listen to them, for example, are we saying that if they don't, we may then have children who respond in extreme ways with extreme behaviors?

N: Yes, that's true. We'd have extremes anyway, as every generation has. It's the light and the dark, the plus and the minus.

However, these children are more comfortable responding in extreme ways. They can be more dramatic. In our generation, we were taught to sit down and shut up. These kids don't know what that means. They see a situation, and they want it changed. They don't feel guilt about how the change is made.

So in the Indigo documentary when they showed only the light side, it really was beautiful . . . when the musician was playing, and the little Down syndrome child was there trying to dance . . . it was very moving. The truth is that we're going to have three different types—the angry ones who don't feel that social life has given them what they expected, those who are going to make it in spite of everything else, and those who come in with physical challenges. Many of the Indigos will come in with unique conditions, which will provide the medical community with something to work on to advance humanity's health program.

J: For instance, the exponential increase in autism?

N: Well, actually, it doesn't seem so much an increase in autism as it is *psychology relabeling autism.*

J: Nancy, just to recap here, when you talk about seeing colors around a person, you're talking about seeing a specific color around Indigos. You also correlate how that applies to certain physiological and psychological aspects. Are you an intuitive, Nancy?

N: Yes, but my special [synesthetic] sight, as related to the colors that I see, is not [intuitive].

J: Can you explain that, please?

N: I have a neurological process called *synesthesia* that allows me to see color and taste form. Synesthesia is a neurological system in which two senses cross to create a sixth sense. You still have five senses, but something is added to two of them.

[In my case, it's] taste and color. For example, when you get through eating you have [either a] sour, sweet, or pungent taste in your mouth. When I get through, I have squares, circles, and triangles.

J: But when you talk about colors, you're also actually seeing a color "field"?

N: Yes, with my eyes. I was in Sedona once, visiting a friend, and we were sitting in a restaurant having lunch. I looked outside and said, "Gee, it's an orange day today." She asked me how I did that, and I said, "It's with my eyes."

J: So for you, it's natural sight. You must have wondered at some time whether everyone had that.

N: I was born with this ability. I don't know where it came from. It's just part of who I am. People ask me to teach them to see color the way that I do, but I can't. It's a physical attribute, not a psychic one.

J: So, you tried to become a pilot? Was that in the Air Force?

N: No, I was in the Army. What I wanted to do was take private flying lessons, and they said I had to ride in a glider first. So I took the glider trip and then came back for a physical exam by a doctor. He asked if I had good eyesight, and I said "most of the time." Anyway, they turned me down because they found the synesthesia when they did my eye exam.

J: Many say that there's no scientific proof about the Indigos. They say that it's just a bunch of psychics seeing an auric color. But you see it without the esoteric quality?

N: I honestly think that when they find out more about the synesthesia and what it actually is, that won't necessarily take it out of the realm of the esoteric but will combine it with science. You see this today: science and parapsychology sort of merging.

There has been a crossing. There have been tests on many synesthetics, but no two see exactly the same thing. They'll all see a color but not in the same way.

There's a funny story that I may have told you: there was a film on *60 Minutes* about synesthesia, and I was watching it with a friend. If you look at a page in a book, I assume you see the type in black. Well, I see it in different colors. Sometimes a letter is a different color, and sometimes a whole word is a different color. I sometimes mispronounce a word or don't see a syllable because of the difference in color.

During this program, they asked a woman what the letter A looked like to her. She said, "Oh, it's a beautiful pastel blue color." Then they interviewed another synesthetic and told her about the blue that the other woman described. The second person said, "She's wrong; it's a beautiful, flowing, light pink color." I turned to my friend and said, "They're both wrong. It depends on the content of the sentence!"

J: Just to confirm this again: within the framework of your color system, based on your experience and your sight, do you consistently see Indigo as the only new color, as of these writings?

N: Yes, that's right. The other colors coming in are "one here and one there," not in any large numbers.

J: Can you talk about the Indigos and their syllabus? [*Note:* The term *syllabus* was used by Nancy in the past in the phrase "the Indigos receiving their syllabus." It simply means receiving their list or intuitive outline of who they are and what to do next.] I believe that I've heard you say that many of them don't really know what their syllabus is, is that correct?

N: Oh, they don't, and they won't for the next year [after the interview]. They're picking it up by what I call "drip feeding," and every once in a while they get an "Aha!" experience. In 2008, they'll start moving professionally into all the fields of influence—business, medicine, law, politics. The one man in politics who I'm watching now is Barack Obama, the congressman from Illinois. He's the only Indigo in Congress [as seen by Nancy's synethesia].

J: And how old is he?

N: He's in the right age bracket, but I don't know his age for sure. I've been watching him, and he's straight talk right down the middle. Tiger Woods is also an Indigo.

J: What do you think will be the difficulty for the Indigos in the workplace?

N: [They'll] talk *straight talk* with people who won't do it in return.

J: If you were an employer hiring Indigos, what would your advice be?

N: Listen to what they have to say. You don't necessarily have to follow it, but at least listen. Talk with them; get their ideas and see how much you can incorporate and how much you can't. Give them some acknowledgment.

You see, one of the things that the Indigos can't tolerate is being talked down to. They want straight talk. Just the fact that you're 20 years older doesn't give you the right to be superior. Just because you happen to be the company president and I happen to be the janitor doesn't automatically give you more authority than I have. For the Indigos, respect [for those around them] must be earned. It isn't an entitlement.

J: What I'm hearing is that these Indigos may not be satisfied working their way up in a company.

N: Well, their basic syllabus is that they don't intend to be workaholics. They want their vacations, and they want to be paid for what they do. They won't sacrifice simply for the good of the company. If their parents had to separate because of work, they didn't understand it. They're very clear that they'll work and earn money, but they won't sacrifice their lives for their work [as their parents did].

J: We've talked about this in an earlier book, but again I'd like to reiterate the left-brain/right-brain balance of these Indigos.

N: The Indigos are more balanced—much more balanced—between the right and left brain.

J: But they're coming into a society that's more left-brain intensive?

N: Yes. Also, we've been trained to believe that we don't use our right brain much, that the right brain doesn't do anything. But the truth is that we always use everything.

J: The right brain is more the creative side, correct?

N: Yes, and it's unconscious also. The left brain is linear and conscious.

J: Nancy, do you have any questions or remarks that haven't been covered so far in this interview?

N: Two things: number one, there's going to be a multitude of opinions about who [Indigos] are, what they are, and what they're doing. In my opinion, that's good because if only one person provided all the information, then that person would be considered a god. We had that with Dr. Spock being the authority on child rearing, remember? This way, parents can peruse the information, listen to it, and make their own decisions. As I said to a woman in Switzerland, "What you really want to remember is that you're the mother." Listen to your heart, listen to what they need, work at giving it to them, or get them to cooperate in getting it.

J: Yes, they'll tell you, won't they?

N: Yes, they'll be very honest and tell you exactly what they need. We have this terrible plight of "want to be." We want our children to be the best because then we can stand up and say, "That's my kid." We don't want to feel like our children aren't succeeding in school or wherever.

The second thing is that these Indigo kids are much better at home study rather than being in the traditional school setting.

J: And why is that?

N: Homeschooling gives them time to do their work. Most traditional classes are 45 minutes long. You work for 45 minutes, and if you aren't finished, too bad . . . you go to the next class. By the time you come back to that [first] class, it takes you 15 minutes to catch up again, and then you have a 30-minute class where you have to get 45 minutes worth of education. It's hard on the teachers, and it's hard on the children. In order to keep up, they often have to borrow work. . . .

With home study, they can do one subject in the morning and one subject at night, cover all of the information, and finish the project. What we need to do in the school system is discover how to give them the ability to learn completion. We didn't get that. We're used to dropping this and picking that up, and dropping that and picking this up.

J: Is there anything else you want us to know?

N: We need to keep an open mind. [The Indigos] are different; they are the future. They'll decide what we do or don't do. We look at places like the Middle East—Iran, Palestine, Iraq—where we see the children fighting in the streets, angry. That's the other half of it, because they're environmentally trained to hate the enemy. It comes from us, the parents.

J: That shows what a mirror they are to our group-consciousness thinking.

N: Right, they show us our mistakes.

J: And as you say, we must realize that they're our future.

N: Yes, they'll change the world. By 2018, we'll live in a world we didn't grow up in.

J: We must understand them and work with them.

N: Yes, but we also have to realize that we're going through changes, too. We need to sit down with them and say, "We know you're changing, but we're changing, too, so how can we help each other walk through this changing time?"

●●●●●

Chapter One

The Educators Speak

"We must be the change we wish to see in the world."
— Mahatma Gandhi

Jan and I want you to examine the qualifications and work experience of each of the contributors in this chapter. Many them are teachers of teachers, and authors. Those in higher education are starting to report on what they're experiencing regarding the new consciousness of children and young adults.

If you still doubt that the Indigo phenomenon is indeed upon us, just read what these college professors and other trained educators are saying. Then take a strong look at their recommendations. Although this book concentrates on Indigos ten years after our original book on the subject, young children are still very much an issue, since they continue to come in as Indigos. So the material has expanded to include new information about the very young, as well as those who are now young adults.

This is where Jan and I take a deep breath and say, "Thank you, God! The educators are finally coming forward, for many have the credibility that may eventually make a difference."

••

The Indigo Children

by Jill S. Porter, Ed.D.

***Jill S. Porter** is a professor of education and university field super-visor at Alliant International University in San Diego, California. As an elementary-school teacher, Jill implemented peace-education strategies to promote unity within diversity, and cultural awareness within the diverse student population, for which she was given the Crystal Apple Award and Saraswati Award for Teaching Excellence.*

Her overwhelmingly positive experiences in Egypt during the Sep-tember 11 attacks on humanity propelled her to be an advocate for peace education within the classrooms of the global community. Jill has lec-tured throughout Europe and Russia, and her Building Paths to Peace project is teaching educators at all levels about strategies they can effec-tively implement to create a peaceful learning environment. It has been published in several international humanity journals, and she presented it personally at the University of Pretoria in South Africa in June 2008.

Jill lives in Escondido, California, with her husband, Russ; son, Will; golden retriever, Socrates; and cat, Aristotle. She's enjoying being a new "Glamma" (Grandma) to William Anthony Reitsma, her first grand-child and gift from daughter Ashly and son-in-law David Reitsma.

••

Children are a celebration of life. They are a combination of our hopes and fears, frustrations and joys, past and future, all rolled into beings who are placed in our care. Unfortunately, they don't come with a clear and coherent instruction manual. So as parents and educators, we struggle. We struggle to make sense of those extreme traits that are common to Indigo children. After we get an understanding of those characteristics, our challenge is how to guide Indigos through this crazy thing we call life. My goal is to give parents and educators a foundation of understanding coupled with specific strategies to help them with this struggle.

In any base of understanding, it's important to have a good working definition of terms. For the purposes of this discussion, these two definitions will apply:

Parent: Any person in the primary role of caregiver or care provider for the Indigo. This could include, but not necessarily be limited to, father, mother, aunt, uncle, grandparent, and the like.

Educator: Any person within the academic arena. This could include, but not necessarily be limited to, parents; teachers; school administrators; and other school staff members such as the janitor, nurse, and secretary. An educator is anyone who enhances the progress of the Indigo's knowledge and search for meaning.

The role of the educator becomes extremely important because Indigos have a solid awareness of who they are and why they're here. The old strategies—based on the idea that children are blank slates, waiting for information to be written upon them—are no longer effective. The role of modern educators is one of guide or facilitator. Our responsibility is to guide the Indigo to make the most positive and informed choices the child can make within a structured and safe learning environment. Therefore, communication is essential. This is a difficult task, for educators normally don't immediately know the needs of the children. Furthermore, while Indigos are definitely not shy about speaking up, most often they're either unable, or don't know how, to do so in a manner that parents or educators understand. An initial period of adjustment occurs as the educator and Indigo are learning how to communicate effectively. It's important to note that during this time, frustration levels on both parts may rise.

It's essential that the educator become a phenomenologist. Phenomenology is usually understood in either one of two ways: as a disciplinary field in philosophy or as a movement in the history of philosophy. In education, the discipline is usually defined as *the study of structures of experience or consciousness.* Literally, it's the study of *phenomena:* appearances of things, things as they appear in our experience, or the ways we experience things—thus, the meanings things have in our experience.

Phenomenology studies conscious experience from the first person point of view. The educator becomes a subjective observer. This field of philosophy is thus distinguished from, yet related to, disciplines such as ontology (the study of being), epistemology (the study of knowledge), logic (the study of reasoning), ethics (the study of right and wrong action), and the like.

Basically, educational phenomenology studies the structure of various types of experience, ranging from perception, thought, memory, imagination, emotion, desire, and volition (choice) to bodily awareness, embodied action, and social activity, including linguistic activity in order to establish patterns within the various types of experience. Once a pattern is established, the educational phenomenologist then determines whether it's positive or negative. Positive patterns are defined as those that enhance the growth of knowledge, learning, and meaning. Negative ones provide meaning, yet hinder the growth of knowledge and learning, which becomes stagnant. Then, working within the learning style of the child, positive patterns can be reinforced and augmented while the negative can be redirected or diminished in such a manner that knowledge and learning can occur and advance.

Parents and educators can use strategies to assist the Indigo child to make positive choices. The following ideas are simply beginning points. They're designed to create a dialogue to further the understanding of the Indigo-child phenomenon. They're divided into two categories—parent and educator—but overlap in many areas.

Parent

Becoming a parent can be one of the most difficult and rewarding choices a person can make, for parenting is the process of learning to let go. When children are young, effective parents protect them while trying to teach them to experience, function, and gain meaning from the world around them. When babies begin to walk, parents allow them to hold on to the grown-ups' hands. As the children grow and mature, the parents patiently and gingerly begin the process of letting the children walk on their own, knowing full well that there will be times when the kids fall or get hurt.

When this happens, we hurt with and for our children. But when they take those first steps on their own, we feel as if they've conquered the highest mountain. Likewise, as they grow, we ache and are frustrated by the negative choices they might make. We may cry or wonder where we went wrong, but we also get to experience the joy in watching them make positive choices. We celebrate and document their rites of passages, such as birthdays, religious confirmations, proms, graduations, and weddings. And all during this process, we read any parenting book or manual and wish for any technique that we feel may help us with the process.

Here are some strategies that might help you with your children. (I've used the plural *children* to avoid awkward "him/her" constructions.):

— **Look for the patterns in your life and the lives of your Indigos.** Try to establish a positive pattern from the moment your children come into existence. For example, it's a commonly held belief that American children are overweight. Further, it's a documented fact that proper nutrition is connected to enhanced learning, so establish good and healthy eating habits that will create a positive experience for your children. By doing so, they'll be less likely to be overweight. Further, they'll be primed and ready for the learning environment.

— **Listen to yourself and your children.** For example, if you consistently demean yourself, most likely your kids will learn to demean themselves and others around them. You need to become your children's best cheerleader and coach. Further, **listen** to your children and their interactions during structured and unstructured time. Indigos don't have the same perceptions of time and reality that you do. Your children's imaginary playmates might not be *imaginary* at all, and your Indigos won't understand why you can't see their friends. Stay open to the experiences they're having. By doing so, you become an active participant in the experiences and provide extra meaning for your children.

— **Read to your children**, for they have wonderful and open minds. There are many books out there that will help them gain meaning. For example, *My Life as a Furry Red Monster* by Kevin Clash is the wonderful story of Elmo. It is a biography for the early years that enhances and guides those ideals that Indigos emphatically hold. For children of all ages, *The Peaceful Warrior Collection* by Dan Millman is also wonderful.

— **Establish guidelines with positive and negative consequences for your Indigos.** Think of this strategy in terms of a spectrum, with one of the extremes being totalitarianism and the other being apathy. You've probably seen those parents who have to be so involved in their children's lives that the kids are afraid to make any choices. Likewise, you've also probably seen the moms and dads who have attempted to be their kids' friends. Both cases result in children who can't effectively make the choices they need to. *Effective* guidelines fall somewhere in the middle, creating a balance so the Indigos can have experiences that will hold meaning for them while feeling safe and secure in a relatively structured environment.

— When your children enter an educational system (whether it's a private or public school) **ask questions of yourself, the school principal and staff, and the classroom teacher.** Ask what their philosophy of education is. Make sure they're all aligned and not in conflict with your philosophy, values, and ideologies. The teacher and institution you choose set the tone for your children's formative years. Most Indigos function best in a *constructivist* learning environment. *Constructivism* encompasses the following premises: knowledge is constructed from experience, learning is a personal interpretation of the world, and it's an active process of "meaning making" that's based on experience. Learning should occur in realistic settings, and testing should be integrated with the task, not performed as a separate activity. The educator creates curricula to match children's learning processes.

— Communicate with your children and the educators. Don't hesitate to pay surprise visits to your children's classrooms, no matter what the age or grade level is. However, don't interfere or dominate your child's time or educational activities.

For example, on one occasion I had a parent who came into our seventh-grade classroom to visit and volunteer. It was a day when the students were doing an art project: creating, painting, and decorating a cultural mask. This mother didn't believe that her son's mask was as nice as some of the others. So during the lunch break, she tried to paint her son's mask. She didn't understand why I stopped her, since she felt his work was substandard. She couldn't understand that the point of the activity was to experience the joy of using the imagination to create.

Further, remain active in your children's educational experiences. After all, middle- and high-school students still search the crowd to see where their parents are sitting.

Educator

Just as the choice to become a parent can be one of the most difficult and rewarding choices a person can make, the choice to become an educator can be similarly challenging and engaging. These men and women dedicate their lives to planting seeds that they might not see grow to fruition. They try to remain idealistic while facing extreme adversities and inequities. They know their salaries won't be comparable to those of other professionals with the same level of education.

Speaking as an educator myself, we know that we'll live and function in a world of paradoxes and paradigms. And with each shift, we're expected to adjust and conform to the new standard. And just when we think we have a good handle on what we do, our students advance to the next grade, and we begin all over again with a new class.

As educators, we look at the possibility in all things. We see the potential veterinarian within the child who lovingly tends the class pet or the botanist within the child who waters the plants. We mourn those students we've lost to abuse, disease, drugs, or alcohol. Yet we still try to see the possibility that all our students have within them, for they manage to get into our hearts.

In addition to this, we see the possibilities that lie in all things. For example, that empty egg carton could become a paint pot, or a crayon or paper-clip holder. An empty jelly jar has the possibility to become a pencil holder. We know that we'll be lifelong learners, continually honing our skills in order to provide the most current information and activities to each student.

If you're an educator, here are some strategies that might help you with your Indigo students:

— **Look for the patterns in the lives of your students.** For the early-development and elementary educators, try to establish a positive pattern from the moment each child enters the learning environment. Then document those patterns you see, putting anecdotal information in the cumulative folder for the student's future educators. When a new class enters the learning environment, use those reports and cumulative folders to get to know the history of the students.

— **Engage the students in the classroom-management process.** Use the development of guidelines with the positive and negative consequences as a learning experience. For example, at the elementary level, you might have a class discussion about what sharing is or how it's important that each child gets along and learns to cooperate with all the others. At the secondary level, a discussion of what democracy is can lead to developing classroom *laws* with positive and negative consequences voted on by the class. By doing this, you guide your students, while each one feels as if he or she has a say in the learning environment. This feeling of inclusion is important for Indigos. And even though this strategy initially takes time, in the long run it will save you both time and paperwork.

— **Emphasize the positive.** Change your grading practices. For example, instead of marking the incorrect answers on a math or spelling test, mark the correct ones. As students progress through the educational system, they learn their areas of weaknesses. By the time many kids entered my seventh-grade classroom, they were already tuned to see the negative aspects of their work.

It was always a pleasure for me to return the first spelling test of the year and see the hands raised to tell me that they'd spelled a word correctly but that I'd marked it wrong. It was fun to see the looks on their faces when I explained that I marked the words they spelled correctly because I wanted them to focus on what they did right.

When grading or editing written work, use different colored highlighters to emphasize those areas that are done well and those that require additional work. Compliments go a very long way in children's lives, as long as the accolades are sincere.

— **Do not use red ink!** Red is perceived as an angry and negative color. Students have a tendency to focus on the color instead of what it's supposed to indicate. Change pens. Use different hues to indicate what you want to emphasize. In today's computer era, use the mark-up function on your word-processing program. Use the different colors available to you when highlighting and making comments.

— **Educate each student holistically.** First, this philosophy advocates a *transformative* approach. Rather than seeing education as a process of transmission and transaction, transformative learning involves a change in the frames of reference a person may have. This shift may include points of view, habits of mind, or worldviews. Holism understands knowledge as something that's constructed by the context in which a person lives. Therefore, teaching students to reflect *critically* on how we come to know or understand information is essential.

Second, the concept of *connections* is emphasized, as opposed to the fragmentation and departmentalization that is often seen in mainstream education. Everything is connected in some way.

Third, along this same thread is the concept of *transdisciplinary inquiry,* which is based on the premise that division between disciplines is eliminated. For example, the process of didactic reasoning or critical thinking is no different in a history course from a science course.

Fourth, holistic education advocates that *meaningfulness* is also an important factor in the learning process. For example, the book *The Grapes of Wrath* by John Steinbeck is read at the high-school level. The meaning of this book would be different for an immigrant student than for one who hasn't had to move to another place. Students gain knowledge when what's being taught is important and meaningful to them.

— **Treat each student in a humanistic manner.** *Humanism* is a broad category of ethical philosophies that affirms the dignity and worth of all beings. As educators, we can sometimes be so focused on the special-education students (that is, gifted, honors, or learning disabled) that we inadvertently miss those children who fall between the spectrums. Or we might accidentally filter ourselves based on perceptions of, and biases toward, those students who we deem to be different.

For example, I was called into a classroom because a colleague felt that a goth student (a member of a subculture favoring black clothing, white and black makeup, and their own "goth" music) was depressed, suicidal, and possibly dangerous. My colleague wanted my opinion on the emotional state of the student. As I spoke with the child, my colleague was surprised to learn that the student was a vegetarian, learning about Hinduism and Buddhism. The student was surprised to learn that his teacher wasn't afraid of him, but truly cared about his well-being.

Finally, try to teach each student to treat others in a humanistic manner. By affirming the dignity and worth of all beings, the student gains an appreciation of others. We can all begin to value the concept of unity within diversity.

As stated at the beginning of this article, children are a celebration of life. They're a combination of our hopes and fears, frustrations and joys, past and future, all rolled into one being placed in our care. Indigo Children come into this existence with specific traits that will challenge us as parents and educators. Unfortunately, they don't come with a clear and coherent instruction manual. There are no easy answers for us, but there is help and hope. These strategies are simply beginning points designed to open a dialogue to assist the Indigos, parents, and educators in understanding the Indigo-Child phenomenon.

●●

Communicating with Indigos: Making Sense for Grown-Ups

by Jennifer M. Townsley, Ed.D.

Here's the wisdom of another college professor, one who works with children and has seen the phenomenon of the new children and worked with it for almost a decade. Now the children are in her college classes!

Jennifer Townsley is a professor at a community college in Arizona, where she teaches interpersonal- and human-communication courses. She works with both children and adults and has successfully facilitated training seminars on a variety of communication- and education-based subjects for the past 15 years. Additionally, she's an active volunteer and enjoys spending family time with her own Indigo son, Joseph. Jennifer holds a master's degree in interpersonal and organizational communication and a doctorate in educational leadership.

••

"Grown-ups never understand anything by themselves, and it is tiresome for children to be always and forever explaining things to them."
— Antoine de Saint-Exupéry

As Antoine de Saint-Exupéry points out in his book *The Little Prince,* quoted above, children are forever trying to communicate and make sense of things for grown-ups. This frustration in *making sense* seems to be a central theme of parent-child communication, especially for Indigo children. I spend a great amount of time watching, evaluating, and researching "communication events"; in other words I try to make sense of the people, the messages, and the approaches of the communication taking place. This is often followed by suggestions for adapting communication in order to develop strategies for a more successful outcome.

In my work, I've spent considerable time discussing, questioning, and educating myself and others on the process of communication and its effects. I've also spent time working specifically with Indigo Children, as I volunteer regularly at preschools and elementary grade levels. Whether I'm sharing family time with my own nine-year-old Indigo, dialoguing with students in a college classroom, talking with child-care workers and teachers, or volunteering in their classrooms, one thing is certain: communication and the sometimes tiresome attempts to "make sense" are abundant.

Examples of attempts to exchange meaning are everywhere. We find them in a smile, a handshake, a tear, and a verbal hello. Communication is the *process* of sending and receiving messages. I wave; you verbally respond by saying hello. You extend your hand; and I smile, perhaps also extending my hand in response.

In any communication event, there are typically a variety of messages being sent through a variety of channels. This is considered an ongoing, continual process; it's transactional in nature, having a back-and-forth process. This is much like the teeter-totter we all played on as a child. Alone, we can't really go up or down; but with another, the game begins. One child starts and another responds: faster, slower, higher, lower, they play this game until one or both decide "enough." With much of our lives spent in this teeter-totter communication game, it's interesting that many communication strategies have either been self-taught or picked up from watching others play the game.

Clearer Communications

Our conversations and dialogues have acted as our playgrounds and classrooms. Generally, it's been hit or miss for most of us—learning and adapting as we go. In fact, we generally "wing it," simply doing our best and, unfortunately, sometimes placing blame on others when a misunderstanding occurs. In communication science, we call these misunderstandings *noise,* and focus our efforts, developing ways to prevent or lessen noise. We develop frameworks to evaluate better styles or more meaningful approaches to communication.

However, when dialoguing with Indigos, the game has changed. To use our playground analogy, we sometimes teeter when we should totter and vice versa. In fact, the Indigo style of communication is more like a teeter-totter that also spins and may at times become multidimensional. This unfamiliar ground with its new rules can cause friction, misunderstandings, and sometimes broken relationships. However, if we acknowledge that the communication game has changed and make efforts to adjust our current rule books, we can reduce challenges and mend relationships. Arguably, the approaches that Indigo Children are using are unique to them. They have a new set of communication rules and expectations. With this in mind, it's past time for us as parents, educators, and teachers to both acknowledge and address the Indigo-communication playground and the realities of their approaches.

Let's look at some of the differences in how children communicate today from past generations. The proverbial "spare the rod and spoil the child" doesn't work today. Children aren't responding to verbal or physical punishment as methods of effective family, peer, or classroom communication. Do these techniques create fear? Absolutely. But do they effectively build relationships and create open and trusting dialogues? No.

Today's children have a stronger, more intuitive sense of community and *"we-ness."* They have an awareness of sharing a common purpose or goal. Indigos see the *value* of being a part of the group and perceive we-ness as being better for the individual than being separate or in a state of "I." Indigos consciously and unconsciously strive to maintain this balance of togetherness and simultaneously honor all participating members of the group, whether they're family members, friends, or classroom peers. These individuals are conceptual and multidimensional, not linear. In turn, their communication approach has also become conceptual and multidimensional.

Social Structure Makes a Difference

Another variation in communication involves the differences in families and family structure. As a norm, mainstream families don't commit to having seven or eight children; instead, parents now economically determine the number of children that define a family. Previously in our society, children were produced as a source of labor to work the farms, fields, and factories. Today, they're brought into the world with the idea that their lives will be better financially and educationally (and hopefully spiritually) than the lives of those who brought them here.

This shift in attitudes foreshadows the shift in communication styles these children are bringing with them when they arrive. In the 1930s, '40s, and '50s, the American culture highlighted the "traditional" family: Mom, Dad, and kids. Today, we see quite a different picture. In fact, when we open the societal photo album, we see several images: *single parent; binuclear* (two separate homes with children spending time in each); *traditional* (the '50s model); and *adoptive* families are smiling back at us from the snapshots. Sociologists acknowledge that family structure has changed, and those of us contributing to this book would argue that the children who make up these families have also changed. The children are arriving and growing up differently. Even as they're socialized in traditional, binuclear, adoptive, and single-parent homes (as well as other variations) with an array of rules, roles, and expectations, the Indigos are unique in their special communication styles.

So what are the communication styles of today's Indigos? This article offers insight and is developed from a variety of observations, as well as experiences shared by parents, child-care professionals, teachers, and the Indigos themselves, who have expanded my understanding in my roles as a professional consultant, volunteer, and parent. Let's look at what they have to say.

Indigos Expect Something Different

Indigo Children anticipate respect. They expect to be spoken to, not talked at or over. They have an inherent expectation that we'll honor each other and *our words* while on planet Earth. This honoring is what occurs when we're in conversation with Indigos—and they'll often remind us of it.

Here's an example of this anticipation for respect. A mom was driving several teenagers (ages 14, 16, and 17) and two 8-year-olds on a shopping trip. While everyone was talking, this mother reported that she unconsciously kept interrupting and answering questions for her eight-year-old son. The conversation went something like this:

"Hey, Nick, what's you favorite movie?" asked 16-year-old John.

"He liked that movie about the turtles who became real. Remember, Nick, we went to see that and you laughed so much?" Mom answered from the front.

"Oh, was that the Teenage Mutant Ninjas? I saw that, too," Lucas (the 14-year-old) responded.

"Nick, you also liked that Incredibles movie with the people with special powers," Mom added.

As they drove and this communication pattern continued for several minutes, the young Indigo, Nick, sternly shouted from the back seat: "Mom, didn't you say you were going to stop telling me my words?!"

This was clearly a demand to have his own words be both heard and validated. And what did the mother do? What would *you* do? Would you penalize this Indigo for shouting in the car or discipline him for back talking? Would you "correct" his thoughts, reminding him why he *really* feels *your* way? Too often, parents justify their own actions by diminishing the communication and thoughts of their children. In this situation, the Indigo Child needed affirmation that his own thoughts mattered and that his desire to be heard and contribute to the conversation was understood.

Another example is provided by a high-school teacher. When asked to describe characteristics she has noticed about her students today, she shared the following:

"I work in a school filled with Indigos. They're a large, concentrated group. It's a unique setting where 'geeks' and 'nerds' aren't uncool, but rather accepted for who they are. Sure, we have cheerleaders and sports and all of that, but these students are accepting of all kinds of people; they're open. . . . When Indigos meet a respectful teacher, someone who accepts them as they are, they shine. They're brilliant and joyful; they honestly care about the course and one another's success in it. Even without a spiritual or metaphysical background, which most don't have, they're innately open, creative, and honoring."

For Indigo kids, respect fosters respect. Let's say that again: respect creates respect, which in turn creates a communication style that's interpersonally successful and satisfying. Here's the foundation for building relationships and preventing communication misunderstandings. Through mutual respect, we can balance the teeter-totter and strengthen ties and partnerships.

Indigo Children Communicate Solutions

In my experiences as a volunteer and classroom observer, both Indigo Children and young adults creatively and divinely make suggestions and offer answers. From an observational standpoint, Indigos seem to have difficulty understanding why their ideas wouldn't be considered, let alone outright rejected, because of something as silly as age, grade level, or scientific proof. This was apparent in one second-grade classroom. The teacher began a science lesson on living and dead objects. Rocks are dead, and plants are alive, she reported. However, when she told the class that water was dead, several children spoke out in disagreement.

"Water is alive—it moves," a girl in the second row offered.

The teacher said, "No, water is not alive."

"But it changes; it changes from hot to cold. Maybe it decides that," a boy from the back row countered.

"No," said the teacher. "Our science book gives a list of what is alive, and water isn't on our list."

Yet another child added, "But water feels stuff—I saw it in a book."

"What book was that?" the teacher asked.

"A book about how water can look like a happy snowflake or a bad day depending on what you do to it," was the response (perhaps a reference to Masaru Emoto's work with water and human consciousness).

"Well, we're not using that book, are we?" the frustrated teacher retorted.

Interestingly, these eight-year-olds naturally and persistently communicated solutions for why second-grade *science* was wrong. They were enthusiastic, engaged, and persistent; teetering and tottering; working in concert to support their ideas. However, in this case, the teacher put an end to that and moved on to page 37, game over.

Indigos Are Intuitive and Have a "Mission"

Indigo children have a *knowingness*. They often prefer certain foods, activities, and even events. Axel, a kindergarten student, will only eat grains and vegetables; he won't eat meat. His mother jokingly says that he was born a vegetarian. And yet this isn't a joke. Indigos just know what they prefer, and in a home where their knowingness is acknowledged and supported, they learn to trust and nurture these instincts. The communication is balanced, the children are honored, and the Indigos grow in strength and truth, becoming their own people.

When five-year-old Matthew's father asked what he was doing, he matter-of-factly announced, "Nothing, Dad. I'm just doing nothing." And there he sat on the floor—just being, simply knowing. After about 20 minutes, his father reported that Matthew got up, came over to him, and shared his reflections about just being and doing nothing: "You know Dad, I sure like doing nothing. It feels good for me."

In a world where we're encouraged to make the most of our time, to consistently be on the go, to achieve a high rate of efficiency, and to multitask in order to be considered successful and even useful members of society, knowing when to do nothing —when not to teeter or totter—is an Indigo communication approach worth exploring.

Another high-school teacher reported that the majority of the Indigos just know that there's something important for them to do in the world: "They have knowingness about being here. They're eager to explore different ways of thinking, even if they've claimed a particular point of view, religion, or mode of thought." Understanding alternative views is important to Indigos and to their overall intention and purpose while on planet Earth.

Indigo Children Have a Spiritual Consciousness

Indigo kids feel a connection to a higher power and consciousness. It's part of their interdimensional wiring. When asked about talking to God, responses from four-year-old Indigos include:

- "God? You just have to listen in your heart."

- "You can say, 'God hear me,' and God will talk to you—it's just like talking to yourself."

- "You just have to be able to hear the words in your own head."

Indigos have a strong spiritual connection, regardless of the religious outlook they're socialized into by parents and family. Over and over, children report: "God is love; God is God; of course there's a God."

One child even shared, "Sometimes my dad yells, 'Oh, God!' kind of mad-like. But then he doesn't even finish his sentence to God . . . that's rude. If you're going to shout to get someone's attention, then you should finish your words. Sometimes I fill in the words for my dad to help him out."

Another example occurred when I was instructing a first-grade class in an art lesson. As these sessions are planned, volunteers are often given questions or activities to get the children thinking about art or art concepts. Ideas and comments are then typically written on the board. When I asked, "What are you here to do?" the class's initial responses included:

- To do good in our world
- Learn all I can learn before I leave
- Make a difference
- Make friends
- Help people
- Have fun

The children shouted the answers, smiling, laughing, and building on each other's thoughts. I wrote the responses on the board as quickly as I could.

The replies flowed from this group until the teacher, thinking we'd lost focus, interrupted and asked, "Class, what are you here to do *at school?*" The communication climate immediately shifted and an audible "Oh" (more of an "ugh") was heard. I could actually *feel* the difference in the children and in the room. It was as if a vacuum had sucked out the energy, enthusiasm, and spirit. The teacher then helped them create a new list. These responses were provided with raised hands, silence, and more thinking than their previous spontaneous replies. They included:

- Do spelling
- Listen
- Don't talk
- Sit and listen
- Write what you tell us

Instinctually, the children initially responded with spiritual concepts and ideas—golden rules, if you will. It was when their communication was redirected that they understood the "expected" responses were desired and thus provided them, although their energy levels and commitment to the task diminished. What would the art have looked like if only we allowed their spiritual consciousness to direct them? I wonder if anyone ever told Monet or da Vinci: "Stop! And color only in the lines!"

Relationships, Not Roles

Indigo children are looking for relationships, not roles. A role is typically defined as a set of expectations for behavior. We expect a nurse to be compassionate, caring, and open to discussing medical concerns. We expect a parent to be kind, loving, and consistent. We expect a coach or teacher to be patient and a positive role model. If you think about it, we actually *expect* a lot based on the "role" we project onto any given person. These expectations include behaviors, communication styles, dress and clothing choices, hair style (length, color), and even activities and interests. We all approach each communication event, each conversation, with these types of preset expectations.

For example, as parents, we may see our child and expect that he needs help; needs ideas; or needs to be told what to do, think, and/or feel. Perhaps we project that he's young, helpless, and knows little about life. If so, we're actually dictating the expected communication between parent and child.

Think about how you speak to someone you believe knows little or nothing. How do you address a person you see as always needing help? In this type of communication event, with these expectations, you'll counter rather than contribute, inform rather than discuss, pontificate rather than listen.

As parents play their expected roles, as well as foster the expectations for their children, they may be disregarding the possibilities of who their children truly are and what they're capable of doing, being, and becoming. What if you saw *your* children as successful and knowledgeable? What if you viewed them as individuals who seek help or information if and when they need it? How would your communication be different? How would the role expectations you have for yourself as a parent change? How might your children change if you let them partner in the communication?

An example of Indigos looking for relationships, not roles, occurred with Ann, an elementary-school classroom aide. She shared with me the story of Susan, an Indigo, and her math lessons. Susan was described as a "child who marches to a different beat" and was perceived as needing help in order to understand what's important. For several weeks, Susan busied herself with crayons, thinking thoughts, or simply talking to herself or others rather than writing down the math lessons that were being given by the teacher.

Ann shared that Susan has told her that she's "bored" with math and that she "already knows how to do this [math]." Susan also openly ignored Ann's attempts to redirect her and bit her crayons in half to make a point, sometimes saying, "Why should I listen to you? You don't even know me!"

Shortly after hearing about this exchange, I was volunteering and observed Susan rolling her eyes at Ann in dislike during lunch. Ann was telling Susan where and how to sit at the lunch table (a preselected seat). Susan simply looked at her and walked away, determined to select her own seat.

Ann later disclosed to me that she's also assigned to help another child during the math lesson (of course!) and has three other classrooms to oversee during the lunch period. She also joked that she has "more than one Susan" which I found to be an interesting validation that Indigos are everywhere!

After spending some time discussing the situation, I encouraged Ann to develop a relationship with Susan based on respect, to use the words *mutual respect* as a simple guide in conversations with the girl. I also talked to Ann about Susan's message: "You don't know me." This was a strong statement, and it seemed to me that Susan was first calling for a relationship. We discussed ways for Ann to get to know Susan so that she could see that Ann wanted to understand her and did care about her welfare and success. Simple questions such as "Susan, how are you today?" and "How's your day going, Susan?" coupled with waiting for a response, became bridges for communication.

Susan began to ask Ann how she was—sometimes making a point to speak first, in an effort that I perceived as a way to confirm her acceptance of this new communication strategy. Within a two-week time frame, Ann reported, "I can't believe how much better our relationship is. It's not perfect, but we've got a great foundation going here."

Within a short time, Susan's participation in the math lessons also improved so that she no longer needed Ann to sit with her. Now they've transitioned into a new relationship phase, and Ann often mentions to me how this strategy has helped her with her "other Susans."

Indigo kids want to create relationships, not validate role expectations. This axiom is key in developing successful and meaningful interactions with them. Whether you're a firefighter, teacher, parent, or peer, Indigos will look to develop a relationship, a partnership free of expectations associated with roles. They encourage others to, as one 16-year-old Indigo said, "really be who [they] are," not what someone else is expecting them to be. How open and spiritually minded to be accepting without judgment of the outcome.

The Indigo approach to communication is to pause and wait for the person and the relationship, rather than rush in with the expectation that things "should be" this or that way. To this end, today's Indigos expect to *partner* in the communication and decision making of the family home and the classroom. Given that these situations haven't traditionally been open to this type of partnering, it's no wonder that Indigos have challenges fitting in, getting along, and doing what is expected. They're looking for a partnership where the rules say there isn't one.

Indigos Are Empathic Communicators

Indigo Children embrace emotions as an all-encompassing aspect of the communication event. Their communication is interdimensional and emotion inclusive. However, many adults (and children) have been taught not to emote, as this is seen as a sign of weakness, vulnerability, and frailty. Our society is now confronted with a group of children who express and share feelings as naturally as they breathe.

Unfortunately, most everyone else's experiences with emotions tend to be simple and one-dimensional. When have we really sat down and contemplated our feelings? We're either happy, or we're sad; we're either angry, or we're peaceful. There often is no in-between place. And yet the Indigos see, adapt to, and communicate from a variety of in-between places. While most of us may not consider the spectrum of emotions found between two polarized words (happy/sad), the Indigos easily teeter and totter among the many emotions in this wide dimension of communication.

In further exploring our emotions, we might pause to consider the many colors of any given feeling. Plutnick's (1980) Emotional Wheel, coupled with his colorizing of intense and mild emotions, provides a simple approach to the various combinations that in turn create shades of emotional color. For example, happiness may include a mixture of optimism, acceptance, and love, with colors beginning at sky blue, moving toward deeper hues, and ending on royal blue—thus depicting the various "shades" and "degrees" of the emotion happiness. And yet for most of us, when we're left to discuss our emotions, we do so either through polarized concepts as mentioned previously or with trite, overused expressions. For example, when asked how we're doing or feeling, we might respond, "I'm fine." What color comes to mind for "fine"? Exactly.

In Indigos' communication experience, the emotion and the color are felt simultaneously. These individuals are able to transcend, "colorize," and feel beyond what we've allowed ourselves to see and accept as the complete picture. The frustration develops when we're communicating in black-and-white and they're responding with color and depth. What's more frustrating is our adult notion that we know better and we know more, a thought process that encourages us to *expect* a particular reaction or outcome. This approach creates tunnel vision in the communication event, often resulting in unmet expectations and disappointment for one or both of the participants. Many of us involved in these types of exchanges tend to engage in surface-level-only communication.

Indigos, on the other hand, have depth and breadth in their communication. There's an interdimensional awareness that creates the event, rather than a simple linear experience with a preset outcome. Indigos communicate using a multitude of colors, feelings, and (verbal and nonverbal) expressions, while many of us tend to be more finite and gray. No wonder they're forever frustrated with us—not only do we not "get it," we don't feel it or see it either.

So What Can We Do?

One of the most important aspects of communication with Indigos is to honor the relationship. Consider your connection a reward—one you've earned together. Partner with the Indigos in your life and build relationships from the seeds of mutual respect. Consider what you can learn from each other and expect this type of growth. Finally, remember that successful interpersonal communication is an ongoing transactional process, one in which you must both contribute and receive. Commit to developing new and better rhythms as you teeter and totter and learn skills to spin toward multidimensional communication. Pause often, reflect appropriately, and respond always in love.[3]

••

The Healing Power
of Children's Imagination:
Teresa's Imagery Toolbox

by Charlotte Reznick, Ph.D.

Charlotte Reznick *specializes in helping children and adolescents develop the emotional skills necessary for a happy and successful life. She's a licensed educational psychologist and associate clinical professor of psychology at UCLA. Charlotte is also the creator of* Imagery For Kids: Breakthrough for Learning, Creativity, and Empowerment *and the author/ producer of the therapeutic CDs* Discovering Your Special Place *and* Creating a Magical Garden and Healing Pond. *Her new book, released in 2009, is* The Power of Children's Imagination.

Charlotte has been featured on national television and published in professional and general journals and newspapers, and she's sought after as an international workshop leader, consultant, counselor, and healer. She maintains a private practice in Los Angeles, California.

••

"Your imagination can help you heal." This simple and elegant statement was the response preteen Teresa gave me when asked what she'd learned from our work together as we were wrapping up our counseling relationship.

Teresa is a beautiful, doe-eyed eight-year-old girl who first came to me a year ago because she was a "goody-goody" who was always sweet and kind and never expressed any negative feelings. Imagine what a wonderful daughter she was. Who would want to change that? Her parents. They were concerned because her younger brother was very expressive—actually a terror around the house—and they didn't want Teresa to get lost. They wanted her to be her own person. They wondered if she harbored truer feelings under the surface that were afraid to come out. And she did.

Teresa lived in a home filled with chaos. Although caring, her parents had serious volatile marital issues. There was a new baby at home, adding to the attention already taken away from Teresa by her four-year-old brother. Nannies were coming and going, partly because the mother was in the midst of starting several new businesses. Teresa never knew who was going to show up at school, take her home, or drag her to some almost-forgotten after-school activity.

I share some highlights of Teresa's story with you because, although she's a very special girl, her problems are the problems of thousands of our kids today: jealousy of younger siblings, trouble with friends, parents fighting, academic struggles, fears of unworthiness, along with headaches and stomachaches—to name a few. In my 25 years as a psychologist working with children from a variety of backgrounds, the most lasting and creative healings have taken place through using the power of a child's imagination. My *Imagery For Kids™* program focuses on teaching children to access their inner wisdom; these imagery tools offer an easy, yet effective, way to get there.

Teresa's healing journey began with her trying to please everyone, including me, and moved on to expressing herself so wildly and strongly that she got into a lot of trouble. Finally, she balanced how to communicate her needs, wants, and feelings, while also considering other people. Imagery was the catalyst, fuel, and vehicle during this process.

During our final sessions, I was delighted that Teresa easily recounted how she incorporated imagery into her life and made the tools her own. Here's her advice (with some commentary from me) on how to use eight of the imagery tools.

1. The balloon breath: Teresa explained how slow, calm, deep breathing (focusing about two to three inches below the belly button) is an imagery-foundation tool: "If you take balloon breaths, it can help. If you're mad, maybe you are able to center yourself and not hurt someone—like for me, my brother. If he does something that upsets me, I may be able to say something instead of hurting him back."

2. Discovering a special place: Teresa learned that a special place is key to creating a safe space for her imagery healing: "My special place is a room that can turn into anything. It starts like a museum, and there's a big remote [control] with dots of color that change the room into different places. Each colored dot means something else."

Teresa created a rainbow of special places, depending on what kind of healing space she needed—from dark green for trees and nature; to blue for waters, ponds, oceans, and lakes; to orange for magical mountains; to yellow where it's really hot and sunny; to black where "it's magical and nighttime," Teresa never ran out of places to go.

She had extra support: "There's a person who lets you use the remote. He helps and is kind of like a security guard, but nicer. My special password is my name backward. And if I want, I can let some of my friends go with me."

3. Meeting a wise animal friend: "If you need help with a problem, then you could ask one of your animal friends to give you a special present that might help you." Teresa's main animals were an owl and a deer.

"My owl is very wise. Owl gives me invisible ink and a pen, so if there's a problem with someone else, I can write it." Her owl's advice helped Teresa get in control of her emotions. "If you're feeling sad, drawing makes you feel better. If you have angry feelings that are bothering you, you can let them out by drawing." One day her owl showed up with a magical pencil that had a magical eraser. "It's really colorful and erases my bad thoughts."

Her deer animal friend introduced Teresa to her wizard.

4. Encountering a personal wizard: "My wizard is very nice and very tall. He has a purple hat, a long white beard that has silver in it, and a magic wand. The wand is blue with gold stripes around it like a candy cane. When I first met him, he said, 'Hello, I will be your wizard.' His name is Wizard E. Wax. My wizard's most special gift for me was kindness so I could be nice to my brother."

5. Receiving gifts: Teresa's competition with her brother often resulted in physical fighting. "I am trying to stop. I know I have to stop, but I just can't. And I yell before I hit him."

So Teresa's wizard came to help and offered the gift of a "magic banana" to help control her yelling and to help her to be able to listen to her heart (another tool). It was a magic banana because: "when you eat it, you think about other things, so you don't pay attention to worries, like your brother bothering you. It makes it like he's not even there." She also received the "magical eraser" (mentioned before) to help her erase her angry thoughts about her brother so that she could be more open to loving him.

6. Checking in with your heart and belly: Another time, Teresa was having particular difficulty with her friends. She felt as though they didn't like her at all, so she sat by herself at lunch-time. She knew to check with the wisdom of her heart. Her lesson turned into wise counsel for others.

"Your heart can be open or closed. If it's closed, it's probably mad and not in a good mood. And if it's open, you're happy to receive love." To help open her heart, this inner knowing suggested that Teresa breath in color (another tool)—the color of love—pink.

With that awareness and a little more exploration, Teresa was able to carry on an inner dialogue about how she felt and what she needed, and then she was able to shift to an open heart and join her friends the next day.

7. Talking to toes and other body parts: Teresa discovered that connecting with feelings that may be living in different parts of her body could also resolve inner conflicts.

"I learned that my feelings are important. Anger is in my head and dark gray, squiggly. Happy is in my arms and is light purple. And love is cherry pink in my heart. If your feelings are bad, you can change them with the 'therm-o-meter.'" This is a special gift Teresa received that looks like a thermometer but can be used to lower or raise the temperature of certain feelings (like lessening anger and increasing patience).

Whatever her problem, some part of Teresa's body had information that could assist her. One day, she was totally distressed and caught up in fear about returning to school. She thought she was "stupid" until she closed her eyes, turned inward, and asked for some guidance.

"Oh—I can wash out my rotting brain with white light and clean it up. My brain rots in summer 'cause I don't think about school; and then right before school starts, it makes me think I should have done more math. After I clean it, my brain feels good and makes me feel lighter. My clean brain is like a flower."

8. Using color for healing: We've seen that Teresa has incorporated color for her healing. She was very clear: "Your feelings have different colors. If you're in a bad mood, they may be darker because they may be gloomier. If you're in a good mood, at least for me, they would be lighter. So if you're thinking about dark red while in a bad mood, then think about a fun color, like gold sparkle, that would remind you to be happy. I prefer to be happy. I hope other kids do, too."

These bits of Teresa's story are meant to encourage and inspire you to share your own personal-imagery toolbox with the children in your life. Kids love to mix and match the tools and find what fits best for their personal circumstances. Please write me with your children's stories; send their wonderful and colorful drawings; and in forthcoming works, I'll share my ninth tool, "energy for healing."

Many blessings.

The Indigo Teen:
A College Professor's
Experience

by Carolyn Hadcock

Now we hear from yet another college professor, this time from Ontario, Canada. She's one of the educators Jan and I often quote and turn to when other educators are throwing up their hands in frustration, asking for answers. Carolyn has practical answers at a time when we need them. She's been able to modify her teaching techniques with great results.

Carolyn Hadcock, bachelor of teaching, ECE.C., teaches courses in early-childhood education (ECE) in Toronto. This places her squarely in a place that can make a huge difference since she's teaching future teachers; and to hear her tell it, her students are mainly Indigos. Her battle isn't with the students but mainly with an old system and the old ways of doing things.

Carolyn has been actively involved in the child-care field of the Greater Toronto Area (GTA) for more than 25 years. She began her journey as a parent and then as a preschool teacher. This experience provided a rich environment to observe and assess children's behavior and development. After five years on the frontline staff, Carolyn was invited to assume the role of supervisor, which proved to be even more enlightening. During her ten years as supervisor, Carolyn witnessed a change in the children's behaviors. At first, she felt it must be caused by poor parenting skills. However, as she became a Way Shower—a mythological term for someone who lights up our path, illuminating the way through life and filling the journey with guidance and knowledge—she slowly realized that the change in young people had more to do with the rising population of Indigo Children than any other factor.

For the past ten years, Carolyn has been teaching at Seneca College in Toronto in the department of early-childhood education. At this time, she feels that she has been instrumental in assisting the future teachers of young children to have a better understanding of Indigo Children and to offer enlightened strategies for successful interactions with them. She has also been offered the opportunity to teach many Indigo teens and young adults in the ECE program, some of whom were her Indigo students in the preschool.

Carolyn also has her own consulting business as an enthusiastic keynote speaker and facilitator of workshops for early-childhood educators and parents, giving them an opportunity to positively interact with the often complex characteristics of the Indigo Child. As an inspirational speaker, Carolyn also presents workshops on self-esteem.

••

One of the most phenomenal aspects of my nine-year career as an ECE college professor has been the opportunity to witness the dramatic arrival of Indigo teens in the postsecondary educational setting. What was once a classroom where everyone had roles to play with clear boundaries between student and professor—students focused and seated at their tables, recording the daily lecture presented by the teacher—is no longer the typical scenario.

The Indigos have arrived. They've entered the scene with an air of royalty, a right of belonging, and a strong sense of self-worth. In my estimation, we can credit the Indigos for shaking up this classical educational setting with their system-busting attitude, and now we as educators have a choice: we can be open to meeting the new needs of the Indigos by modifying our teaching techniques, or we can attempt to simply repeat our old methods and face the consequences.

When I first became more cognizant of the Indigo personality in the classroom, it was the result of a series of wake-up calls. One day, for example, a student approached me after class with that air of Indigo confidence and declared, "I really liked your presentation today, miss, but if you'd given more personal examples, the class would have enjoyed it more." Comments like these can make me question my role as a professor and my delivery technique! It wasn't long before I learned to quickly suppress any reflex response of defensiveness, take a deep breath, and reply, "Why, thank you so much for your suggestion. I appreciate that, and I will take your comments into consideration for next class. Anything else I can help you with?" That seemed to be the ticket.

The Indigo student had an opinion, and I gave her an opportunity to be heard, as well as the sense that her point of view really mattered to me . . . and I made sure it did. I also quickly learned that if you fake your sincerity to the Indigos, they can sense it. They demand, among many other things, that you be genuine with them. This is paramount to building student/teacher rapport. The more respect you have for them as individuals with their own opinions and values, the deeper the rapport. Respect begets respect . . . compassion begets compassion. Look them in the eye and let them feel your sincerity about being on their side and wanting them to be successful. Make sure that it's a team approach in your class, not a professor-versus-Indigo situation.

Ultimately, this rapport makes your job as professor much easier because the students become more open to the knowledge that you're sharing with them. They will trust you to take the lead when you know best because of your years of experience in the field, if you've opened the door to listening wholeheartedly to them. This can even be as simple as really hearing their requests for extensions on assignments. They, as Indigos, have a "surety" about themselves to ask for such things, sometimes even en masse with one Indigo as a spokesperson for the entire class.

They're also forthright in questioning the purpose of assignments or the overall course content. Giving the Indigos the opportunity to express their opinions doesn't mean that you're always willing to give into their requests, but it does mean being open to negotiation. This is the key. Becoming a negotiator meant that my role as a teacher shifted from an authoritarian to an authoritative role. This alteration has gone a long way to restore a sense of balance to the Indigo student/teacher relationship so that the learning can unfold, uninhibited by the drama that tends to manifest when a more authoritarian approach is in place.

It has been my observation that those educators who continue with a more authoritarian approach with their Indigos spend more time in the staff room seeking sympathy from their co-workers. They express their woes about the struggles they experience in attempting to get the students to conform for the sake of conforming. A 14-week semester can seem like an eternity to these teachers and their students.

Professors perpetually hurl the rule book at these "systems busters," and predictably, the tug-of-war energetically ensues between Indigos and professor. Late papers, for example, are given deductions without exception. It is the "without exception" clause that's the potential source of the rift between students and teacher. When there's no room for flexibility, negotiation, or discussion, the Indigos will continue to be vocal about their opinions, often to the point where the learning atmosphere is compromised for everyone.

Regarding late submissions in my classroom, for example, an Indigo who's working as both a full-time employee and full-time college student may request an extension. I'm very inclined in such instances to grant one without late penalties. To me, it's more about demonstrating compassion and understanding for a fellow human being, rather than forcing a student to adhere to the rule book. I get the distinct impression that Indigos truly appreciate a gesture such as this, and it's my hope that they're more likely to turn around and demonstrate that compassion in their own careers in ECE or to their fellow human beings in general.

I've come to think of this demonstration of compassion as my higher purpose in teaching. Those of us who are willing to modify our techniques to meet the needs of the Indigos are in for the most enriching teaching ride of our lives . . . and when the semester is finished, we actually lament and know in our heart of hearts that we're going to miss those students as we hug them good-bye and send them on their way into the next term.

There are a number of other ways that ECE professors are trying to modify approaches to teaching in order to meet the needs of the Indigos. This has been inspired by the relatively new ECE teaching techniques of Reggio Emilia and of Sylvia Chard's Project Approach. Both of these philosophies address the whole child and base their curricula on the child's interests and needs. I feel that we can apply these philosophies in postsecondary education for the benefit of the Indigos. Asking students for opinions—what they'd like to learn, what their feedback is at the end of class in regard to what they learned, and what was missing for them in the lectures—gives the students an opportunity to actively participate in determining, to a degree, the content that's covered in class.

Consideration is also given to the fact that Indigos become restless easily, so although lecture formats are sometimes necessary, it's best to vary the modes of delivery. Emphasis on small-group work is an alternative that gives Indigos an opportunity to practice their skills of interacting with peers, taking turns, and cooperating. Students taking responsibility for their own learning through chapter reviews and research projects are also very effective teaching alternatives to the podium lecture. Wherever possible, hands-on learning opportunities both in the field and in the classroom are highly emphasized.

Therefore, I've come to realize throughout my career that learning takes place via a variety of modalities. From a broader vantage point, we can also see that our efforts to meet the needs and interests of the Indigo students have caused postsecondary instructional techniques to evolve to new heights . . . many thanks to those "system busters" for doing their job in inspiring us to make changes!

••

Assisting Indigos to Connect for a Higher Purpose

by Pat Childers, M.Ed.

Pat Childers is a doctoral candidate whose dissertation is her book, The Indigo Grandmother: Communication Among the Generations. She holds bachelor's and master's degrees in education, and also has her certification to teach gifted and talented students. She has taught in junior high, high school, and college.

Pat started helping people with their problems and situations when she was in grade school and everyone wanted her advice. When she was seven, she even set up an office on the playground at recess. She is living a full life as a minister, teacher, healer, lecturer, mom, grandma, life coach, promoter, networker, and event coordinator.

She has assisted at many conferences, lectures, and seminars with groups such as Hay House, International Coach Federation, Omega Institute, Celebrate Your Life, International New Age Trade Show, New Life Expo, and The META Center in New York. She has also traveled with Deepak Chopra and has assisted Sylvia Browne, Ted Andrews, and Starr Fuentes, to name just a few of the authors she has worked with.

Pat enjoys sharing information through the written word, TV, radio, live lectures, and individual sessions. She recently contributed to an anthology called Conscious Entrepreneurs.

••

The question is: "How are the Indigos faring in the world today?" After interviewing superintendents, assistant superintendents, principals, classroom teachers, special-education teachers, and alternative-school teachers, I've discovered that all of these people want the best for every student. But in dealing with the rules of the new system and interacting with the parents of these children, many of whom have placed their kids on drugs such as Ritalin, I've realized that the parents may not fully understand the consequences of their choices. For instance, the schools may invite them to participate in learning and growing activities with their children, and many parents choose not to become involved. Unfortunately, some of them are totally irresponsible—doing drugs themselves or just being too lazy, busy, or uncaring to send their kids to school at all. The main responsibility lies with the parents, who need to do the best for their kids while working in "cooperation" with the school system.

Unfortunately, the No Child Left Behind Act *is* leaving more children behind because it attempts to set up a system to make everyone follow the rules and do all the lessons and classes in the most boring way by only using the mental, left-brain style of teaching, especially "teaching to the test." Each year, the students have to pass the MAP test, which designates funding for the schools according to the results. This doesn't allow time for these children to bring to the classroom and school experience what they truly have brought with them since birth, which is their connected knowledge and creativity. They assist the world in evolving to a better, highly esoteric place for all of humankind to realize we're one and that we don't benefit from being in competition.

Communication is the key to success. The parents and teachers all need to be ready, willing, and able to do what I've always done with each and every person I talk to, no matter how young or old, which is to look into the person's eyes while truly caring about what's being said, and talk things out until there's a pathway to success lined out and followed daily to enhance learning, growth, and a responsibility toward happiness and joy for all concerned. Realize that everyone needs to be willing to truly "listen" in order to understand where the others are coming from, then come to a consensus of agreement and go from there toward success in all endeavors. Don't be selfish with time, ideas, caring, and especially love. The results will be phenomenal and last throughout life.

Because I was born an "Indigo Scout," I've always truly been connected to what kids are attempting to communicate. I can see and understand where they're coming from. When I taught junior high and high school as an English teacher, I met the students where they were and allowed them to expand and grow in my classroom by taking the initiative to connect whatever projects we were working on. I let them bring in their own creativity, ideas, thoughts, and concerns; and then we worked together toward a satisfying "life lesson." Whatever came up for them, we worked it out together. That's why I'm so thrilled when I now see "my kids" around town. They always come up to me and share what's going on with them in their life *now*. The connection will always be there. Everyone needs to be willing to love, share, trust, and care; and together we can change the world for the better.

An example of individual students doing a good deed because they wanted to is found in a brother-and-sister team whose parents are both teachers. This junior and senior are highly involved in school activities and created the idea to collect old cell phones to turn in for credit to purchase calling cards for soldiers. They've gifted over 100,000 cards and transacted $1.4 million in cooperation with AT&T, via 1,800 drop-off sites.

The expression "What goes around comes around" certainly does apply here, because the company they've been working with (AT&T) gave each of them a scholarship of $100,000 to the college of their choice in order to honor the students' love, concern, and dedication. This was a fantastic reward for these kids "being who they truly are" and doing what they're here on Earth to do.

Einstein said that we can't solve problems by using the same kind of thinking we used when we created them, so it's time for everyone on Earth to live up to his or her full potential. It's now time for the innovative school systems to utilize the teachers' "intuitive knowing" to truly see and work with the kids to allow their creativity and interests to come together in order to raise the consciousness for the world. Embrace the "old soul" knowledge to create a new world peace. Seek answers within yourself and then lovingly share with others. Work together as a team for the greater good.

I'm personally pleased to report some other cool things that Indigos have initiated for themselves and their schools in the area where I live in Missouri. Yes, the "Heart of the Dove students of the Ozarks" are taking the initiative by creating their own drama clubs, working with a concept called *character education,* helping newborns in need, and raising money by selling bracelets for a cancer cure and working with the Relay for Life teams. They're also actively participating in an after-school program that joins with the community for hands-on activities that promote educational concepts. One example is a program that utilizes outdoor classrooms to focus on nature, wildlife, and conservation techniques in order to teach more about the "greening" of America.

Another initiative that really suits the needs of Indigos gives them the chance to create their own videos—editing sound, choosing animation, and broadcasting live. Practicing these procedures encourages the students, affording them more opportunities to develop their speaking skills. This group has won national awards for its work.

"Incentive learning and cooperation" between students and the town they live in is truly shown in this next example, which was encouraged by teachers. It allows the students in a computer-business class to earn credit for creative ingenuity and growth of knowledge. This is done by matching up these kids who have computer skills with business owners who'd like to have new Websites. This is a win-win situation, where everyone is working together and acknowledging how wonderful cooperation can be.

I'm especially excited about the school system that connected with its state representative to present a proposal to the state House of Representatives to seek more funding for music and the arts for *all* Missouri schools. These students did the research, drafted the resolution, and wrote the House bill themselves. Programs in the arts, as well as gifted-student programs, are often the first to be cut by school boards when taxes don't meet costs.

This project was a hands-on learning project where the students showed the government what they could do for themselves with the coaching they have received from their teachers. The kids wanted to give back in appreciation for what the teachers did for them. These students also realized that it was important to get all the younger grades and other schools involved in this project, so they sent everyone an e-mail explaining the objectives and asking their opinions. They found that 99.6 percent of the people responding believed that fine-arts extracurricular activities had a positive impact on students' academic performance. They also believed that such programs allow individuals to look at concepts and ideas with a wider perspective, broaden their horizons, and help them move forward in a positive way.

I have always believed in the "100th monkey phenomenon," which theorizes that the "knowing" passes along from being to being (the idea being that once a certain number of "monkeys" know something, it spreads to all monkeys). I believe that the Indigos have the ability to connect with each other on a soul level to heal the world, and they live in peace to see what miraculous achievements can be attained. I'll leave you with some words of wisdom from our former President from Missouri, Harry S. Truman: "I have found the best way to give advice to your children is to find out what they want and then advise them to do it."

••

Soul-Connected Teaching: The Alchemy of Deep Honoring

by Sue Haynes, M.S. Ed.

Sue Haynes *began her teaching career as the teacher/director of the Newtowne School in Cambridge, Massachusetts after receiving a B.A. from Tufts University and a M.S. Ed. in special education from Wheelock College. Following her two years at the nursery school, integrating special-needs children into her program, she spent a year as a play therapist at Children's Hospital Boston where she consulted with T. Berry Brazelton, M.D., (the author of a number of child-development books) about the specialized growth needs of failure-to-thrive and battered children. In 1987, she completed a master's in literacy at the University of Maine.*

Throughout her teaching career, Sue has focused on empowering her learners to achieve their inner potential through honoring and encouraging their strengths, interests, and creative expression. Many of the students in her classrooms and the vast majority of the students she has tutored have struggled with standardized education. Often they've been mislabeled as "learning disabled" or having attention deficit disorder (ADD). Through honoring their uniqueness, she witnessed their highly creative orientation and began identifying them as "creatively gifted." These learners are indeed not dysfunctional; they're beacons of authentic learning.

The following article is an adapted excerpt from her book, Creative Mavericks: Beacons of Authentic Learning.

••

We all know that what will transform education
is not another theory or another book or another
formula but a transformed way of being in the world.
In the midst of the familiar trappings of education
—competition, intellectual combat, obsession with
a narrow range of facts, credentials—we seek
a life illumined by spirit and infused with soul.
— Parker Palmer[4]

Over the past 30 years of teaching, I've had the privilege of working with a unique population of learners who are attuned to, and compelled to be true to, their internal agendas. These agendas haven't meshed with the goals of traditional education. I've termed this population of learners—often labeled "learning disabled" or as having ADD—*creatively gifted.* In researching Indigo Children, I've noted these same qualities. Both the children I've worked with and those individuals described as Indigos have a deeply sensed life mission that they're compelled to be true to. My work with creatively gifted children (who are no doubt in the broad band of Indigos) offers a teaching approach that supports both the unusual drive and awareness of the Indigos and the growth in consciousness of all children.

My maverick learners explore the frontiers of possibilities "outside of the box." In their resistance to paying tribute to the superficial and often-bogus learning agendas of traditional schooling, they're beacons of authentic learning; they have the potential to transform education.

The qualities of authentic teaching and learning described in this chapter can't be translated into the scope and sequence curriculums utilized by most schools. Predetermined learning goals are informed by the philosophy of acculturalization—training individuals to perpetuate the cultural status quo. A teaching philosophy that honors each learner's internal agendas espouses a radically different goal. Maxine Greene (1988), a professor of philosophy and education at Teachers College, Columbia University, warned in a *Language Arts* article:

There is a growing tendency to describe children as "resources" rather than persons, with all the implications of "use value" and even "exchange value." Proposed improvements in their education are argued in the name of the nation's economic competitiveness, not for the sake of the growth of persons viewed as centers of choice, agents of their own becoming.

A curriculum that supports the growth of persons as "agents of their own becoming" can't be predetermined. It must grow organically and be responsive to qualities sourced from the "bejeweled self" of our innermost being, which flower on their own timetable of unique expression.

In contrast to the philosophy of acculturalization, I believe that the purpose of education is to awaken and support this bejeweled treasure within us and to infuse its creative vitality and wisdom into our functional personality. The role of the teacher within this new paradigm changes radically:

> Once we acknowledge a new set of assumptions regarding the innate capacities of students, we find a new role for the teacher emerging. From being a dispenser of information and knowledge, the teacher becomes a gardener whose responsibility is to nurture growing children so that the innate potential of each organism is allowed to blossom and bear fruit. (Clark, 1991, pp. 26 and 27)

In my own career as a literacy specialist and special-education teacher, I've worked primarily with children who show dysfunctional behaviors within a school curriculum that has denied them access to their natural learning. I've operated from the premise that the core of my students' learning requirements stems from their need to be engaged with authentic learning—learning that feels personally interesting and relevant, learning that gives them creative initiative to explore and express their self-determined learning agendas.

There's a different lens through which we can look at their "deficiencies." For example, Thomas Armstrong, Ph.D., in *The*

Myth of the A.D.D. Child: 50 Ways to Improve Your Child's Behavior and Attention Span Without Drugs, Labels, or Coercion, suggests that we reenvision the negative behaviors of ADD/ADHD in a positive light. He writes:

Instead of thinking of your child as . . .	Think of him as . . .
hyperactive	energetic
impulsive	spontaneous
distractible	creative
a daydreamer	imaginative
inattentive	global thinker with a wide focus
unpredictable	flexible
argumentative	independent
stubborn	committed
irritable	sensitive
aggressive	assertive
attention deficit disordered	unique

Armstrong's positive spin on the behavior characteristics indicative of possible ADD/ADHD also describes the highly creative learner.

As I sit beside my highly creative learners, I sense a waxing and waning of their focus as we explore learning that both does and doesn't resonate with their inner agendas. As I'm able to increasingly invite these learners into experiences that relate to their personal interests and invoke their creative expression, I witness their joyful, focused absorption in the place of their previous distractibility. When I honor *their* learning missions, I witness miracles of empowerment. An example is the following case study of a student who tested as learning disabled and, in fact, is creatively gifted.

Christina

Christina, a fourth-grade student in a small outer-island school off the coast of Maine, had just about given up. She felt intense frustration with her classroom work; she felt like a complete failure as a learner. Christina's teachers knew that she was bright, despite her various learning difficulties, but they felt powerless to ease her frustration and dispel her belief that she was stupid. Even an assessment affirming her high IQ did nothing to alter her belief.

At a PET (Pupil Evaluation Team) meeting following testing, Christina was identified as "learning disabled" in the areas of reading, writing, and math. I was asked to work with her one afternoon a week in my capacity as special-education teacher. After talking with her other teachers and working with Christina during our initial session, I expressed my belief that she was, in fact, "creatively gifted." Applying this lens is the first step I take in revaluing a highly creative, troubled learner. Along with seeing Christina's obvious challenges with her schoolwork, I could see, on another level, her highly creative orientation in all aspects of her learning.

Christina loved to draw; and her pictures displayed wonderful line, perspective, color, details, and expression. She was, in fact, driven to progress artistically, exploring drawing at any given opportunity. I allowed Christina to draw as we worked together to both honor her talent as well as heighten her focus on our task at hand. I also arranged for Christina to have an art mentorship with the teacher's aide, Gail, (who's an artist). Two years later, Christina's weekly visit to Gail's home continues to be the highlight of her week.

In our work with reading, writing, and math, I gave Christina choices of the resources we used, the topics we explored, and the formats for our practice. Creatively gifted learners have an intense need for ownership in every aspect of their learning; they make intuitively excellent choices in line with their needs. I've always been amazed to see these children sort through a considerable pile of book choices, for example, rapidly prioritizing them into categories of "maybe now," "at some future time," and "let go."

Along with giving Christina a choice about the books we read together, I also encouraged her to more fully utilize her rich language sense and fabulous prediction—the core of the reading process. As she shifted her perspective on reading to personal transaction, I reveled in her identification with the characters and situations in the stories and her deep understanding of the themes. Christina's rich bonding with narrative included books with sophisticated themes, like David's growth of self-identity in Anne Holm's *North to Freedom* and Cusi's journey to embrace his ordained destiny in *Secret of the Andes* by Ann Nolan Clark. These are the kinds of books she chose and delighted in, stories that resonated with her astute perceptions.

I engaged Christina in spontaneous conversations about our responses, refraining from questioning that would assess a mere mental understanding. Her personal connection to the stories would lead her to argue sometimes with the characters. One day while we were reading *Secret of the Andes,* she became impatient with Cusi's wandering and commented, "I think he should try to find out who he is rather than trying to find a family." When we watched the PBS video *The Incas,* following our reading, Christina transformed this rather dry documentary by exclaiming, "That's Cusi's mother's hut," and "That's his llama, Misty." When I shared her responses with her art mentor Gail, she commented, "And for her, they really were."

In writing, I encouraged Christina to brainstorm a story idea that would spark an "organizing vision" compelling enough to encourage her risk taking. Her previous attempts at writing had been frustrated by her difficulties with spelling, punctuation, and penmanship, as well as assigned topics with which she felt no personal connection.

I invited Christina to write on my portable computer in order to bypass her transcription angst; and while this novelty helped, she was still unable to find an appealing idea. In order to start *somewhere,* I suggested that she continue with a piece she'd written for her school newspaper about a young Russian girl emigrating to this country in the mid-1800s. Reluctantly, she began, placing the girl in

Texas. Plodding along, she wrote a few lines each week with many pleas for typing help from me.

One day, Christina had her main character escape from her chores to travel with a friend to a nearby creek. At the creek, the girl saw a man. "Or was it a boy?" I suggested. "Oh yes," she said, "a young black boy who has escaped from a cruel master." Fueled by this compelling idea, Christina set off with full wind in her sails. She had a strong sense of social justice, and this story gave her a creative opportunity to explore this. "Natasha's Adventures," the story of how a young girl helped an abused slave boy connect with the Underground Railroad, became a beautifully illustrated little book. Christina's transition from writer's angst to empowered author was a beautiful unfolding as she began to reenvision herself as a capable author and illustrator.

Christina and I still had the potential tedium of math facts and spelling words to work on. Within my developmental approach, I assessed where Christina had become stuck foundationally in both subjects. In math, she wasn't using number sense in computation and thus had difficulty learning facts. Often with "learning disabled" students, this difficulty is deemed a short-term memory problem. It's my experience, however, that a creatively gifted learner generally doesn't retain memory for any fact isolated from personal understanding or relevance. One must ask, "Memory in what context?"

For math-computation work, we co-created games to practice number sense. First, we reviewed the "10 + any number" rule and doubles. I also had Christina develop a fluent sense of counting up and back by twos on odd and even numbers. Once she was fluent in these areas, I taught her how to quickly figure out almost any addition fact by beginning with doubles or +10 and adding or subtracting 1 or 2 as necessary (for example, 9 + 7 is 10 + 7 - 1, and 8 + 6 is 6 + 6 + 2). Multiplication is multiple addition, so I encouraged her to go back to a fact she knew and use her addition strategies (for example, to get 8 x 7 remember that 8 x 6 = 48 and then add +10 - 2). Once she solidly learned addition and multiplication, then subtraction and division could be figured out by reference to the former (17 - 8 turned into 8 + what? = 17).

After I assessed Christina's developmental level in spelling, drawing on guidelines in Bear, et al's (1996) *Words Their Way,* we brainstormed rules and practice words that would build a solid foundation for future spelling growth. Christina would have rebelled against endless, boring drills of math strategies and spelling features, but she was quite motivated to practice with games she created, varying the rules to keep us on our toes.

Today, two years later, Christina is a far more confident learner. She has grown in her reading, writing, spelling, and math skills, although she still tends to go into a shorthand version of spelling in writing "on the run." She has her own AlphaSmart portable computer for use with classroom assignments and homework. The computer helps her focus on expressing her thoughts, bypassing her handwriting struggles. While not as fluent a reader as a classmate she works with, Christina amazes her teacher with her depth of understanding inference, characterization, and theme in the books they read. She writes more easily, but still needs that spark of inspiration to create a story with strong voice and energy.

On one recent day as Christina and I sat together on the mail boat that services her island, I noticed her absorption in reading a babysitting handbook for an elective course. I smiled because I'd been wondering how her independent reading was developing. At one point she looked up at me and said, "Sometimes I really love riding on the boat because I get to read a lot and relax."

In discussing my work with Christina, I've described aspects of facilitation employed by many Whole Language teachers: the honoring of developmental level, the offering of personal choice in all aspects of learning experiences, and the offering of opportunities for creative initiative. But beyond these tenets, I applied a lens through which I "saw" Christina as a child who had an intense need to be true to her passionate interests and who *had* to employ creative initiative to effectively energize her learning. I understood that her obstacle had been her inability to connect to curriculums that felt both developmentally intimidating and personally irrelevant.

Highly creative children often wilt within the acculturalization model of education, with its thrust toward "fitting in" and "measuring up." When rigidly interpreted, today's prescriptive-learning results and standards can further squeeze out the "growth of persons, agents of their own becoming." How would it be, I wonder, to articulate a learning result of: "The learner will feel a deep resonance with self-selected stories," or "The learner will grow in making choices sourced from his or her inner knowing."

I believed in Christina, in her strengths, talents, interests, and passions. I honored her need to be true to her compelling internal agendas. More than the choices I gave her or the games we created together, I feel that this lens of "seeing" and honoring *Christina* was the catalyst for her empowerment.

Creatively gifted and Indigo Children are forthrightly aware of their internal agendas. We all, however, have a unique calling. We all have the bejeweled self within. Teachers who are living from their authentic core are in a position to awaken self-awareness in all of their learners.[4]

• •

Seeing the Difference—
1974 to the Present

by Quinn Avery, Ph.D.

Although Quinn doesn't say "Indigo" in this brief report, the very fact that he submitted his comments to the Indigo book is a strong statement that he is indeed speaking of the new kids.

This article is short but very telling. These kids are far more cerebral than the older generations were, and some are even sensitive to what's coming up (intuition about future events). Before you laugh, remember that this very thing was proven at Princeton University by Dr. Nelson (see my comments in the Introduction on page 9). Could it be that these children are "picking up" on the same thing?

Quinn Avery has a degree in special education from the University of Arizona. Quinn has taught in the public-school system since 1974 and worked in retail sales from 1977 until 1985. He returned to teaching in 1985 and has been working with children ever since. His experience gives him license to report on what he has seen about evolving children, and the space between teaching stints gives him a window of comparison often not experienced by other educators, who simply get used to small changes.

• •

I presently teach sixth-grade students with learning disabilities —the mildest of disabilities—at a middle school in Hawaii. Of course I've seen many changes in the children year after year, but I experienced an event this year that surprised me.

I was teaching four students in a language-arts class when one of them stated that he knew when something would happen. He proceeded to tell me that he would have a dream, and a while later, his dream would happen. I believe in dreams and prophecy, so I told him this was a good thing and not to be afraid of it. Then the other three students in the class said the same thing happens to them. I've never heard any of the students I've taught previously mention anything like this.

There are also two students who keep journals of the drawings they make. They take every opportunity to draw when their work is finished, and they appear to be very serious about what they do. One wants to make videos; the other wants to write a story and make a movie. They each have a dream and motivation to pursue that dream.

I've had other students mention something they were interested in doing but none who had a plan and then executed that plan at so early an age.

●●

Emotions and
the Indigo Child

by Julie B. Rosenshein, L.I.C.S.W.,
psychotherapist and
school consultant

It was difficult to decide which of many articles of Julie's to use. They were all stellar and right on point. So Jan and I chose the one that so many parents have asked about: emotions!

Julie B. Rosenshein is a psychotherapist, parent educator, and teacher-consultant who specializes in ADHD, Indigos, and highly sensitive children. Julie uses her medical intuition and channeling abilities to bring practical information to parents and adult Indigos, even over the phone. She's affectionately known as "The Indigo Doc" because she lectures nationally sharing her experiences as a highly sensitive child and teaching tools for kids that work. Her work has been featured on CNN, the Boston television show Chronicle, and the A&E Network. She is the author of The Highly Sensitive Kids Guide.

••

Are they ADD? ADHD? Bipolar? Oppositional defiant disordered? What label will be next for the Indigos and highly sensitive children of today's world?

Sam is a four-year-old in a preschool where I'm the behavioral consultant. He displays strong emotions, tantrums, crying jags, oppositional behavior, inattention to subjects he doesn't care about, and extreme noise sensitivity. He also has the wonderful

Indigo qualities of a master LEGO builder, musician, computer whiz, and multitasker. He has developmentally "delayed speech" that's common among many Indigos.

Sam has hit classmates, hidden under desks, and refused to be a part of song-circle time, especially if he's not given the choice of sitting on the letter "S" on the rug. He was switched from one preschool to another because the teachers couldn't deal with his emotionality, severe mood swings, inattention, and aggressive behavior. His profile is very similar to many of the children and teenagers I see in my private practice.

After taking a thorough psychosocial history, we came up with a working behavioral plan with privileges he could earn if he didn't hit other students or teachers. We encouraged using the "music center" often, and set firm and loving limits with respect to any kind of aggressive behaviors such as throwing things at kids or grabbing children and trying to push them off swings. We also encouraged him to take frequent cool-down break periods in the occupational-therapy room. When he got overloaded, he learned to ask for a break so he could swing, dance, march, climb, and use yoga balls to process his feelings and energy before he got so out of control that the negative behaviors surfaced.

They Can Learn to Balance

Whenever Sam showed me his "Let's Take a Break" card, I would stand up with him; hold his hand; and march, stomp, or skip with him to the break room. I often saw signs of his emotional world crumbling on the way to our sanctuary, such as stuttering in his speech, yelling at me about other kids, and having to rub his body against the walls leading to "our room." Once we got to our room, though, another child emerged. After turning off the harsh fluorescent lighting and opening the window to let in fresh air, we jumped on the trampoline and bounced on yoga balls on the carpet. He built a fort with pillows to block out the loud noise and other sensory stimulants that were intolerable to his system.

Sometimes he just screamed, punched pillows, or swung back and forth. Sometimes he called out, "Ball smoosh! Ball smoosh!" Then I knew to take down the large yellow-rubber yoga ball while he lay down. I rolled the ball up and down his back and legs with just the right amount of pressure.

I watched as he went from complete overload to "in the zone," usually within 15 to 20 minutes. When he walked in, steam was coming out of his ears; and when we walked out, a smile was usually spread across his face. In the beginning, he took four of these breaks a day and managed to make it until 1 P.M. for parent pickup. His mom reported that immediately after getting home, he took a nap for almost two hours each day.

Within three weeks, however, this child had gone from two or three crying episodes a day to just one episode each day. He was no longer using physical aggression and was starting to join in the song circle if he was able to have his choice of seat and stand up if needed. He was still quite impulsive and inattentive, but he was on his way toward balance in these areas.

After a month, his parents called and asked the teacher if she'd seen improvements within the last seven days. She replied, "It's hard to say. The improvement has been progressively better in small increments all along. We're quite proud of him, and so glad that there's steady progress."

The parents then informed the teacher that seven days earlier, the child had been put on Ritalin by their pediatrician who said that ADD was probably the culprit here and that medication would help the child's inattention and impulsivity.

Words can't describe how my heart sank when the team told me this at our weekly meeting. Not only was our intervention now clouded by a second variable that would confuse our findings, but what would come next for a child who had been put on stimulants before he could even speak full sentences?

Causes, Not Symptoms

In this case, I knew we had to look at root causes, not symptoms. We were dealing with a highly sensitive Indigo Child who was experiencing energy overload, overstimulation from fluorescent lighting and noise, and anger/boundary authority issues. He required lots of movement for his body to process all of the stimuli in a place like school. He needed help with anger management and frustration tolerance. He also needed help with the family issues that were taking place at home.

Three months later, Sam was scared when he'd misbehaved at school. He was crying inconsolably. "If Daddy finds out, he will put me in the garbage pail!" He said this a number of times between his sobs.

As it turns out, this child had been verbally threatened by his father. The roots of his emotional ups and downs and inattention weren't ADD or any other psychiatric label. He was a highly sensitive Indigo—anxious, distracted, and scared for good reason—and needed help with his emotional regulation and family issues.

It's very important to know that just because a child is inattentive, they aren't suffering from "ADD." There are many causes of inattention in children. Haven't you noticed that your child can actually sustain hours of attention looking at animals in the woods, building models, or playing music, even though the school has said he's inattentive? These kids aren't *in*attentive, they're *selectively attentive*. When they're made to focus in coercive or disempowering ways on things that are meaningless to them, they just plain tune out or lash out.

No Quick Fix

Sam is still on Ritalin. His mother and father were forced to go to a parenting class, and they were educated on appropriate discipline techniques. I wish I could report that the end of this story was better than its reality. I also wish I could say that this is an isolated incident. It isn't. I frequently see these kinds of kids at the schools I work in, and they're usually at the mercy of uninformed, old-paradigm parenting; schools that want kids to be under control; and pediatricians who are looking for quick behavioral fixes. (In my private practice I can do much more intervention; but in schools, because of legal constraints and various levels of parent/school readiness, I sometimes have fewer options.)

The chances are that Sam will continue to have attention problems and that his mood swings will continue to escalate. By first or second grade, his parents will probably take him back to his pediatrician and say that the medicine must not be working because their child is still inattentive and having mood swings. By this time academically, he'll have to do much more work and won't be allowed to take the movement breaks he was able to in preschool, due to time constraints. His unprocessed feelings will drive the moods and anger issues even more aggressively toward inappropriate behavior.

At some point, Sam will probably lose it in class and hit someone. The school won't know what to do because the behavior plan isn't working anymore; and besides, the child's system is too overcharged for him to make good choices for himself. Unfortunately, what usually happens next is that he's given a new diagnosis: bipolar disorder. He's then given a mood stabilizer (which he takes along with the stimulant) to help with the mood swings and emotionality.

He'll continue to struggle in school and with authority figures. As time goes on, he'll probably become more full of rage and feel powerless over the way his emotions overwhelm him and over the limited choices he's given. He'll usually have many medication tweaks along with doctor visits, and maybe try several different kinds of pharmaceutical "cocktails." (One child I worked with at a public school had tried nine different psychotropic-medication combinations and then wound up in the hospital.)

Tomorrow's Problems from
Today's Misunderstandings

By about the fifth grade, Sam will be even more mistrustful of adults and authority in general—and with good reason. He'll probably hate doing what he's told and have verbal outbursts in class. His teacher will have tried everything but won't know what to do besides call home and send him to the principal's office. He won't want to go to school—or be at home for that matter. He'll be angry at everyone and everything.

At this point, he'll probably get his last label: oppositional defiant disorder. This is a label that could probably fit all of the Indigos I've ever seen when they haven't been given fair choices, freedom, appropriate boundaries, and frequent movement breaks at school. "We just can't seem to manage him. He won't do a thing we say. Maybe it would be good to consider a different kind of school where they can give him more personal attention. . . ." And on and on it goes.

In high school (if he stays in school), he may experiment with other types of drugs. He'll seek to self-medicate his feelings of isolation, anger, despair, or academic failure. Many times, I see these kinds of kids end up in hospitals due to drug abuse, addiction, or overdose.

Bipolar or Just Sensitive?

As a clinical therapist and diagnostician, I have to be very emphatic about this: just because children have mood swings doesn't mean they're bipolar. Children's moods (Indigos and non-Indigos alike) can be caused by a combination of very logical, biochemical, and temperamental reasons. They can be dealing with emotional issues; mismanaged anger; high, energetic sensitivity; thyroid imbalance; nutritional deficiencies; family issues; and academic difficulties. They also can be dealing with a lack of sleep from night terrors or unprocessed anger from past-life memories.

Frequently, Indigos are carrying around the "rage of our planet," the anger from their households, and unprocessed energy from all the kids they come into contact with during their school day.

Indigos are highly sensitive energy magnets, and when this energy isn't cleared and processed, it wreaks havoc on their system. Usually, I find that these mood swings and frequent meltdowns come from the unprocessed anger, which causes the child to swing from rage (anger turned outward) to depression and despair (anger turned inward). If we help these Indigos properly deal with their rage, we give them the fuel to power their life's mission on this planet. If we don't, then by adolescence, they can end up shooting outward with guns (like Columbine) or shooting up inward, with drugs, to end the pain.

Making Sense of the Chaos

I frequently receive e-mails from teenagers or twentysomethings who tell me stories similar to that of Sam. After years of struggle, they find an article on Indigos that "blows their mind," and they ask me: "Am I an Indigo? It sure sounds like me. . . . Do you think that was it from the start? Am I not bad or stupid, just different?" And then they weep on the phone. Their lives suddenly make sense to them in ways they never have before. At this point, 20-plus years of struggle click into place internally, suddenly knowing the new information. They feel so connected to it in their gut that they know it's the truth.

All these young adults need are proper emotional and spiritual supports, outside-of-the-box educational resources, and encouragement. Then these wise souls can go on to lead productive, creative, meaning-filled lives, one step at a time.

Many of these teens finally quit school and either start homeschooling with a grandparent or find a training program or internship where they can learn a trade. They come back to their interests and dive in; and having survived the school scene, they walk on. They find the courage to do what they were meant to do all along: their life purpose.

What We Can Do

So how do we stop the downward spiral in the case of Sam and others like him? It isn't insurmountable. It just takes patience, and you must know that as a parent or teacher of an Indigo, you know things that traditional doctors and professionals might not know. You must trust yourself and your guidance to know what's right for your child. Don't leave it up to other people to determine, even if they're in positions of power. (That will change as time goes on.) In the meantime, hold your ground and ask for inner guidance and opinions from your own child to guide your compass. Most of the time, children will know the best things for themselves if they're in their center.

Following are some interventions, tips, and tools that may be of use to you and your child to help process the important anger that Indigos carry. Please know that many of these interventions are best done with a professional who's trained in mental-health issues and knows how to work with Indigos. Some tools are purposely simple and user friendly so that you can empower yourself and your child in the privacy and safety of your own home.

Ways to Help Children Process
Their Emotions . . . Especially Anger

— **Rule out underlying biochemical imbalances.** Find a naturopath, allergist, acupuncturist, or kinesthesiologist who can help you determine whether there are biochemical imbalances that are creating mood swings or irritability. Quite often, deficiencies in magnesium, B vitamins, calcium, vitamin D, or thyroid levels will throw children's bodies off balance. If children are allergic to foods or their environment, they'll be on an emotional roller coaster. (Almost always white flour, sugar, colas, NutraSweet, dairy, or environmental sensitivities are the culprit.)

— **Rule out any learning disorders at school.** See if your children's learning is creating such frustration that they can't keep it together at school. Homeschool if you have to as a way of making learning tolerable.

— **Explore bodywork.** Chiropractic, Reiki, hands-on healing, and exercise are all wonderful ways to help your children process feelings. The energy gets locked and needs unblocking.

— **Get an Indigo book for the teacher at school.**

— **Allow for as much choice as possible.** These children are at their best if they have a say in their lives and future. If they don't have a chance to participate in their own welfare they become full of rage and frustrated. It's hard to be an old soul in a young body.

— **Use sensory integration when possible.** Find out about what occupational therapists do with kids who are sensitive. These exercises are particularly helpful for Indigos at school and at home.

— **Make a place in your home for processing and decompressing.** Your children will need a place to come home and "crash" from their day. Make a place in the house with pillows, an old mattress, blankets for fort building, and maybe even an enclosed cubby or cardboard box for them to curl up in and block out the stimuli of the world. This helps their bodies get back into balance. Let them romp, crash onto pillows, scream, journal, or be silent—or just hold them there. They need this!

— **Help them choose some activities.** Journaling, drawing, hitting pillows, jumping, crying, using a punching bag, beating a drum, doing martial arts, kicking a ball around, asking for hugs, receiving Reiki, swinging, doing yoga, scribbling their feelings, draw their feelings with color, taking an Epsom-salt bath, weight lifting, getting into/by the ocean or the woods, talking about things, jumping on a trampoline, creating poetry, and singing are all good options.

— **Find out what led to their meltdown or frustration.** The problem probably started growing way before the meltdown happened. Be a detective and find the causes that led up to the feelings.

— **Look for underlying *clinical depression*.** Depression looks very different in children and teens than it does in adults, and boys show it differently than girls. If they're suffering from depression, it can be masked by anger, hyperactivity, lethargy, or indifference to life.

— **Be a detective.** Keep a journal or chart that tracks your child's days, moods, meltdowns, and frustration levels. If you can eliminate the triggers for their mood swings, you spare them the agony of having all the ups and downs of their emotions. Have them start to realize these causes, too, and be advocates for their own well-being.

— **Relax.** Your child will be picking up on all of your moods, too. The more balanced you can be, the better off they'll be. If you need your own emotional space, explain that and honestly tell them what you're feeling. They'll intuitively know, so you might as well help them know that you're human, too, and simultaneously model good ways of dealing appropriately with your feelings. You can't expect your Indigos to do anything that you don't carry out yourself, so practice what you suggest to them—or better yet, do these things together. You'll see a world of difference if you allow your child to guide you along your own path as you guide them. They need your consistency, emotional availability, and structure to feel safe in their own skin.

Peace and blessings to you on your choice to be a guide to one or more of these special children. Be well, and know that when you raise an Indigo, you're really helping to bring not only that child, but also the whole planet, a step closer to the kind of place we all want to live and love in.

••

Jan and Lee: We can't stop here. Julie is so prolific and accurate! Here's more from Julie from one of her other articles:

Usually, Indigo Children will feel the rushing around or undercurrent of pressure from family members, school, or the world around them, and they'll want to balk at it. They're meant to do so, and we must listen to their misgivings if things are to change. They're here to transform the systems of our society that aren't working, which include our family systems. Your Indigos probably need to feel a connection with their home, and also a link to a larger community of children or teens who share their views and passions. Many Indigo networks and groups are forming throughout the country and the world, so there's a place for these special souls to feel validated and appreciated by those who really understand them and share their experiences. The Internet and your local healing or metaphysical center are places to find like-minded souls. Ask that the Universe provide you with the right people, places, and things so that you and your family have the support and connection you need.

Some simple things to try with your Indigos:

- Keep a shoe box filled with clippings from newspapers and magazines of fun things you and your children would like to do. On a Sunday, randomly pick one out of the box and just go!

- Make a gratitude list or play "High Point/Low Point" at the dinner table (telling the best and worst things that happened to each person that day), and add pictures if you have artistic-minded kids. Put the project up on the refrigerator.

- Be as authentic as you can with your kids without being inappropriate for their age. Explain your

thinking or feelings about things in a candid way.
Tell them the reasoning behind your decision-making
process. Listen to how they feel about things, too. Let
them know that you hear their points of view, but you
still aren't going to change your decision or boundary.

- Ask questions more than giving answers.

- When your children are aggressive or acting out,
  look for the pain or hurt behind their actions. Try to
  address the need underneath the behavior.

- Remember that *no* is a very important word, even
  though it's met with disdain. When you stick to your
  no, then your children respect your boundaries and
  trust that you can't be manipulated. This feels safe to
  them, even if they rail against it.

- Remember that people are more important than
  things or schedules. Do half of what you think you
  must do in a day and give the extra time to yourself
  and your family.

- Eat a home- or family-cooked meal at least once a
  week together. Invite your neighbors over to share in
  the fun. Stay up late on a school night!

- Have regular meetings where family members air their
  feelings or problems. Model using "I statements" such
  as: "When I'd just finished cleaning everything and
  then it was all messed up five minutes later, I felt really
  frustrated. I need help in figuring out a better solution
  here. Any ideas?"

- Give as much choice as possible within every
  situation.

- Don't sound like a broken record by yelling at the kids over and over. Yelling loses its efficacy the more you do it. Chances are, your kids are so used to it that they don't even hear you anymore. Say something once while putting your hand on their shoulder, establishing eye contact on their level, and asking them to repeat back to you what you've just said. Then stop.

- Remember that your Indigos may actually know what's best for them more than you do. Ask them first what they think, and if appropriate, follow their lead.

- Make each weekend a time when your schedule slows down and allows for organic play and connection. Limit computer and video time and get outside.

- Make exercise part of what you do together as a family. Let your Indigos choose the activity out of three that you offer. If you see that the environment of one activity is too overstimulating, limit time and provide for a cooldown afterward to help them process and decompress.

- Remember that time is a human construct; it really doesn't need to dictate your life. Try turning back all the clocks in your home, or get sleeping bags and do a camp in or camp out under the stars. Take an old-fashioned road trip where you get in the car and ramble on routes you don't know. Ask people for directions. Let Spirit guide you. Allow the kids to pick which way you turn. Buy things that are less than a dollar. Have a picnic. Forget your cell phone.

●●

The New Children: A Closer Look

by Carol Crestetto, Ph.D.

Carol Crestetto knows about child education! After more than 25 years as an educator and consultant providing services for children, youth, and young adults with a variety of learning abilities and challenges (from severely disabled to highly gifted), Carol conducted original research and completed a doctoral dissertation entitled The "New Children:" A Multidisciplinary Study of Humanity's Shifting Sensitivity.

Holding both traditional and Montessori education credentials, an M.S. in holistic education counseling, and board certification as a senior-disability analyst and diplomate from the American Board of Disability Analysts, Carol is well qualified to assist people of all ages with the challenges they face in learning and education. She has worked to bridge practical learning and behavioral needs with a broadened understanding of her clients' often remarkable, but unrecognized, gifts and abilities.

Retired now, Carol is working on a series of stories for young children (and the young child in all of us) that introduce, bridge, and strengthen understanding of, and connection with, the fast-paced changes and underlying spiritual shifting of energies and sensitivities that so many are now experiencing.

●●

The "new" children (very wise spirits in children's bodies, placed in a challenging family, school, or world scene) are in the spotlight today. We say that they've come to change the world. They're healers and psychics. They're the new badge of motherhood. Soon, we may even replace the "My kid made straight A's at such-and-such school" bumper sticker with "My kid's an Indigo." There's a very legitimate need and desire to understand them; and there is, unfortunately, also a lot of hype. How do we sort it all out? How can we help? What follows is one view.

I'm not sure when it was that I began to realize that what I was seeing in many of my students and private clients went beyond their diagnoses. I'd always been fairly intuitive, and I knew that I saw my students and clients differently from others' views. As an educator and consultant for more than 25 years, I spent the last 15 or so years working mostly with children and youth (kindergarten through grade 12, along with young adults) who were seriously struggling to deal with the schools and educational processes in which they found themselves. The local school district assigned students to me as a home instructor. Most were ill or had other issues that kept them from attending regular classes for an extended period. As a private consultant, I also met with children who were wrestling with various learning, behavioral, and health issues. In addition to these difficulties, youngsters were also challenged with questions of who they were and how they fit into their families, their social environments, and the lives they were living. Each had a different story, yet many shared a common thread. Some were diagnosed as variously disabled: learning disorder (LD), nonverbal learning disorder (NLD), ADD, ADHD, or AS. Others had a variety of different challenges that kept them from regular participation in the traditional systems. One was simply described by a school administrator as "odd."

But there I was in the mid-1980s, beginning to see children who I thought were a departure from most I'd worked with before. They still bore the usual diagnoses and labels; they were still tested and treated in the same ways. But to my way of thinking, they were different—not necessarily "disabled" so much as "differently abled." These were children who learned differently, functioned differently, perceived differently, and were frequently not understood by one or several of the adults in their lives.

This isn't to diminish the diagnoses they'd been given. Some were definitely diagnosed correctly. Others were certainly quite "disabled" for the circumstances in which they found themselves. Many had grown so frustrated and disillusioned by their parents, teachers, or society that they'd developed poor behaviors and "disabled" school functioning as a result. Nor would I begin to suggest that parents hadn't done or weren't doing all they knew how to do in order to make life work for their kids. Most mothers and fathers devoted every bit of energy they had to that end. But what I kept seeing with many of these clients was that something else was going on that didn't fit into the typical diagnostic definitions as we know them.

Correct diagnosis or not, even administrators at the school district began to notice that I seemed to reach these youngsters at a level others didn't. It was fairly easy for an intuitive person to "see through" some of their behaviors. I saw more of who they really were—and on some level, they knew it. Parents would say things such as, "You can get her to do things that she won't do for anyone else," or "He seems so much calmer around you." There was even the young client who told me once, "If everyone who had problems came to you, we'd sure live in a nicer world."

For a long time I didn't use the labels (Indigo or the like); I just worked with the kids as they came to me. Then I, too, began to use (probably overuse) them. However, I learned fairly quickly from these youngsters that such characterizations aren't really helpful. As my son used to tell me, "Mom, it's all just labels!" As a general rule, I don't see energy, so I had no idea if they were really Indigo or not. I could readily identify what I saw in my students and clients from the descriptions given in the "Indigo books." Yet I also noticed patterns that weren't really mentioned, or maybe I just saw some traits differently.

In any case, these youngsters thought "outside the box." Some seemed to understand complex issues or processes without going through the usual steps to get their answers. They would simply know things. Some—even at a fairly early age—would see social or educational conflicts, or political or environmental issues from a very unusual perspective. They seemed to have solutions that soared beyond current rhetoric and rules.

Many of these children seemed truly uncomfortable or uncertain of their physicalness, as though no one had ever instructed them in "How to Be in Your Body." Some were very dexterous for one or two activities (usually a physical skill combined with mental passion), but were quite clumsy and awkward elsewhere. Others weren't very coordinated no matter what they were doing. Still others had visual-spatial issues, yet not the "usually diagnosed" ones. It seemed as if they could take in information visually in a format beyond our grasp, yet they had difficulty seeing in the usual ways. But they also had no idea that everybody couldn't see the way they did. (Typical visual-integration activities helped some of them to a degree but never quite got the job done.) They just couldn't get their body (or vision) to do what others expected—or what most of us take for granted.

Still, the problem was often more in others' perception of them than in their own concern about being able to do as others did. The story of "Kirby" (not his real name) illustrates beautifully both what this could look like and what could make all the difference in the life of such a child.

Kirby: Disabled or Different?

This was a child who, in nearly any public-school classroom, would have been labeled with some "diagnosis" very quickly. Watching his energy, some might have called him ADHD. Others (after much testing and trial) would surely have said he had nonverbal learning disorder (NLD). He had all the "signs and symptoms." His father described him as "accident-prone" since he constantly fell over furniture, tripped over nothing, and fell sideways out of his chair. Both parents reported that he'd had numerous mishaps, broken bones, bruises, and even a couple of concussions. He was an avid reader and loved to pursue his often-mature interests, although math and handwriting were a struggle. He was clearly challenged to sit still and get his work done in a classroom. In addition to these, Kirby could talk—faster and more excitedly, and on a wider variety of subjects than any kid I'd ever seen! He seemed to have a rote memory of every fact or figure he had ever heard or read.

We've probably all heard the statement: "He can't walk and chew gum at the same time." Well, this was true of Kirby. I watched him daily sit and try to do paperwork activities such as math or writing tasks. He perched like a bird, with his toes on the seat of the chair, wrapping them around the front edge of the chair seat. (He just couldn't sit on his bottom in a chair.) He then leaned over the table or desk, and as soon as his hand picked up the pencil and started to write, he fell out of the chair onto the floor! If you picked up any book on NLD, you'd think you were reading the story of Kirby's life.

But Kirby was a fortunate boy. He was the only child of parents who not only loved him very much, but also were blessed with enough wealth to provide an unusual but interesting life for him. The family spent about half the year on the southern end of the eastern U.S. coast and the rest of the year on north-central part of the western U.S. coast. His father spent most of each week working in a third location at the far north of the eastern seaboard. He "commuted" home on weekends. This certainly wasn't the average American childhood.

Kirby went to a private school most of the time, but around spring break each year, he and his mom moved back to their home on the far shore. There, Kirby was homeschooled for the remainder of the school term. At that point, his dad would commute to the opposite side of the country, so the spring and summer could be spent in that other home. His parents had begun Kirby's early education in a Montessori school, where he learned to work independently, following his own interests. The current private elementary school he attended, structured more traditionally, was the sort of place that encouraged pursuing personal academic interests, as long as it could be done within the curriculum and the parameters of the class requirements. The staff willingly made some adjustments so that Kirby could leave before the completion of the year, bringing some specific work and general requirements to the homeschool situation for completion.

Because in a Montessori school, children typically have the choice to work on their activities on the floor (on small mats or rugs), no one really noticed him falling out of chairs in those early years. His parents accommodated his quirky way of sitting, allowing him to read, work, and play on the floor as he chose, so again, it didn't come up too much. (Both parents did mention that meals were often a struggle because he would perch in the chair, pick up the fork, and fall off the seat.) He was a happy child, and obviously so bright and well spoken that no one ever considered that he might have a disability.

Because Kirby was born into a family with means and with a relaxed view of his differences, they saw him as unique, very bright, and quite *able*—not *dis*abled at all. As a result, they supported his gifts and abilities and simply didn't fret over things he did differently. He's probably an Indigo, although of course, I never saw his energy field. He functions very differently, perceives equally differently, and is certainly not disabled! He was fortunate to be born into the circumstances he was. With another set of parents, other school circumstances, or a family determined to find out "what's wrong with him," he would most likely have been "in trouble" with his teachers, tested by the school psychologist, diagnosed, and labeled. Had this occurred, he might have been given designer drugs to control his oddities and ultimately, in frustration and depression, have developed some very challenging behaviors in order to cope.

How We Understand

This is a key for all of our children. Each of them—each of *us*—is unique. While there are, of course, many devastating disabilities, many of the ones we call learning disabilities are, at least in part, some manifestation of the inability to fit late 20th- and early 21st-century youngsters into the structure, rules, and curricular demands of schools still built on principles from late the 19th- and early 20th-century. Often, very bright or differently gifted students become bored, disillusioned, or stifled by suffocating and controlling school environments. Others are held captive by their circumstances in inner-city schools and neighborhoods where mere survival keeps them from even wondering about life or consciousness beyond "right here and right now."

Many leaders in the field agree that our schools are a causal breeding ground for many of the difficulties we see in our children. How much worse is it for those kids who actually perceive from a higher perspective? How difficult must it be for the ones who see energy around people, read the thoughts and feelings of their teachers, and have sensitivities that aren't understood by the adults who care for them? Can it be that this is a large contributing factor to the problems and frustrations many of these children and young people experience?

We learned at first that these new children were "systems busters"—kids who'd come to shake things up and change the world. But before long, some people began to paint with a broader brush, calling every childhood difference a new Indigo trait. Some began to suggest that they were all psychic or could do laying-on-hands healing. That certainly wasn't my experience of them. Children like that were certainly out there, but most of the ones I encountered had different distinctions. They perceived the world differently, but presented as having great difficulties—they just didn't fit into our obsolete systems and mind-sets.

Sadly, children with serious challenges in school or legitimately diagnosed health or learning issues were often relabeled as Indigo (by desperate parents or misguided teachers) to salve the pain that came with "being identified." It's certainly natural to want to know that your child is unique in a "good" way, or to be stunned by a diagnosis and wish to avoid disability labels. To call them "Indigo" might be the perfect way out. But not all children with disability labels are Indigos, and not all Indigos are seen as disabled. Like *all* children everywhere, each is different in both abilities and gifts. "New" children have the same full range of possibilities as other children. And we must remember: in spirit, they chose their parents and their circumstances as a way to bring their messages to us. When our children have "good" gifts, like telepathy or healing abilities we're thrilled (if, perhaps, somewhat frightened at first). It's the ones who don't fit our "perfect pictures," who don't excel, who will always cause us the most pain.

As a society, we've tried to integrate a higher level of understanding of our children into an "old thinking" brain. We turned Indigo Children into a "separate," "better," "higher" kind of child—a status symbol among soccer moms. But the kids today show us that the new vision can't readily integrate into the old ways and the Old World. In the same way that the hippies of the '60s tried to integrate the ideals of true freedom and unconditional love into the consciousness of their day but couldn't quite change the world to what they saw, we now try to idealize "Indigo-ness" into our old paradigm without upgrading how we do parenting, education, and the business of the day. The hippies couldn't yet integrate what they saw into their old programmed way of thinking. They turned it into bra burning, flag burning, and "free love" (promiscuity). They saw something new, but could not put that "new wine" into "old wineskins," as stated in the biblical books of Matthew and Luke.

What they *could* do—and *did* do—was to open the door, to break down the tightest controls, and shed a new light into some dark places. We now see the vision of "new kids" and "higher consciousness," yet many are still trying to put that vision into the old skins of our lower consciousness. We're going to have to change much of how we live our lives before these children (or any new children) can be free to share all of their gifts.

How Do We Help?

Over the years, I did find some things that helped those early children and youth who were trying to bring a higher awareness into our lives. Much like Kirby's parents, the first thing I did was to acknowledge their gifts and strengths and accept their differences as their own unique signature. When I met with them, I did my best to treat them not like people I was "in charge of," not as being less than myself, but with the respect I would show to younger peers or colleagues. When one had an idea that completely differed from the required class assignment, we discussed how she could do the work in her own way while still meeting the school's demands. When another felt a rule was "stupid," we explored together why the rules and requirements were there, what they were for, and why they were necessary. We even laughed sometimes over how absurd an occasional rule really was! But we always persevered and worked on problems until we could reach an agreement and in some appropriate way complete the work that the school required.

When needed, I acted as a liaison with the teachers and administration to open or broaden their understanding of ways that rules or curriculum could be approached uniquely for different children, with no extra teacher time, while still meeting all education requirements. By helping these kids understand "the system" and recognize that there are different acceptable ways of fulfilling demands made upon them, our work together allowed them to express who they were at their core. This helped them learn how to work within the boundaries needed to keep them safe and at the same time meet the specific expectations of home and school.

Through many years of observing and listening to children (and their parents), I also studied and practiced different modalities that showed promise. I was eventually guided to develop a protocol, Integrative Repatterning, that has been extremely helpful for many children challenged by anger, frustration, body disconnects, and learning issues, among other difficulties. I believe it's so successful because it addresses their needs on several levels. It works with body, mind, emotions, and spirit. Although I put together several components to effect a broad and lasting change, I believe that *any* of the individual components, if matched to the needs of the child, could be quite effective.

Integrative Repatterning is a gentle, noninvasive, emotional-processing activity that allows a person to reframe and release the distracting and debilitating patterns of behavior that stand in the way of personal success and well-being. This process relaxes mental and emotional tension, which may then free personal energy to be used in more productive ways. Specifically guided eye movements, acupressure release points, coached breath-work, Interactive Guided Imagery^{SM}, and conscious verbal guidance form the core of this deeply relaxing process. The sessions take place with a background of specifically created music that has been shown to promote the integration of the right and left hemispheres of the brain. There are additional vision activities for those who have vision-related imbalances.

Clients have reported relief from anxiety, fear, upsetting memories, phobias, depression, feelings of powerlessness, low self-esteem, and lack of self-confidence. The process is received and used differently by each person. In many cases, learning disabilities also improve as relaxation and fuller access to the self became available. This natural and holistic process assists those who are feeling the effects of traumatic occurrences and everyday stresses. It stimulates a self-healing response and can restore perspective, making it integrated, appropriate, and functional. Most people describe a deep sense of relaxation and well-being as a result of their participation with this work. I continue to learn and add new information to the process as it becomes available to me.

Any child born into today's world is bound to feel the tension and turmoil of the economic, political, and personal circumstances of our times. Being a "new kid" (as I said, a very wise spirit in a child's body in a challenging family, school, or world scene) simply adds to that tension and turmoil. The individual pieces of Integrative Repatterning each bring their own kind of help. Certain guided eye movements appear to desensitize or "unlock" the intense feelings that are locked into the neural pathways in the brain. This can free up those routes for more peaceful and creative uses. It can also stimulate new neural pathways to form, giving greater access to one's possibilities and potentials. Acupressure release points and coached breath-work have been used by Indian, Chinese, and other cultures for centuries to release the blocked chi (energy) in order to bring healing and balance to body, mind, and spirit. Breath-work also assists relaxation and the release of debilitating emotional "baggage" while bringing clarity and well-being. Interactive Guided Imagery^SM is a way of using a person's own inner images in an interactive way for self-education and self-healing.

Doctoral Research

I began to wonder, even back then, what it was that made the perceptions of these young people so unlike what we were accustomed to seeing in our homes and classrooms. Was there an objective way to understand what we were seeing intuitively? This curiosity led me to a new exploration. I'm currently doing research for a doctoral dissertation and a subsequent book on the *science* of understanding these children. I've been gathering data on today's children and youth, and even adults, looking at several aspects of life. My questions explore areas such as educational and learning experiences, social awareness and social experiences, health and wellness issues, feeling and emotional responses, and perceived identity (if any) as one of the classifications of "new children" (that is, do they or their parents perceive them to be an Indigo, Crystal, Star, or the like?).

These questions will allow me to ascertain initial general information from respondents. From this, I expect to discern patterns (if any) between the various components of subjects' lives and their possible correlation to the classification as "new children." Of course, these questions are answered by parents for their children, or by older youth and adults for themselves, and are therefore very subjective. *All* interested participants are invited to fill out the questionnaires, whether they are or aren't (or don't know whether they are) such a "new person." This encourages more varied comparisons, and *allows me a window into people's understanding of these concepts.* (Many individuals of all ages have reported themselves to be Indigo, Crystal, and several other possible choices.)

From this initial research, I may contact selected individuals for follow-up interviews to gain further in-depth understanding of their subjective experiences. The questionnaire is available on the Website: **www.placeoflight.net**, through the generous assistance of Susan Gale, co-author with Peggy Day of a book about Edgar Cayce and the Indigo Children.

Although the research is in its infancy, there already appear to be trends in the data regarding general understanding of the "new children." Of course, it's way too early to draw any conclusions. At the time of this writing, the questionnaires are still coming in. Until all are received, recorded, and evaluated, it will be impossible to know what patterns will emerge. It appears, however, that even at this early date, there's much confusion and misinformation about the true nature and characteristics of these children. Perhaps people are still *very* confused about the terms used to describe these kids. Maybe myths and tall tales are being perpetuated by the well-meaning but misinformed. Or conceivably, as the world gets more chaotic every day, we all yearn for a "new" group of people to "save us all." Is this just the sort of promise we need to get through the day? Or could there be another possibility? Could the children and youth be changing things right now—not just as "systems busters," but in a way we haven't yet noticed? Maybe their higher vibrational energy, their new awareness, is having an effect on us that's easily explained by simple physics.

You've probably heard of "entrainment." In physics, it's a "process whereby two connected oscillating systems, having similar periods, fall into synchrony." In psychology, it refers to one person responding to or mimicking another person. Explained differently, it means that when two forces, fields, people, systems, or the like are in close proximity to each other (living or working together), they'll tend to synchronize their vibrational frequencies. Pendulum clocks placed together will start to swing at the same time, women who work together will begin to have their monthly cycles simultaneously, and so forth. It's my belief that these children, even while they're still young, are lifting our vibrational frequencies, our consciousness levels, to match up with their own. This is part of the reason that many older adults, who by the definitions given couldn't be "Indigos" or "Crystals," feel as though they are. This is human evolution in the making. It's this notion that my research intends to explore.

Conclusion

There's a definite need to really look at what we're experiencing with this ever-expanding awareness of our new children. Intuitives have provided a great service by introducing us to these individuals. They continue to assist our understanding by bringing books and Websites to our attention. What began as people on the "fringe" knowing that something had changed has now moved on so that mainstream professionals are looking more closely at the phenomena and traditional media are bringing it to the public. We can hope to see more legitimate research and study as more and more information is shared. Soon enough, it will be impossible to deny the change. It's up to us, the grassroots movement of real people, to open perception around us.

When we adhere to rules and regulations without questioning their appropriateness, follow the school structures that have come to us from the early 1900s and before, and then make the same parenting mistakes that were made by our parents and theirs before them, we begin to realize that there's a lot of room for improvement. Aware parents and educators have begun to try different approaches. But it is *not easy* to treat kids like peers or colleagues when you have 20 to 30 bustling and clamoring students before you. Neither is it always possible to sit down and explain rules when you need to get dinner on the table, help with homework, finish the laundry, and put a child's younger siblings to bed.

We must still do the best we can to make time to listen to the children and to allow them to express their ideas and concerns. We have to teach them to express themselves respectfully and then create ways of working that actually allow their true brilliance to come through. Anything less is allowing ourselves to think in 19th- or early 20th-century ways.

Where once we saw children as those who "should be seen and not heard," we now understand that young people have a legitimate contribution to make. Those who came of age in the '60s were probably the first generation who, as a whole group, publicly rejected the notion of quiet, complacent youth who blindly followed the rules. Today's children take us to the next level. Young people today have a lot to say and much to offer—even more than in the '60s. But to hear and understand them, we must first *listen* to what they're saying. They won't always be right. They may not even be close! But if we don't listen, we can't know what they're thinking, or how to direct them to a clearer understanding. And worse, we'll miss the times when they have a revolutionary idea that could bring about real change. When we control, schedule, rush, or ignore them through their days and their childhoods, we stifle, or miss out completely on the gifts they have to share.[5]

• •

Ten Ways We Misunderstand Children

by Jan Hunt, M.Sc.

---

*Jan Hunt is the director of The Natural Child Project at **natural child.org**, a parenting counselor, and the author of <u>The Natural Child: Parenting From the Heart</u> and the children's book <u>A Gift for Baby.</u> She and her son Jason have just co-edited a new book, <u>The Unschooling Unmanual,</u> a collection of essays by Jan and seven other writers, including Daniel Quinn, the author of <u>Ishmael.</u>*

*Jan has more than 20 years of experience writing about attachment parenting and unschooling issues. She offers telephone counseling worldwide, with a focus on solutions that meet the needs of both parents and children. For more information or to schedule a session, visit: **www .naturalchild.org/counseling**.*

••

1. We expect children to be able to do things before they're ready. We ask an infant to keep quiet. We ask a two-year-old to sit still. We ask a four-year-old to clean his room. In all of these situations, we're being unrealistic. We're setting ourselves up for disappointment and setting up the child for repeated failures to please us. Yet many parents ask their young children to do things that even an older child would find difficult. In short, we ask children to stop acting their age.

2. We become angry when a child fails to meet our needs. A child can only do what he can do. If a child can't do something we ask, it's unfair to expect or demand more, and anger only makes things worse. A two-year-old can only act like a two-year-old, a five-year-old can't act like a ten-year-old, and a ten-year-old can't behave like an adult! To expect more is unrealistic and unhelpful. There are limits to what a child can manage, and if we don't accept those limits, it can only result in frustration on both sides.

3. We mistrust the child's motives. If a child can't meet our needs, we assume that he's being defiant. To determine the truth of the matter, we need to look closely at the situation from the child's point of view. In reality, a "defiant" child may be ill, tired, hungry, in pain, responding to an emotional or physical hurt, or struggling with a hidden problem such as a food allergy. Yet we seem to overlook these possibilities while thinking the worst about the child's "personality."

4. We don't allow children to be children. We somehow forget what it was like to be a child ourselves and expect the child to act like an adult instead of acting his age. A healthy child will be rambunctious, noisy, and emotionally expressive and will have a short attention span. All of these so-called problems aren't really problems at all, but are in fact normal qualities of a normal child. Rather, it's our society and its expectations of perfect behavior that are abnormal.

5. We get it backward. We expect and demand that the child meet our needs—for quiet, for uninterrupted sleep, for obedience to our wishes, and on and on. Instead of accepting our parental role to meet the *child's* needs, we expect the child to care for ours. We can become so focused on our own unmet needs and frustrations that we forget this is a child who has needs of her own that she can't meet herself.

6. We blame and criticize when a child makes a mistake. Children have had very little experience in life, and they'll inevitably make mistakes. This is a natural part of learning at any age. Instead of understanding and helping the child, we blame him, as though he should be able to learn everything perfectly the first time. To err is human; to err in childhood is human and unavoidable. Yet we react to each mistake, infraction of a rule, or so-called misbehavior with surprise and disappointment. It makes no sense to understand that a child will make mistakes and then to react as though we think the child should behave perfectly at all times.

7. We forget how deeply blame and criticism can hurt a child. Many parents are coming to understand that physically hurting a child is wrong and harmful, yet many of us forget how painful angry words, insults, and blame can be to a child who can only believe that he's inadequate, incompetent, and unloved.

8. We forget how healing loving actions can be. We fall into vicious cycles of blame and misbehavior instead of stopping to give the child love, reassurance, self-esteem, and security with hugs and kind words. As Mother Teresa wrote, "Kind words can be short and easy to speak, but their echoes are truly endless."

9. We forget that our behavior provides the most potent lessons to the child. It's truly "not what we say but what we do" that the child takes to heart. A parent who hits a child for hitting, telling him that hitting is wrong, is in fact teaching that hitting is right—at least for those in power. It's the parent who responds to problems with peaceful solutions who's teaching the child how to be a peaceful adult. Problems and challenges present our best opportunities for teaching values, because children learn most effectively when they're learning about real-life situations.

10. We see only the outward behavior, not the love and good intentions inside the child. When a child's behavior disappoints us, we should—more than anything else we do—"assume the best." We should assume that the child means well and is behaving as well as possible, considering all the circumstances (both obvious and hidden from us), together with his level of experience in life. If we always assume the best about our child, the child will be free to do his best. If we give only love, love is all we will receive.

• •

Lee: Jan and I have to tell you that although this is the official end of the "Educators" chapter, we received many more submissions to this area than we could ever print. Some of the contributors you've just read presented several articles! We've been overwhelmed with good, positive input from the educators of the world, and we wish to go on record in thanking them all for their work, especially those who submitted articles that space didn't allow us to include.

• • • • •

Chapter Two

Indigos at Work

"Oh my God—they're in the workplace!"
— Lee Carroll

I'd like to attribute the above quote to someone really important, someone whom history might recognize as wise. However, the statement was made by *me*, Lee Carroll, as I slowly realized that my professional life was being affected by Indigos who were invading my space everywhere I went.

Jan and I travel a lot, but I'm the travel king. I'm on 12 airplanes a month, doing at least 50 meetings in the United States a year and about 10 more in foreign lands—really exotic places, like Moscow and Latvia. So over the years, I've become accustomed to navigating through airports. I know what to expect, how to maneuver within the travel industry, how to make it comfortable for all, and how to have it work for me . . . until the Indigos arrived, that is.

Now, I'm going to offend some folks here, but hey, it seems I do that for a living anytime I present this bizarre proposition that the human race is shifting. So I'll apologize up front for being insensitive or politically incorrect as I tell you that the new kids are finding jobs in places that are taking a big "hit" in terms of their company's service. You see, the Indigos aren't born to serve. (Did I really have to say that? You knew that, huh?)

They Simply Don't Want to Be Servers

I'm finding Indigos taking my orders at fast-food counters, trying to check me in at hotels and motels (hotels are using them at the front desk!), being pseudowaiters in restaurants, and taking other "service" jobs. The employers giving them these positions are obviously clueless that they've hired human beings who have no intention of following in the footsteps of those who learned to "serve with a smile."

This isn't an indictment of Indigos at all, just a fact! These kids are *not* here to hold these jobs, and they aren't suited for them. In fact, they don't even know they *can't* do them. They just know that they get fired a lot for . . . uh . . . "lack of motivation." What they actually have is "lack of any desire to do a service job." When they're told what's wrong, they can't believe it.

They say, "You want me to lie, not be myself, pretend I like my surroundings and my co-workers, bow and scrape to people who don't deserve it, clean the toilets and like it, not argue with the customers even though they're fools, and do it all fast and efficiently?"

"Yes we do!" the boss says. "Others before you did so. That's the job!"

"Forget it!" they exclaim, and off they go to apply somewhere else to repeat the process.

I can't tell you the number of times I've rolled into a city after 11 P.M. and tried to check into a hotel. Out comes the front-desk agent with the word *Indigo* practically stenciled across their forehead (at least in my eyes). I'm holding two bags, a projector, and my coat (in my teeth). I've just had to forcefully back into the lobby through obstinate double doors. Even some of the best airport hotels often don't include doors that actually open automatically. Go figure. There I am, facing the only link I'll ever have between me and the president of the hotel chain. The young person usually isn't exactly what that first contact used to be, or at least what the hotel would like it to be.

"What happened to your hair?" I want to ask.

"Wow . . . how did that piece of metal get in your lip?" I want to say. "Is it hard to eat spaghetti?" I've always wanted to ask that . . . and the big one about how to position yourself for kissing without becoming tangled. However, I don't say any of those judgmental things. After all, we had our stuff when I was young, too. The difference is that we stopped with the pink and green hair and long sideburns right about college, and never (ever) took it with us when we applied for a job at the bank.

"Wow . . . what is that long white strand of spaghetti coming out of each ear? Are you listening to the ball game?"

I don't say that either, but I'm aware that I'm competing with some kind of music on an MP3 device, and this young person isn't going to miss a beat of it because of me. Unless, that is, I earn it.

First interaction: silence, but with eye contact.

This is when I know who I'm dealing with. Silence with eye contact isn't normal, unless you're being carjacked, but an Indigo will size you up and wait.

Continuing contact: the Indigo, waiting to find out what I want.

You'd think that my presence with luggage at that hour, in a lobby that has no other persons in it would be a giveaway, but this desk official is going to wait until I state my needs. There used to be a day when protocol words would spill out of the clerks' mouths: "Can I help you?"

Now, I've gotten used to walking straight up to the counter and saying: "I'd like you to help me."

"Are you checking in?" the Indigo asks.

"No, I'm a luggage salesman and wish to knock on the door of every room in your hotel until someone buys one of the beat-up suitcases I have in each hand," I'm tempted to say. But instead I say, "Yes, please," and give a big smile. "I'm so glad you're here!"

Bingo! Things start to change. When I start to show respect to whoever is in front of me at that moment (male or female . . . sometimes hard to know due to the hardware, odd hair, and bulky clothing . . . they know but we don't), attitudes begin to change. I've just done something that's counterintuitive to travel: serve the servers! I never place myself above them, even though I know I'm the client and they know that they're the desk clerks. Then I start my Indigo-communication drill.

"Boy, it must be hard on you to have to stay up and work this late."

I mean it. I would never want that job! But how often do we verbalize that? I ask about their lives, where they're headed, and what they want to do (never about their hair).

Smile with eye contact—I'm in!

Then a barrage of verbiage begins, no matter what the age difference between us (normally vast). They've found a friend in the middle of the night. I get water, I get an extra pillow . . . and on it goes. Imagine that! And all I did was to treat them as an equal and *not care* about protocol—an Indigo attribute to the max!

This is harder to do when you're ordering a hamburger. Oops! I just got busted, but yes, sometimes when traveling, you just have to get what smells the best at whatever airport gate you're going to live at for a while, and the golden arches beckon. In those cases, just talk to the order takers as though you're collectively disgusted with having to be there (even if you're really enjoying yourself in the airport). It isn't hard, and you'll get your smile. They just want to know that you're *not* going to look down on them, and that you're all in the same boat . . . er, airport.

What you should *not* do is have expectations of service! Don't believe me? Watch for it. For someday, you're going to have to work for things you used to assume would naturally happen. Trust me. The days of "Can I help you?" are slowly slipping away. You're going to have to learn to say, "Here is how you can help me" quite a lot—and with a smile, not a snarl of disappointment. You're going to have to earn that service. What a concept!

If you complain? Forget it! It doesn't work. Instead, you earn a zero in the department of "needing to be alive on Earth," and you'll get the opposite reaction than you expected. Remember the phrase "the squeaky wheel gets the grease"? That means if you complain and raise your voice, you'll probably get what you want faster than the guy next to you. Not with an Indigo! With them, it's "the squeaky wheel gets the boot." At least that's the way it feels. I've watched so many instances where the complainers make it worse and worse at the hamburger counter, digging holes for themselves that only the manager can get them out of. They don't get results; they get a cold hamburger with limp fries. And the Indigos? They're nowhere in sight. They simply turned it over to "someone who's paid to care."

What Bosses Have to Say

Added to this is something that several business owners have recently told me, and normally without any knowledge that I was "the Indigo author guy." These conversations took place on airplanes and at dinners, generally with managers and owners who just wanted to talk about how things were changing for them in the workplace. Almost without exception, their complaint about the "new workforce" was the same: the kids don't want to "pay their dues." They want raises after 90 days! This gets back to what appears to be a spoiled "entitlement" attitude, but it really isn't. That's one of the keys to understanding these new young people. They aren't spoiled, wanting things just because they exist. Instead, they have a consciousness of *having already paid* their dues. In other words, they don't want something for nothing. They have an innate sense that their mission is far beyond what's being asked of them at the hamburger stand. They have a feeling that they've "been there, done that." Ask them; they'll tell you . . . if you gain their trust, that is.

This is all part of the "respect" theme that you're going to hear over and over in this book. Throw away the protocol, the age differences, and the social status. These new humans don't care about any of that! And if *you* care and expect things to be the way they always were, then you're in for a wild and frustrating ride.

A Confidential Story

Let me tell you a funny story about Indigos in the service business. Shhhh . . . it's a secret, so don't tell anyone you heard it here. It's a story that only the travel agents know and only those in a certain state of the Union, which is surrounded by water and where you pay to watch someone bury a pig and another someone dances with a grass skirt (not the pig).

Let me describe our annual cruise. We take one each year for those who wish to join us for a week of travel and fun. We have seminars; talk about subjects such as Indigos, metaphysics, and science; present wonderful music; and generally have a great time. We're experienced cruisers, having gone on many trips with many cruise lines over the years. We know what to expect, but on the trip I'm thinking of, we were about to have a very unusual experience.

The setup was this: the cruise lines were using massive amounts of fuel and wasting days of excursion-profit time going from this U.S. island state to a small atoll in the Pacific, located near the equator and called Fanning Island. By law, each foreign-flagged cruise ship had to touch a foreign (non-U.S.) port. As you might also know, most of the cruise lines are based out of Norway, since the Norwegians are the only people on earth who know how to run a cruise ship. (Hey, I'm just giving you what I was told by the captain!) Therefore, the ships traveled 1,200 miles in each direction to fulfill the rule. Imagine the fuel they used! Somebody once told me that it was about a gallon a foot, or something outrageous like that.

So the cruise-ship companies made a deal with the bury-a-pig-in-a-grass-skirt island-state officials. If the cruise lines would stop using the traditional Filipino, Jamaican, and Romanian stewards and servers and instead employ the local island young people, the ships wouldn't have to do the "touch a foreign port" trip anymore. What a deal! And the Norwegians all said, "Ja" (unless they were from Sort-land, and then they said "Jo"—sorry, another cruise joke).

On this specific cruise, we, the unsuspecting passengers, didn't know that we'd be some of the first to experience the "new breed" of servers who'd just been trained. And you guessed it: they were mostly Indigos!

On board this new cruise, we spent a week trying to figure out why each meal was taking up to three hours, and the sheets in the cabins were never smooth and sometimes not even white. And there were no towel animals! (These are towels twisted into animal facsimiles and left on your bed at night when you return to your cabin.) That's enough to make you want to jump overboard. Towel animals—that's why you cruise!

The "waiters" in the fine white-glove restaurants were having trouble pronouncing the names of the dishes, not to mention the wines, and probably had great difficulty in putting on the gloves, too. Salad dressings were arriving up to 30 minutes after the salads. Then, when the much-requested dressing finally came to the table, we realized that the servers were clueless about the fact that it actually belonged together with the greens. We were all in formal dress, but we had the feeling these young waiters were all wearing jeans under their serving outfits.

They tried. They really did, since they wanted these coveted jobs. But Indigos just don't work as servers. As we spoke to them, we had to laugh. Not one of them was going to do it again next year! They were all "trying it out," and most didn't care to try it again. At this rate, a crew of more than 1,000 servers per ship would be impossible to recruit from the island state! They might actually have to find someone else to work these jobs.

I don't know what the final result has been, for that was more than a year ago. Someone told me that there was a sudden influx of Filipino, Jamaican, and Romanian young people moving to the islands to be eligible for their old jobs . . . a very funny thing if it's true.

Those Who Follow in this Chapter

So what follows is a more authoritative discussion on Indigos in the workplace. It's from the pros: the ones who hire and fire and who are watching all this happen. Believe me, it's making an impact. My funny stories are fodder for boardroom discussions all over the world, for they're happening to everyone.

Again, take a good look at the credentials of the authors in this chapter. The few Jan and I selected here aren't just managers. They're captains of industry who have graciously agreed to step out and be part of this book. Our great thanks to each of them.

••

Insights from Indigo High-School and College Students

by Bruce I. Doyle III, Ph.D.

Bruce I. Doyle III is the president of Growth Dynamics International (GDI). GDI is focused on providing interim "C" level management, business consulting, leadership development, and executive coaching to forward-thinking leaders in order to facilitate business transformation that's driven by values, integrity, and employee passion.

Bruce held positions at GE as engineering manager and venture manager; at Ingersoll Rand as worldwide marketing manager; at Varian Semiconductor Equipment Associates, Inc., as general manager for semiconductor equipment; at Pulse Engineering, Inc., as division manager and director of emerging technologies; at Scientific Control Systems as senior vice president for strategy development; at Systems Control as COO; and at Impres as president and CEO.

As a business consultant and executive coach, Bruce has worked with clients such as IBM; Nortel Networks; TI; Apple, Inc.; Sumida Corporation; WD-40 Company; Tres-Ark, Inc.; Smartmicros; TCG Energy; CuraPharm, Inc.; RDX Technology; and Maxim Systems, Inc., on strategic planning, leadership development, executive selection, leading organizational change, and Six Sigma business-process improvement.

He holds B.S. and M.S. degrees in electrical engineering and a Ph.D. in leadership and organizational transformation. His doctoral dissertation was titled "Indigo Leadership and the Invisible Link: The Key to Bridging the Gaps in Business."

Bruce served on the boards of directors for Systems Control (Palo Alto, CA), Impres (Austin, TX), and The Center for Creative Living (San Diego, CA). He also served as vice president and board secretary for the San Diego Leadership Initiative and is currently on the Board of CuraPharm, Inc.; the business advisory board at UCSD's Rady School of Management; and National University's Leadership Advisory Board. He is board secretary for the Corporate Directors Forum.

In addition to Bruce's corporate background, he has a passion for human development—driven by his own personal work. He has completed the Warner Erhard Training (now Landmark Education), the Avatar® Masters Course and Wizards Programs, Hakomi Method, and is certified in Jin Shin Jyutsu®. Bruce is also very interested in how the Indigos will impact our future—especially in the workplace. His book Indigos in the Workplace: Paving the Way for Tomorrow's Leaders was released in 2008.

He recognizes the need for coaching individuals and businesses on the principle that "life experience is self-created." This understanding brings with it tremendous personal power. Bruce is dedicated to helping individuals achieve their full potential through the realization that their beliefs create their lives.

His 1994 personal growth book, Before You Think Another Thought, has been translated into Spanish, German, and Portuguese. His Website is entitled Indigo Executive, and you can find it here: **www .indigoexecutive.com.**

●●

"The responses to Bruce's survey reveal the best information about the Indigos that I have seen."
— Nancy Ann Tappe

There's an abundance of documented evidence that the Indigos are being recognized for their uniqueness, demonstrating their gifts, and making an impact on society at very young ages. Having spent more than 25 years as a senior executive in global corporate-leadership roles, I asked myself, *I wonder what's going to happen when the Indigos increasingly populate the workplace?*

I figured that the best way to find out how they think, what drives them, and how they see their future impact on the world was to ask them. To do so, I took the opportunity of fulfilling a portion of the requirements for completing my doctoral dissertation, "Indigo Leadership and the Invisible Link: The Key to Bridging the Gaps in Business," by conducting a survey of high-school and college students. This was done via a questionnaire that addressed the students' personal values, anticipated career choices, desired work environment, leadership preferences, and generational expectations and contributions. It also included a list of traits—attributed to Indigos—developed by Wendy H. Chapman, M.A. educational psychology, University of Connecticut, magna cum laude, and director of the Metagifted Education Resource Organization in Nashua, New Hampshire. The students were asked to select those characteristics from the Indigo list that best described them. The intent was to determine the extent to which the survey audience matched the Indigo attributes.

The questions were designed with open-ended responses to prevent any generational bias on my part. Questionnaires were distributed via hard copy and e-mail to friends and business associates around the world who had access to students; directly to students whom I encountered that were working part-time at banks, restaurants, and coffee shops; and by attending student-leadership events. One hundred completed questionnaires were tallied, analyzed, and profiled. A synopsis of the survey follows. The complete survey can be viewed at **www.indigoexecutive.com**.

Survey Synopsis

The survey audience of 100 students included slightly more college students (51 percent), slightly more females (57 percent), and a majority of Caucasian Americans (59 percent). Students participating from other countries included those from Mexico, England, France, Australia, Japan, Korea, Indonesia, Laos, and the Philippines.

Indigos have a strong passion for self-expression. In response to the question "What do you have a passion for in life?" 29 percent of the student responses related to self-expression through art, music, and writing. Self-expression related to helping and giving to others accounted for 21 percent, while 17 percent chose self-expression through athletics and outdoor activities. The remaining categories reflected the students' passion for expressing individuality, achieving life goals, and having loving family relationships.

Indigos are committed to facilitating change. In response to the question, "What are you committed to in your life?" 57 percent responded with statements that dealt with making changes and championing causes that would make life better for others. Commitment to reaching their personal goals was key for 30 percent of the students, and 13 percent were committed to being true to themselves—"being me" and "being myself."

Indigos have strong values. In response to the question, "What are your most important personal values?" 25 percent responded with statements that reflected positive self-defining attributes such as "staying true to my self," "freedom and independence," and "open-mindedness." Values related to integrity, trust, honesty, and loyalty accounted for 23 percent. The third-largest response category (19 percent) reflected ideals associated with displaying positive personal characteristics when relating to others: "caring/loving/compassionate," "empathy for others," and "respect for all—no matter what." The remaining categories reflected values related to family, friends, faith, and obtaining a good education.

Indigos have a strong inner self and aren't addicted to material possessions. In response to the question "What in life is really not important to you?" 29 percent responded with statements that reflect the triviality of things that would normally impact self-confidence or stature. Sample responses about what was unimportant included: "Being famous—I would prefer not to be," "Fitting in certain distinct groups of people," "What others think of me," and "The popular choice." Not caring about material things accounted for 26 percent of the responses, which included: "money, because it can't buy me happiness," "materialistic achievements," "fancy cars," and "amassing wealth."

Indigos want to work for people who care about them as individuals and are more interested in who the leaders are "being" rather than what they know or do. In response to the question "What are the most significant skills and personal attributes that you want in your company's leaders for you to feel supported in expressing your skills and talents?" 58 percent responded with comments that articulated the desire to have leaders who would develop a personal, caring relationship with them. Frequently mentioned qualities were: "open-minded and approachable," "cares about me," "good people skills," "supportive," "respectful," and "friendly/kind." The second-largest category (13 percent) reflected the need for leaders who demonstrate integrity, honesty, and trust. The answers covering intelligence and knowledge of the business came in third at 7 percent.

Survey Samples

Marc, a high-school student in San Jose, California, wrote the following response to the leadership question:

> For one, they must be very confident in their decisions. They have to be very social and open to debate and discussion upon any issue brought up while working. I believe they must follow guidelines, but enforce them in an environment that's friendly. They also must be human and have a comical side to them, so they don't feel intimidating. They must make themselves feel as equals to all in the company, not someone superior and top of the line. To push around with authority would only stress me out and make me want to leave the company.

Annette, a student in France, wrote:

He has to care for me, to want to teach me things or give me the information I need without resistance. He must delegate interesting tasks. Clear out tensions, have a sense of humor and not be stressed out each time there is a problem. Be trustworthy and be like a guide and help me to progress by showing me the way and giving me the opportunity. A good communicator that gives me feedback and that is patient. Know his job and do it well with integrity.

Indigo Desires

Indigos are diverse in their choice of future careers: 22 percent will be seeking to impact the world of corporate business, 19 percent will choose to make a difference in the field of education, 14 percent will pursue the freedom of self-employment, 11 percent will share their gifts in entertainment, 10 percent will contribute to health care and social work, 9 percent will work in small businesses, 8 percent will got into government, and 7 percent will go into law.

Indigos want to have fun in an efficiently run organization where self-expression and autonomy are nurtured. In response to the question "What are the desired characteristics of your working environment that will allow you to fully express your skills and talents and allow you to feel fulfilled?" 43 percent responded with answers that reflected the desire to work where it's "fun, peaceful, and well organized, with opportunities for self-expression and autonomy." Another 36 percent chose characteristics related to flexibility; teamwork; opportunities for continued learning; and the desire to interact with professional, honest, hardworking coworkers. Representative responses included: "lighthearted and not serious," "optimally running," and "somewhere I can be myself and not have to put on a fake front."

Sensitivity to Those Who Judge Them

Indigos see their challenges as being related to the diversity of values, limiting attitudes, and the need to address major social and economic issues. In response to the question "What do you feel are the biggest challenges facing your generation?" 37 percent responded with answers that reflected their concern for others unfairly judging them. Sample responses included: "Everybody looking at the negative aspects instead of the positive ones; judging people of my generation; making assumptions without knowing the whole story," "Our generation has been labeled with so many stereotypes that we've lost our real identity," and "Insecurities in general and lack of role models." The second-largest category (25 percent) reflected the harsh realities of the students' personal challenges. Responses included: "Discovering our self-worth and applying it to the harsh realities of life as we try to fit a niche within the political atmosphere around us," "Keeping up in school, saying no to the peer pressure (drugs, alcohol), and finding the right job," and "Competition with others." The third-largest category (20 percent) reflected the need for fixing major social problems: "Handling what's laid before us," "Finding ways to lead to unity which is becoming crucial—unity within ourselves, unity within our families (divorce rate is just too high), unity among countries (the military weapons are just too destructive), and unity with nature (healing the earth)."

New Ways of Thinking and Doing Things

Indigos want their generation to contribute their vision, skills, and intellect to create new thinking in the global workplace regarding diversity, values, ethics, technology, and purpose. In response to the question "What major contributions would you like to see your generation make that will positively impact the workplace and significantly enhance personal satisfaction in the workplace?" 39 percent responded with statements reflecting their desire to contribute to valuing people, promoting equality and diversity, and fostering cooperation among workers. Sample statements included: "Supporting a more diverse work environment," "Remember what it means to respect others," and "I would like to see the workplace look up to the team and not the hero, for without the weakest link there would be no strongest link."

The second-largest response category (20 percent) voiced the desire to contribute to change by driving new purpose and utilizing their skills and intellect to create vision with new thinking. Responses included: "I expect our generation to make an effort in helping make this world a better place and make a difference in people's lives, and the thing that could change is the Army—we don't need war," "A fresh new look or way of doing things," "Have a clear purpose of why?" and "Perhaps people of my generation being selected for jobs not based on appearance or leisure activities but on what they can bring to the company and their work ethic."

Indigo-Attributes Profile

I tallied the number of students who indicated that their behavior matched items on the Indigo-Attributes List (which follows) in order to determine the degree to which the survey audience matched the Indigo Attributes. An analysis of the students' self-defined behavior versus the questionnaire's Indigo Attributes approached a full normal distribution (bell curve), with the peak at 55 percent. It's expected that a larger survey sample would reveal a full normal distribution and that, as more Indigo children become students, the distribution will shift to the right due to the fact that the number of Indigos (as a percentage of those born) has steadily increased since the mid-'70s.

One student, Maria Hilario, matched all of the Indigo Attributes. A truly delightful Indigo, she scored a 100 percent match. This beautiful, energetic young lady stays very busy with her part-time job at a California Pizza Kitchen in San Diego, California, and her studies at Grossmont College. Maria wants to be a clinical social worker when she finishes her education. She's committed to "inspiring others and helping them create meaning in their lives with health and positive changes." Her favorite quote is by Elisabeth Kübler-Ross: "People are like stained-glass windows. They sparkle and shine when the sun is out, but when the darkness sets in, their true beauty is revealed only if there is a light from within."

Indigo-Attributes List

- Have strong self-esteem.

- Have an obvious sense of self.

- Have difficulty with discipline and/or authority.

- Don't like to follow orders or directions.

- Are very impatient.

- Get frustrated by structured systems, routines, or processes that require little creativity.

- Often see better ways of doing things at home, school, or work.

- Resist conforming to others' desires or trends.

- Always want to know "why," especially when asked or told to do something.

- Get bored easily with routine tasks.

- Are very creative.

- Are good at mental multitasking—can do many things at once.

- Display strong intuition.

- Have strong empathy for others, or have no empathy for others.

- Developed abstract thinking very young.

- Are gifted, talented, and/or highly intelligent.

- May have been identified or suspected of having attention deficit disorder (ADD) or attention deficit/hyperactivity disorder (ADHD).

- Are talented daydreamers and/or visionaries.

- Have spiritual intelligence and/or psychic skills.

- Often express anger outwardly and may sometimes have trouble with rage.

- May need support to facilitate self-discovery.

- Are here to help change the world—to help us live in greater harmony and peace with one another and improve life on the planet.

This list was adapted from attributes originally developed by Wendy H. Chapman, M.S., at **www.metagifted.org**.

I determined the predominance of each attribute—the number of students selecting each one. The top five were:

1. "Have strong empathy for others" (selected by 84 percent of the students).

2. "Have an obvious sense of self" (76 percent).

3. "Often see better ways of doing things at home, school, or work" (74 percent).

4. "Are a talented daydreamer and/or visionary" (72 percent).

5. "Are very creative" (70 percent).

It looks as though the Indigos in their teens and early 20s still sport the Indigo traits listed in Lee Carroll and Jan Tober's 1999 book, *The Indigo Children.*

Survey Conclusions

The survey results provide additional perspective on the Indigos, the maturing insights of the children described by Jan and Lee, and the hunter-gene behavior described by Thom Hartmann in his book *The Edison Gene.*

Indigo students have a very strong passion for uninhibited self-expression and are committed to serving others so that they, too, might experience their right to a life of equality and self-expression. Their values reflect a strong self who's committed to being guided by personal integrity in the pursuit of freedom, alignment with truth, openness, inclusiveness, respect for all things, and self-expression through service. Their strong understanding of who they are facilitates a self-directed life where success is measured by what they *experience* rather than what they *accumulate.* They'll pursue career options that provide unlimited self-expression and the opportunity to bring truth to situations that are not aligned with integrity.

We might assume that the recent floods of controversy surrounding large corporations would cause the Indigos to avoid or show disdain for the corporate world. Fortunately, the data indicates that this isn't so. They see this trend as a necessary step in a larger evolution. We need the Indigos' creativity and keen insight to help bridge the gaps of unmet expectations. Many will, however, choose entrepreneurship as a way to attain the autonomy they need to bring their creative endeavors to unencumbered fruition.

Indigos work best with a leader who demonstrates a personal interest in their lives and professional development. A leader is perceived as someone who's there to serve, guide, and coach them. To be effective leaders of Indigo employees, we must demonstrate impeccable integrity, be excellent communicators, and inspire the team to excel for the benefit of all concerned.

The Indigos want to work in an environment that's fun, well organized, and efficient. They want responsibility, autonomy, and an atmosphere of flexibility. They'll develop strong personal relationships with their co-workers. Community is important to the Indigos, and they'll support each other with integrity, openness, transparency, and compassion.

The survey results, coupled with literature review and interviews, indicate that the Indigos are "bridge builders," ready to construct—from a platform of truth—the new infrastructure required to span the gaps in our business, economic, and social institutions. They'll drive new visions, unfurl unlimited creativity, and deliver with divine purpose the solutions required to move civilization to the next level of consciousness.

The question at hand is: "How can today's leaders support the Indigos as they strive to develop and express their inherent gifts?" This question is addressed in my forthcoming book, *Indigos in the Workplace: Paving the Way for Tomorrow's Leaders.*

••

Indigos in the Workplace

by Gates McKibbin, Ph.D.

Here's one of those industry professionals we speak about who can really see what's happening in the workplace.

Gates McKibbin is the founder and president of McKibbin, Inc. She has exceptional experience as a consultant in strategic planning, leadership development, organizational effectiveness, and change management. She has superior coaching, communication, team-building, and interpersonal skills.

Gates has worked in the corporate-consulting arena since 1982, when she joined McKinsey & Company as a research consultant in the firm's San Francisco–based organizational-effectiveness practice. Soon afterward, the business book In Search of Excellence was published, which described many of the practices at McKinsey & Company. As a result of this publicity, Gates spent the subsequent six years conducting leading-edge research, producing management-training videos, and giving international speeches and seminars.

Gates's most recent consulting has involved working with CEOs, boards of directors, and senior leadership teams to develop first- and second-curve strategies for business success. Since 2001, she has served as a member of the board of directors of TrueBlue, Inc. (NYSE). In addition to being a member of the compensation and governance committees, she has helped the company develop strategies to grow revenues from $1 billion to $2 billion in five years.

A decade ago, Gates took a sabbatical from consulting and reentered the corporate world for a "reality check." She served as the vice president of education at the Health Research & Educational Trust at the American Hospital Association. She followed that experience with a position as vice president of change management at Bank of America.

Gates has published eight business articles on leadership and change. She has also published a series of seven personal-development books on topics such as courage, hope, love, and faith. She has three degrees from the University of Illinois, including a B.A. in liberal arts and sciences (Phi Beta Kappa and Bronze Tablet), an M.S. in library and information science, and a Ph.D. in organizational theory and research.

• •

It's epidemic. In the past few months, I've received almost identical phone calls from many of my business clients. Their concerns are the same, whether they're managing a small business or leading a multibillion-dollar corporation. In short, they're experiencing culture shock with their new hires, especially the ones under 25. These young employees are rubbing their managers the wrong way. They are:

- Unrealistically confident in their abilities, given that they have little or no prior work experience

- So anxious to learn that they proclaim that they're working to improve their abilities first—and contribute to the business second

- Determined to leave work at five o'clock, even if it means that critical tasks won't be completed

- Adamant that they should be considered for a promotion after less than a year

- Unabashed about demanding more money to keep pace with their peers

- Ready to resign at a moment's notice if their expectations aren't met

The word that most managers use to describe these new hires is *entitled*. Their attitude about work is summed up in these statements: "I know who I am, and I'm not about to compromise any aspect of myself to fit in at work. If I'm pierced or tattooed or wear flip-flops, that should be acceptable. My life outside of work is my priority, so don't expect me to sacrifice my leisure time to the gods of profitability. I'm a valuable employee, and I expect to be given opportunities to stretch and grow. If you assign me the same tasks all the time, I'll soon become bored and unmotivated. I expect to be promoted quickly and constantly given new opportunities to expand my talent—and thus my marketability."

As I listened to my clients, I had to admit that this indeed sounded like an acute case of entitlement. My intuition also told me that this was a predictable result of the older Indigos entering the workplace *en masse,* with all of their independence, impatience, skepticism, and self-absorption. And business was definitely feeling it.

Company cultures have been built on the opposite values and attitudes. For decades, baby boomers and then Gen Xers have been grateful to have a job, ready to work hard, and willing to adapt to the character of the company in order to succeed. They've learned to live with some degree of bureaucracy, and they accept the hierarchy of control as necessary, if not optimal. They've also invested their time and energy in becoming better leaders, streamlining processes, and improving the workplace environment. Nonetheless, the new generation seems intent on not just challenging this status quo, but lobbing a barrage of grenades into it. What to do?

I went to the Internet to see what insights I could glean about "Generation Y," the label used to identify this young demographic group. I expected to find a connection between Gen Y and Indigos. And in fact, my research proved that Gen Y is just another term for Indigos born between 1980 and 1994. Without a doubt, the members of this group, all 60 million of them, are radically different from their predecessors:

- One in three is not Caucasian.

- One-half come from single-parent homes.

- 80 percent have working mothers.

- More than 2 percent have one or both parents incarcerated.

- More than half of those aged 20 to 24 leave their jobs in less than 12 months, and 78 percent of those aged 16 to 19 do so.[6]

Members of Gen Y—Indigos—have lived in the belly of the beast. They're acutely aware of the vicissitudes of the human condition, be it the corruption of power by unethical leaders or unchecked violence within the underclass. Indigos see integrity as the exception, and they believe that justice can be bought. They skate a fine line between being in-your-face realistic and cynically disillusioned. Whereas boomers thought that questioning authority was revolutionary, authority is so pointless to Indigos that it doesn't even deserve to be questioned.

Faced with an inconceivable national debt and a generation of boomers ready for government-supported retirement, Gen Y lives for today, keenly aware that the future is up for grabs. They've grown up with accessible pornography and the threat of AIDS, and they've been exposed to almost eight hours of Jerry Springer–influenced media a day. Masters of technology, they communicate with each other constantly via pager, cell phone, text messaging, e-mail, and chat rooms.

Recognizing this, what value do Gen Y employees provide to a typical business—and how can managers make the most of their contributions? Here are a few perspectives and approaches that have worked for my clients:

— **Explore their world.** Watch Gen Y in action at the mall. View their movies, read their magazines, and turn on MTV every now and then. You'll witness both aspects of their worldview—their almost reckless independence and their deep need to be inspired by something relevant. Talk openly with them about their lives, and be sure to pepper your conversations with provocative questions.

— **Constantly challenge them.** If Indigos in the workplace want to be on a steep learning curve, then create one for them. Identify what they do best and give them plenty of opportunity to get even better at it. Be willing to expand the scope of their duties. That way, they'll keep growing while they also contribute more significantly to the organization.

— **Coach and mentor.** Unlock their full potential intellectually and interpersonally. Provide honest feedback on attitudes and behaviors that enhance or erode their credibility. Help them understand how to develop their professionalism without compromising their sense of self. Guide them to build strong working relationships and contribute to team effectiveness.

— **Question self-evident "truths."** Be willing to recognize sacred cows in the workplace and openly challenge their validity. Engage in candid dialogue about sources of ineffectiveness and how to improve working conditions and processes. Remain open to the Indigos' perspectives, even if they're frank and irreverent. Challenge yourself to be more flexible and open-minded.

— **Encourage their values.** Self-sufficiency is their mainstay, and their autonomy is nonnegotiable. Recognize that these qualities can be advantageous in a workplace that thrives on the energy of self-starters. Uncover what gives Indigos meaning, and then find ways for them to derive more of it from their work. Reinforce ways in which their values are aligned with your corporate culture.

— **Keep finding a new edge.** When you've challenged them to explore a limit of their capability—and they've succeeded in surpassing it—challenge them again with yet another one. Remember that they love to experiment and that trying and failing doesn't feel like a career-limiting move to them (even if it does for you).

— **Focus on validity.** Refrain from exerting your control as an authority figure. Indigos will disrespect you for it, and any trustworthiness you may have built with them will evaporate. Instead, when something needs to be done, explain how it will contribute to the company's success—and to theirs.

— **Acknowledge their contributions.** Like everyone else, Indigos need to feel appreciated and respected for who they are and what they're doing at work. Leverage every opportunity to catch them doing something right and immediately recognize it. You'll find that underneath all of the bluster, they still want to be sure that you know they're doing a great job.

The manager's role is to unlock the potential of each employee. In many respects, Indigos are no different from anyone else. It's just that their potential manifests in a different way from what we're accustomed to seeing at work. When managers affirm that their company has a lot to learn and gain from Gen Y, even if the contributions are contrarian, they're in a position to bring out the best in everyone.

••

Learning to Learn

by Kimberly Kassner

This author's life is a testimony to the power of learning to learn. Jan and I wondered if her contribution should be in the educators' section . . . and it could have been. However, Kimberly comes right out of corporate America with a message for our newest young adults, who have often been diagnosed with "learning disabilities."

Kimberly Kassner began to master her ability to learn by her senior year at Central Michigan University, taking 22 credit hours, getting a 4.0, and never studying past 5:00 P.M. or on weekends. Prior to her senior year, she struggled with her differences and had to put in countless hours of study time just to pass a test. Then she uncovered the secrets of how she learns. She graduated cum laude with a B.S. in communications and psychology.

In 1982, Kimberly began her career in sales with PepsiCo, Inc. She was promoted five times in seven years and was one of the top-ten performers in the country in her last four positions. In her final job, as a national account district manager, she was responsible for managing the Pepsi-Cola local bottlers and national food-chain accounts. She was ranked number eight in the country and number one in her region for two consecutive years. She worked less than 35 hours a week while teaching the 14-week Dale Carnegie Training course "How to Win Friends and Influence People in Business." During that same time, she was awarded

Young Careerist from the Michigan Business & Professional Women's Foundation, Inc.

In 1994, Kimberly wrote and published a book, <u>You're a Genius and I Can Prove It!</u> It was Baker & Taylor's top seller in its fourth month in print. She appeared on more than 100 radio and TV shows promoting her book and workshops, including two national shows. <u>Family Talk,</u> a show on public radio in San Francisco, received the greatest number of requests for their show's tape when she was a guest.

In 1998, Kimberly produced <u>EmpowerMind for Teens</u>®, a three-video, five-audiotape series accompanied by her book. Because of the strength of her product and testimonials, two award-winning infomercial producers pilot-tested Kimberly and her <u>EmpowerMind for Teens</u> product on national TV. In 1999, Nightingale-Conant began distributing the video, and it was the number one–selling series in their catalog the first time they ever advertised it.

Kimberly is currently in the process of finishing her second book, <u>Discovering Your Child's Divine Purpose</u> and is planning to start filming a documentary called <u>You're a Genius and I Can Prove It!</u> The film will examine EmpowerMind's philosophy, techniques, and amazing success stories.

Kimberly is pleased that she and her work have earned the endorsement of the California Association of Student Councils and the Educational Media Group of California. She currently resides with her husband and seven-year-old son in Commerce, Michigan.

••

Is this the solution to our educational crisis or just more hype? I've spent 16 years trying to solve the riddle of "learning disabilities." After working directly with over a thousand dyslexic, hyperactive, attention deficit disorder (ADD), and "hopelessly learning disabled" students, I now believe that what some label as "learning disabilities" may instead be a shortcoming of some teaching methods and school curriculums.

I'm one of those "learning disabled" students. I couldn't take a multiple-choice test well or read and retain information effectively in school. I struggled with all the signs of ADD. I was a daydreamer and a compulsive talker, and I couldn't stay focused on any subject unless I was stimulated by the material or had an internal desire to learn it. I was never formally diagnosed with ADD and didn't understand that I was a kinesthetic learner—one who learns by doing—until ten years after I graduated from college. My husband teases me often by saying, "You may not know where Bhutan or Tanzania are, but you're pretty smart when it comes to living life." I learn by doing, so I guess I make things happen by default!

By my second semester of college, I learned what time of day my brain received information best and how to switch my negative self-talk to positive. I also learned how to effectively communicate with some of my professors about my learning style, which resulted in two of them giving me a different testing format from the rest of the class. Because of these few insights, I studied almost half as much as I had in the past. I went from a 2.3 GPA my first semester of college to a 3.5. I didn't get smarter; I just learned an aspect or two of *how I learn.* I agree with the adults who have graduated from EmpowerMind: "If I'd only known then what I know now, after taking EmpowerMind."

Let's examine an analogy. Let's say that brains are like computers, and we have classrooms of computers (students). Many teachers are cramming Apple software into IBM machines. But there's no converter to make a connection; therefore, learning doesn't take place. However, as with a computer, if a converter is created for students that helps them discover *how* they learn, then they *will* learn. Figuring out how to learn creates that converter and facilitates effective education. It helps students *learn to think* for themselves.

If a student is a visual learner and has a good imagination, then that person can take auditory information and convert it into mental imagery. For example, I taught 12 "hopeless" students the prologue to *Romeo and Juliet* using this method. Once they were shown how to imagine the words as pictures in their heads, they remembered them. We also put the prologue to a rap-music beat, so those who learned rhythmically could also be reinforced by the beat of the words in addition to the pictures.

The more senses people use to learn something, the better chance they have of retaining the information. These students learned the 14 lines of the prologue verbatim in only one session and retained 100 percent of it four weeks later. Because the students learn *how* to do this *for themselves,* they *own* their own mental converter. I don't need to be there for them to process the information; they can do it themselves and take responsibility for their own learning process, no matter who their teacher is, what school they attend, or what material they're given.

Here's an example of the conversion process taking place within the student and without my physical proximity. By the end of third grade, eight-year-old Zach didn't know most of his multiplication tables. This was because he'd been taught in a left-brain style, when in reality he was a right-brain learner. So he just learned to convert the information himself. Zach looked at two 7s next to each other in 7 x 7 and the numerals looked like upside-down feet to him, so he pictured that in his mind. Then he looked at the answer, 49, and thought of the San Francisco 49ers football team in his mind. Then he attached the two pictures together. He saw the feet as belonging to the 49ers, and they were all running upside down. So when he saw 7 x 7 in the future, he went through the same thought process. He used this method of association and mastered the eight multiplication tables he couldn't previously learn. He got them in less than ten minutes, in fact, and he retained the answers without much review.

Here's another example: I just tutored Garrett a few months ago, and at the age of ten, he still couldn't recite 12 of his multiplication tables. His mom was at her wit's end. She'd tried once-a-week tutoring since kindergarten at great expense, hours of painful homework, and extra help that the school was trying to provide, yet nothing was working. Garrett was easy for me to understand because he's a kinesthetic learner and he's 10, so if I associate anything with bodily functions and we act them out, it's like magic. For instance, I asked him what a four looked like, whether it reminded him of anything. He loves dogs, and they have four legs, so he said, "A dog." (It may sound like a stretch for you, but if it works for him, it works.) So I had us both get down on the floor next to each other, on all fours (4 x 4) and bark like dogs, then we looked up and imagined a "sick teen" (16) coming into the room. (Fortunately, I don't have video cameras in my basement or this could get hard to explain!) Anyway, after the 75-minute session, Garrett learned all 12 multiplication tables perfectly and performed them for his mom when she arrived. His mom got teary eyed and just couldn't believe it. It's so easy for all children to learn when they're taught in the way they learn best.

A 12-year-old boy named Donald had an IQ of 168. The school system said he was "learning disabled"; he was labeled ADHD and was an incessant talker. When I gave him the opportunity to doodle and build a clothespin model while listening to an auditory exercise, he got 22 out of 24 questions correct after hearing the tape only once. If he hadn't been allowed to doodle and keep his hands active, he would have reversed his score, which is what he was experiencing in the classroom. When he went back to school, his teachers were astonished! They called his mother to find out what had happened. The secret was that he'd uncovered the mystery of *how* he learns. The authorities now let Donald doodle.

When schools have curricula that help students discover their *own ways* of learning, children's chances for success increase. This can start in early elementary school and be reinforced in middle and high school. When students learn and think for themselves, they can use the skills in all aspects of their lives. Students are less likely to drop out of school and have degrading labels attached to their learning processes. These tools for success can be applied to any field of study that they choose to explore, regardless of the constantly changing needs of our society.

○○○○○

Chapter Three

Other Lands

When Jan and I created the first Indigo book ten years ago, it was obvious that this was a worldwide phenomenon. It had to be. The evolution of the human race can't appear only in North America! So we knew it would only be a matter of time before the stories came pouring in from around the globe, and we were right.

From the Culture of Harmony

One of the most gentle societies on earth is the Japanese. We've been there a few times now and continue to be impressed by this culture of harmony, as they call it. Yet Japan now holds the world record for the most teen suicides. How can this be? It's due to the Indigo consciousness. These children are taught from birth that the well-being of the group is everything. Then many teenagers realize they aren't fitting in! Rather than risk the harmony of many, they sacrifice one life . . . their own. This is typical of an

Indigo mind, weighing all the possibilities and choosing the one that's best for the group instead of themselves. Now apply this to those young people who strap on bombs and kill themselves. They're told that doing so will create peace and that it's for the greater good . . . and they're ready to go.

Way Too Many Submissions!

We received many international submissions, but we could only use a few due to the other categories we were creating. We had slots for only four, so here are the ones we most wanted you to see. We begin with a very strong woman in Chile—a driving force who has single-handedly placed the Indigo subject on agendas throughout South America.

••

My Testimony

by Mariella Norambuena
CHILE

---

*In 2002, **Mariella Norambuena** founded the Indigo Children Center Chile (Niños Indigo Chile) and is the current director. This institution, located in Santiago, is dedicated to diffusion of information and education about Indigo children. It's also dedicated to their personal development and supporting Chilean families with a transpersonal therapeutic approach.*

In 2005, Mariella founded an international Indigo organization for South America, the Indigo Network (Red Indigo) whose members are Argentina, Brazil, Colombia, Venezuela, Guatemala, and Chile. The objective of this network, in its first phase, is to unite the Latin-American region in a common educational model.

Since 2006, Mariella has been a member of the editorial committee of the online bulletin "EDU-futuro Amerikalatina." She's a teacher at Instituto Profesional de Chile, IPECH, 2006 (Professional Institute of Chile), an undergraduate school of educational counseling.

*She gives conferences and seminars, and evaluates children. You can see her Website, and the scope of her work at **www.ninosindigochile.cl**. Oh, and it might help if you speak Spanish!*

••

In 2000, I came across the book *The Indigo Children* by Lee Carroll and Jan Tober. I'd never heard about this subject before, and as I was reading it, everything that was written made sense to me in terms of myself and my relationship with my children, ages seven and six at that time. I'd always had the idea of working with kids, but I never knew how. I wasn't an educator or someone who had experience in the field. I was an engineer; however I'd already started preparing to become a transpersonal therapist.

While reading the book, I kept thinking the same thing: *This is it!* This is the information I need to know in order to start working with kids. It was so easy to understand each one of the testimonials in the book that I decided to research even more about the subject. It took six months of studying every document I could find about this on the Internet. I needed a lot of patience, since most of what I found wasn't really helpful for the children. I could tell that there wasn't specific information on how to help parents guide and support their kids. I wanted to approach the subject by giving information, guidance, and support to the families and children from a transpersonal and educational point of view.

During the time I was researching on the Internet, I found two Websites about people who reflected the same opinion I had about how to relate to the Indigo Children. One of them was the Spanish educator José Manuel Piedrafrita, and the other was from Fundación INDI-GO, Ecuador (Indigo Foundation, Ecuador), which unfortunately doesn't exist anymore. I got in touch with Mr. Piedrafrita to bring him to Chile to talk about his experience and knowledge of the Indigo and Crystal Children. These terms weren't very well known at that time. After this experience with him in 2002, I opened the Centro Niños Indigo Chile (Indigo Children Center, Chile) in Santiago, the capital of Chile.

Not a Popular Thing to Discuss in Chile

Talking about the Indigo Children in 2002 was very daring since no one had heard about them before. Even riskier was opening a center totally dedicated to this subject. I felt so confident about what I wanted to give to Chilean families that I didn't care if everyone thought it was a crazy idea. Also, it wasn't the first time I'd heard that criticism. Ever since I was a little girl, I've always been ahead of my time and was quite mature for my age. My projects were always rather futuristic, and I was usually told that I wouldn't get any results.

When I understood that I was an adult Indigo, I knew this was the path I wanted to follow in my therapeutic work. I opened my center and gradually started giving informative talks to parents. I wanted to help them form a new view of their Indigo Children. I wanted them to guide their kids respect their own abilities and needs.

Little by little, families started coming to the center. We used to meet once a week to share experiences and our own views about the subject. My mentor, Omar Romo, who is also one of my dearest friends, was always supporting me and has been by my side since the beginning of this project. He's a senior Indigo (75 years old) and a visionary, and I deeply thank him for his guidance and support.

As time went by, parents started to feel the need to bring their children in for individual sessions where I could talk more about their needs and specific abilities. I could help them understand their children's behavior, feelings, and ideas. I've been working for five years as a transpersonal therapist, and I deeply appreciate the thousands of wonderful experiences I've had with these children. They've helped me better understand this world.

Identifying the Kind of Indigo

When I first have a session, I discern whether the children are Indigos or Crystals, according to their characteristics. (I use the plural "children," although some families may bring in just one child.) We go through a 90-minute interview where I ask questions about the children's personal histories. How were the pregnancies? What were the types of delivery? How was the mother emotionally during pregnancy? How were the first years? Did they have any accidents, surgeries, or the like? This is all important information from the transpersonal point of view.

There can be important traumas that stay in the body memory and many times are the cause of behavior problems. Therefore, they aren't biological problems. I also look at the family history. What has happened inside the family since the children were born? How are the relationships between the children and the people they live with? Finally, I ask for the parents' backgrounds, which help me determine the influence they have on the children. After the parents answer my questions and explain why they're seeking advice from me, I offer details about how I work.

In the meantime, I've already felt the frequency of the children's vibrations. Sometimes I talk with the children one-on-one, usually when they're older than seven. This way, I can have a better understanding of their lives. I can also give better support and guidance to the parents. I make suggestions about the school system, healthy eating, behavior, physical activity, and holistic therapies. I might even suggest psychotherapy for the children and the parents when it's necessary.

The Specialists' Support System

I've invited a group of specialists to Indigo Children, Chile. They're psychologists, educational therapists, and holistic therapists. All of them have extensive knowledge about Indigo Children, so they're open-minded about these new generations. They can support them and help them deal with their psychic abilities.

This is how we've organized the support system for the whole family, not only the child. We've established that the change we expect from children has to come first from the parents.

We've also started an information system for the community. This consists of giving conferences and seminars in schools, and private and public institutions in Chile and abroad. We created a Website for all the people who can't come to our center or who have no information near their homes. This site is in Spanish and is visited by approximately 2,000 people around the world. It ranks first on the most popular Web browsers, with an estimate of 50 online visits per day.

All of the preceding information shows how we've been working to guide and support parents, educators, and health professionals. We have to recognize that we're facing changes in the new generations; and as adults, we need to quickly adapt to these changes.

The Inner Child

Every day that I work in the center, I learn something new from the kids. I realize that the best gift they've given me is being able to see my inner child. Every one of them, with their personal histories, difficulties, sadness, and happiness, is like a mirror. They help me heal my own childhood pain and guide my children better. Each kid who comes to my office is a master to me; they're all here to give us love and compassion.

As an adult, I've learned how much damage we've caused our children. We don't "see" them or respect them, and many times we forget our own childhoods and aren't capable of getting in touch with our inner children. It's important for previous generations to learn that each child is like a reflection and result of what goes on inside the home. After all this time, I don't really need the parents to tell me what's going on with their kids at school or at home. I just need to look at the children, and I know. Indigo Children speak with their whole being—with their body language, behavior, words, and inner strength. If we adults are aware of these signals, we'll know how well we're doing raising our children.

Most parents bring their children to my office because they're failing at school (90 percent). Some want to know if their children are either Indigos or Crystals (7 percent), and the last group are the ones interested in raising healthy and happy people and who are willing to work on that (3 percent). Children in the main group are usually stressed out, having difficulties at home and dealing with adults, emotionally hurt and unstable, and unwilling to go through personal therapy. Their parents don't realize that children aren't the problem; rather, the issue is the way the adults are acting. As a consequence, the children are misbehaving, failing in school, and ending up misdiagnosed and taking medications.

This is a very common situation, unfortunately. I admit that some families have come to my office referred by teachers, pediatricians, psychologists, and even neurologists who see healthy children and suggest that they might be Indigos. However, these professionals are still few in number. Most decide to treat the external symptom (biological), which is the result of a certain situation, but this doesn't resolve the cause, the origin. This is where we focus our work. We're sure that Indigo Children aren't troublemakers in their essence, so the origin of this problem is the "emotional damage" usually caused by an adult. Most of the children I've seen in my office through the years are between five and ten years old. I can certainly say that, sadly, only a few of them aren't emotionally damaged.

Issues Starting Very Early

When I began my work in 2002, eight-year-olds were coming to my office because they had problems at school. In 2004, I started seeing six-year-old kids. After studying this situation, I thought that maybe in five years, I'd be seeing two- or three-year-olds. However, reality was harsh. In 2006, I started receiving preschoolers referred to neurologists by their teachers because the kids were considered hyperactive or ADD. Then I thought, *We adults are really crazy. How can a professional even think this about a young child, full of life and potential; curious; and with a need to explore, discover, and learn?*

That's when I started seriously researching the ways these children have been stigmatized. I began communicating with different professionals from other countries in South America. I wanted to know the reality on our continent about this subject. To my surprise, I found that other nations had the same situation as in Chile: children were abused daily at school, destroying their self-esteem; and they were being medicated in their own homes to become "normal."

All of this information led me to create the Indigo Network (Red Indigo) in 2005. The main objective was to develop a new educational model for our region, which would be used by every country-member of the network. We're currently working together with Argentina, Brazil, Chile, Colombia, Guatemala, Peru, and Venezuela. In the near future, we'll expand to work with Israel. The professionals in charge of each country know how to work directly with children and their families, guiding them and supporting them with therapies.

We've developed special seminars and lectures for teachers and health professionals, but more specifically for parents. Our goal is to spread the information in synchronization with one another.

A New Objective for Chile

I have a new objective today, which I'm currently working toward in Chile. I'd like to build school in the mountains, on the east side of Santiago. It will be called *Para Educativo de reserva ecologica multicultural Indigo* (Multicultural Indigo Educational Park and Ecology Reservation). The slogan will be: "We bring the future education to the present for our children to develop in harmony."

Indigo Park will be open for all children; and the "education," as it's called in the traditional system, will be "to share the future." The true knowledge will come from the inner self, not from the intellect. Children will be the main participants in their own learning experience. Adults will only guide them and support them in the process of learning, not be instructors who tell them what to do. This educational model will be used in every country-member of the Indigo Network and also in every place where we can find adults interested in working from the heart for childhood development.

We need to trust our children. Their conscience levels are many times better than those of adults, even if the adults have great academic knowledge. Children have innate wisdom, so we must admit, accept, and respect that they need to learn through concepts and experiences, not only through their intellect.

We Need to Create a New View as Adults

Nowadays, all kids are intellectually brilliant, and we adults need to approach this from a new viewpoint, with new knowledge. We need to know about multiple types of intelligence and neuroscience. We need to understand how they're using most of their brain capacity, using both brain hemispheres at the same time or separately. We should research physics and mechanics in order to understand most of the miscalled "phenomenon" like the power of intention-thought. Let's learn why our children see reality or the world a certain way. Why, for many of them, does their behavior, language, expression, and posture have nothing to do with their parents, family, or upbringing? They have their unique ways, and these are what I call "conscious levels." As the days go by, I see more and more of these kids and feel thankful for being part of this big change in the evolution of humankind. I'm certain that our race is evolving, here and now in front of our eyes, in our homes, and we must be amazed and thankful for being alive to witness it.

Someone might wonder: *How can she say that we're evolving? Those are really big words.* Yes, they *are* big words, and this is why we must act quickly. We need to adapt because children are already born adapted to this changes. Happily, I have a lot of hope for the children of our planet. They'll make it. Even when everything looks negative and hopeless, they're showing their evolution through their generous and compassionate hearts. They're expressing this to the adults who are still trying to understand and, most of all, to believe.

I trust humankind. Children have taught me to have this hopeful perspective, full of colors. I hope to say to myself in 30 more years: *It was true. They made it, and I'm alive to see it.*

For this to happen, we as adults need to help to create places for the children to grow. We must stand strong against the system that's hurting them. We need school and health systems that include, not exclude, children. We need to raise them with respect, not repression.

You can do something about this, too—I can assure you of that. If it wasn't true, I wouldn't be writing this article. I wouldn't have dared to talk about this seven years ago; I would have just listened to the society that told me: "You won't achieve anything with that idea."

This is the Indigo strength that allows us to move anything necessary to achieve our purpose in life. My purpose is to help alert adults, to make them aware so that the children of today will become the conscious adults of the future.

Today, nothing is impossible. I learned that from the children. This is a beautiful moment to live within the history of our planet. Don't miss it. Feel the present with your whole being and share it with every kid in the world.

I thank every one of the "little Masters" who have come to my office day after day for the last five years. Thank you for the opportunity to learn something from you. Thank you for healing me and your parents and for trusting in my work.

●●

An Alternative Approach to Learning Disabilities

by Karin Roten, speech therapist

Karin Roten *is a qualified speech therapist in the French-speaking part of Switzerland. She has worked as an independent speech therapist since 1991 and is also the mother of two little girls.*

In addition to her academic background, she has received training in aromatherapy, flower and mineral essences, and energy work. Being quite an outsider in her profession, she mainly works with "new kids" and their parents.

In her part of the world, as in America, speech therapists take care of children who have difficulties learning to speak (speech delays, stammering, pronunciation defaults, and the like) or difficulties reading and spelling (such as dyslexia).

••

Children are increasingly being diagnosed with learning disabilities of some kind: dyslexia, dysphasia, dyspraxia, ADHD, ADD, autism, and so on. One way of addressing this is to follow the researchers who are trying to explain in detail how the brain misfunctions in each of these pathologies. Focusing on what kind of dyslexia a child has, trying to figure out how the brain analyzes information, and so on, is one way to approach the issue. I believe there are also other paths. I don't deny the symptoms that the child exhibits. They exist, and I think there are many ways of understanding them. The risk is to identify the child with a diagnosis, forgetting to focus on the whole being and on the child's potential.

In order for a child to learn, he needs a safe physical, emotional, and energetic environment that helps him build good self-esteem. In order for the brain to function properly, it needs proper nutrition.

Over the years, I've come to some conclusions. They aren't definite because I still learn every day! Kids with learning challenges often need help in three main ways:

1. Rebalance their diets to impact their biology and thus improve their emotional and cognitive functions; lessen environmental toxicity.

2. Use energy-based therapy with Emotional Freedom Techniques (EFT) to release emotional, mental, and energetic blocks toward learning and self-esteem; use mineral essences from Indigo Essences (**www.indigo essences.com**) to help on all energy levels.

3. Teach them what they need to learn in an appropriate way.

I'll develop each of these three points and help you see how they work with each other. Because we're complex beings, a synergy of approaches is often necessary.

The Diet and Environment

We're becoming more and more aware of the impact of food and environmental pollution on our physical, emotional, mental, and energetic health.

A child's body is often subjected to toxic products since conception or birth. It starts often with vaccinations at an early age, when the immune system is immature. This is followed by a few courses of antibiotics; clouds of pollution; regular doses of food colorings, preservatives, and glutamate; heaps of sugar, pizza, pasta, and white bread; and on top of that, synthetic cosmetics full of undesirable chemicals such as sodium lauryl sulphate, propylene glycol, and the like. This is the perfect recipe for inducing gut dysbiosis—an important imbalance in the gut flora. The consequences of gut dysbiosis range from allergies and eczema to learning, emotional, and behavioral disorders.

How is this possible? An impaired gut lining won't be able to guard the body from pathogenic invaders, nor absorb the nutrients from food. In addition, the gut wall will become "leaky." Undigested food and chemicals will get into the bloodstream, thus causing different ailments: allergies, ADHD, ADD, dyslexia, dyspraxia, autism, depression, and schizophrenia, for example.[7]

Energy-Based Therapy

Our physiology interacts with our energy bodies and vice versa. We're holistic beings. Clearing toxic interference by rebalancing the diet and suppressing unnecessary pollutants is the first step toward a healthy body and mind.

One hypothesis holds that a cleansing and restoring diet allows the first layers of toxins and memories to be cleared. We then have access to older memories stored in our cells. Working energetically on those old memories may result in a very deep healing, which wouldn't be accessible if the first cleansing—through diet—hadn't occurred.

Next we need to look at possible blocks in the energy system that were created by recent, old, or timeless events (which we call memories). Examine how they result in negative emotions that stop us from tapping into our real potential. Learning problems can be triggered by memories that have led to erroneous conclusions, thus keeping a child from accessing his brain potential and his immense creative capacity.

In order to have a learning disability, people need certain limiting beliefs about themselves. More often than not, children with such challenges come very quickly to false conclusions about their potential and their value. "I'll never make it," "I'm just an idiot," "I can't spell," "I'm dyslexic," "School is boring." Do these complaints sound familiar?

In fact, being weak in English or math isn't inevitable. Limiting beliefs can only exist if there's a block in the energy system. Dissolve the block, and the belief is gone! Sounds too good to be true, doesn't it?

How do we accomplish such a miracle? This is where therapy such as EFT, for example, comes in. It consists of tapping a sequence of acupuncture points while focusing on a problem. The limiting belief or negative emotion is then released, and the child's perspective is completely different.

I love EFT because it's so easy to learn and is quite efficient. It can be used with any age group. The effects are often quick and long lasting. Any emotion (fear, anger, sadness, shame, and so on), limiting belief, or physical symptom can be addressed. This is very helpful for the challenged learner and his parents.

As if this wasn't good enough, when you free energy blocks, you facilitate the flow of life energy in the whole organism and in the whole being. The result is finally stronger health and a happy and creative child (or adult) who will experience a much better emotional state.

In addition to therapy like EFT, I like to get the child to choose mineral essences from Indigo Essences (**www.indigoessences .com**), which will help him fine-tune his emotional and overall energetic balance. The essences will often work at levels we aren't even aware of. This is why we let the child select his own essences: he knows what's good for him. Let's not forget that our new children are highly intuitive.

Learning

A rebalanced physiology, feeling safe in himself, a solid self-esteem, and a fluid energy body are all major ingredients that are interconnected. These are the best assets for optimal learning. Now the child is receptive to pedagogy!

The majority of children will naturally resume learning when they feel good inside their bodies and about themselves and when they feel safe, provided that the learning environment is respectful and interesting. We must remind ourselves that these kids learn quickly and hate boring repetition. They'll happily get involved in meaningful and creative learning. What suits one kid doesn't always fit the next.

As pedagogues and therapists, our skill is to present information at the right pace and in a way that suits the child's learning pattern. EFT, essences, or diet won't miraculously make the child learn what he's missed out on, but he will be able to learn easily and more quickly once the physical, emotional, mental, and energetic blocks aren't in the way anymore.

Conclusion

Sometimes rebalancing the diet will be all that's necessary for the child to start learning. Other times, working on the limiting beliefs will be enough. There's no rule. What's clear to me is that our new children are born with increasing sensitivities, be it to chemicals of all kinds or to energetic interferences. Experience shows that when energy therapy doesn't give the expected results, there's an interference of some kind of toxins; and the answer is often in changing the diet and eliminating environmental toxins.

It's important to give easy but effective tools to the whole family —children and parents—which they can use by themselves so that everybody takes control of their own well-being and life.

● ●

Indigos: Leaders of the Future

by Ingrid Cañete

SMALLBRAZIL

Brazil is a huge country in South America (in case you haven't looked at your map lately). It's the fifth-most populous country in the world, and Portuguese is the national language, isolating the people a bit from their neighbors, who mostly speak Spanish.

This article from Brazil could have come from any large American city. The Indigo situation is universal and global. You might say that this piece should have been placed in Chapter 2, which addresses Indigos in the workplace, and you'd be right. But I wanted you to see the congruity of these issues from far away places and have a better understanding that no matter what the culture, those who are working in the field have many of the same challenges and solutions.

＊＊

Ingrid Cañete is the champion for the Indigos in Brazil. She's the author of Humanization, a Challenge in Modern Enterprise *(1996);* A Way through Exercise at Work *(2000);* A Shine in the Eye *(2001); and* Indigo Children: The Evolution of the Human Being *(2005). She's the co-author of* Me, Stressed? *(2004) and* Contemporary Management of People *(2004).*

Ingrid was born in Porto Alegre (RS-Brazil) and is a psychologist, specialist and master in human resources management, specialist in

161

transpersonal psychology, specialist in stress management and quality of life, founding partner of ISMA-BR, university professor, therapist, and business consultant in health and quality of life. She has worked for more than 20 years in the clinical and organizational fields and is fascinated by human beings and their behavior, with her main interest being to help them discover and reveal their potential.

Ingrid started studying the subject of Indigo Children nine years ago through information received over the Internet. She inevitably wanted to learn more about the subject after she found that she was an adult Indigo.

••

"We are waves longing for the sea which is unity.
Yet we forget that we are the sea. The spirit is the great visionary,
we cannot search along for the searcher . . . he is inside.
What we are in search of is the observer which is inside, which is us.
We forget that we are the sea."

These words by Pierre Weil from a talk in 2002 in Brazil deeply moved the hearts of those who heard and later read them, and they still rock the cradle where our thoughts and imaginations grow. From his soft and pure words, I was led to a passage in a book by Eduardo Galeano, *The Book of Embraces,* from which I quote:

Diego had never seen the sea.
His father, Santiago Kovadloff, took him to discover it.
They went south.
The ocean lay beyond high dunes, waiting.
When the child and his father finally reached the dunes
after much walking, the ocean exploded before their eyes.
And so immense was the sea and its sparkle that the child was
struck dumb by the beauty of it.
And when he finally managed to speak, trembling,
stuttering, he asked his father:
"Help me to see!"

162

I begin in this rather poetic form to talk about a recurrent theme in the perspective of a fairly new subject. The recurring idea is the eternal quest of the human being along the path of history for the answer to so many questions:

- Who are we?
- Where are we going?
- What is the purpose of life?

The new theme is the revelation of the presence of more evolved beings on our planet. Different names have been given to them, but they're internationally best known as Indigos, according to Nancy Tappe. This also corresponds to a certain frequency of vibration and a specific mission on planet Earth.

In my most recent book, *Indigo Children: The Evolution of the Human Being,* published in Brazil in 2005, I wrote about this theme in the final chapter. This was an exercise in imagining intuitively the future world under the leadership of Indigos. How will governments, education, the economy, business management, and families appear? My view about this is positive, optimistic and even passionate, although I'm not ignoring that right away there are challenges, conflicts, and suffering to overcome in order to build a more evolved society.

In this article, I'll amplify that exercise based not only on my studies, observations, and intuition, but also on a real case: an enterprise brought forth by young Indigos and a team of other young people. I was contacted by one of the young founders of this company, who asked me to help out as a consultant with a focus on health and the quality of life. After having read my book about Indigos, he was filled with emotion and had the intuitive feeling that I could help him with the healthy development of his enterprise. He was 24 years old then and had a one-year-old child. Here's the letter he sent after having read my book:

Hello, Ingrid,

Here I am, writing to you 24 hours after having experienced something that seems to have the potential to change my life and my conception of what's coming to us. Divine wisdom, hidden in chance (which doesn't exist), made me get to know a special person who was carrying a book that caught my attention. Curious, I asked to have a look at it while this person was engaged in conversation with somebody else. A marvelous experience started right there. Within 15 minutes, I could identify in your book characteristics, virtues, and defects that are the essence of my life. My first feeling was to cry because to carry these characteristics isn't easy, as you yourself point out in the book. At that moment, I experienced a feeling of freedom in which certain doubts withered and new ones sprouted.

I've just come back from the book fair, where I bought your book Indigo Children: The Evolution of the Human Being. I'm reading it while my son is crying, and the TV is blaring at high volume. (That's normal, isn't it?) I had the impulse to write to you in the hopes of getting some orientation to my question: what now?

*Ingrid, I also learned from your book that you work with companies to improve quality of life. I'd be grateful if you could inform my partners and me about how you develop this kind of work and how our company can count on your support. I always say to them that what we do is only half of what our real goal is. Our real activity aims for something nobler and more sublime, and I'd like to pass this message on to other people. Please visit our site: **www.paixaopeloquefazemos.com.br**.*

Thank you, congratulations, and God bless you for your initiative!

When I received this letter, I was happy and moved. It's impressive how quickly synchronicity works. Even being aware of that, I couldn't help but be delighted with its magic and precision. After all, I'd just launched *Indigo Children*, in which I wrote about leadership in the future. Right away, I was getting contact from an

Indigo indicating that his time isn't in the future, the time of the new leaders is *now!*

This was a present from the Universe. In recent months, I've worked as a consultant to this company. I shall write about that later in this article.

Manifest Leadership of Indigos

In my book *Indigo Children,* I finished the chapter about Indigos as leaders of the future as follows:

> . . . and we will create new functions for them, functions and positions that never existed before because of their genius, their shine. This the case with Russian conductor Valery Gergiev, for whom the Metropolitan Opera in New York created the function of General and Artistic Invited Maestro, a function that never existed before, just to have the talent of this genius of contemporary music with the orchestra. Gergiev is somebody so different in his behavior and whose attitudes defy all established rules and patterns but with such gifts that nobody can do without his talent. In the name of his fantastic geniality, we let go of rigid rules. Tolerance is enhanced and the path opens! This is unconditional love . . . the love we all need to live.
>
> Or they will create these new spaces themselves according to necessity. Maybe one of the first challenges and main missions of the Indigos is in education. They will have to propose new models and methods to teach and learn, becoming new and lively models of a new education and new educators. They will have a humanistic base and a holistic transpersonal and multidisciplinary vision. Overall, they will be guided by Ethics, Love and Truth.

Let's wait and see what kind of companies they'll create and what solutions they offer to a new world!

A characteristic of Indigos is breaking the system. This gives a clear idea of their mission, which is to question, to poke, and to de-arrange, always for the best. They're coming to accelerate destruction of walls that separate the old from the new energy, thus clearing the way for the expression of consciousness, evolution, and freedom of being.

The Universe is wise, as it evidently provided Indigos with a fundamental gift to fulfill this mission—leadership. In other words, leadership means a capacity to influence others, which translates as power, personal power.

Indigos bring with them the distinguished characteristic of leadership from early childhood onward. I heard from a grandmother about her four-year-old grandson who has the gift of talking with animals, which then protects him from any threat. He researches in libraries, and he travels abroad with his parents, affirming that he'll be a scientist. According to his grandmother's report, he's extremely determined and takes everything very seriously, especially the care and protection of animals.

His parents, teachers, and schoolmates are interested in, and taken aback by, his attitude and conviction. What passion he has as he defends his high, healthy values! In this way, he shows natural leadership when interacting with his classmates, who end up interested in the subject, asking questions, and being on his side to help in the cause he defends. They respect him, accept and follow his ideas, and noticeably love and admire him. According to his grandmother, this boy also attracts adults, always being himself without any effort.

I had the opportunity to talk to this four-year-old and was impressed. His look is deep, serious, and concentrated. His countenance magnetizes, and he speaks very little, but he says a lot through his eyes and attitude. When I pointed out that his mission was very, very important and that I wished him success in caring for and protecting animals, he looked deeply into my eyes, nodded, kissed my face, and hugged me. Then he left, as if to say, "All right, we understand each other. Now, let's work." His grandmother was surprised, especially because he usually doesn't kiss anybody but her and his parents.

Well, according to this and other reports and books, Indigo leadership is spontaneous and charismatic. It usually manifests through the knowledge of certain themes. Their way of being in the world delights people. Apart from these characteristics and natural gifts, they're also surrounded by a special colorful atmosphere, which attracts admirers and followers. Their traits include humility, cooperativeness, solidarity, integrity, spirituality, sensitivity, and the facility to create a consensus about higher values. Among their gifts and talents, they have the capacity to instantly read people's thoughts, as well as understand electronic-equipment manuals. They also show great creativity, telekinesis, and the capacity to foresee the future and to capture these visions.

Indigos are normally concerned with the well-being and life conditions of other people, known or unknown. They show an interest in volunteer work and social responsibility, and they're very humane. They question the world and are annoyed with hypocrisy, falsehood, and incoherence between speech and action. They often show indignation.

When they come from rigid and repressive families, it may take some time for them to express themselves openly; but once they overcome the barriers and are pushed to their limits, they go against the system, surprising people as they present themselves differently from what they were before. Then their relatives will say, "What's happening? He (or she) never behaved like that before and always seemed so calm and peaceful."

In fact, these Indigos—for their own reasons and because of a sense of responsibility—controlled themselves until they couldn't stand it anymore and decided it was time to be who they really are. As they let go of self-control, they may have scared their families. But if we look closer and see their relationships with friends, colleagues, and co-workers as well, we'll probably find out that their spontaneous leadership is manifesting fruitfully and positively in their lives.

A Profile of These Leaders of the Future

The leaders of the future will have vision and will be guided by intuition, centered in the power of the now, and exist in true love, which comes from the one and only Source. They will not only be leaders, but will inspire and be inspired by a clear, pristine vision—the vision of life as a divine kaleidoscope, multifaceted and multicolored in infinite nuances of colorful possibilities and shiny forms. Looking into the kaleidoscope, each of us will see exactly what we dream about, aspire to, and long for.

Leaders will stick to their own values and principles as being evolved and superior. The center of these values will pulse tirelessly and will be visible to all people with pure souls and clear auras. They'll undoubtedly be as the light of the sun is to any living being.

The leaders of the future will vibrate mainly in the Indigo, Crystal, and Rainbow frequencies. They'll be evolved human beings who feel deeply, are easily moved, talk openly, and have eyes to see. They'll have all their senses activated, balanced, harmonized, and unified in their hearts. So the heart center will be the true locus of the expansion of consciousness. These leaders will know that and will invest their energy in developing this center in everybody they're leading.

Business management will not be inspired by external economic indicators such as the GNP, national risk, or commercial balance. It will be totally reoriented and restructured, and will be based on and inspired by internal indicators. These will come from a collective vibratory pattern and a platform of multicolored and multifunctional energetic signals. They'll supply all companies and institutions with different needs and expectations, such as fresh and clean air, solar energy, the pulsation of the earth, oxygen, chlorophyll, water and light in different forms, gamma rays, proximity, distance, acceleration, activation, subtlety, and denseness of energies. From that information, distributed by such a leadership platform, all business will be guided and self-organized daily in a cyclical form.

Industries involving raw material and manufacturing won't exist anymore, at least not as they do in the present. Pollution and environmental damage will be controlled or banned with wisdom from new management techniques inspired by the leaders of the future.

The true challenge won't be to compete for better products and services in order to make more profit, but to cooperate more and more for the integration of our individual cells and consciousness so that eventually, no significant differences between human beings will be noticed. Essential characteristics of our being will be focused, exercised, and developed to generate new configurations in the fields of art and advanced science, which will be very different from current science. *The ultimate goal* will be evident to future leaders: growing cooperation and permanent evolution in cosmic union.

Disciplines studied and applied in lower schools, universities, and companies will be, among others: fundamental ethics, spirituality, art and creativity, unity and diversity, ecology, cosmology, energy in its different forms, and bio-psycho-social-spiritual beings.

The pact for peaceful living will be like the pact a veteran musician made with Bob Dylan: "No evil, fear or envy, so we can work together."

A Real Case of Indigo Leadership

My aim here is to show a real case in which young adult Indigos are doing business. They're managing people; technical, financial, and material resources; and relationships with their partners, suppliers, and society. The company was founded by the young man who wrote the letter I quoted, together with two partners approximately his age. They work in the field of informatics, and because of ethics and secrecy, no names or work focus will be given. I will just identify it as *Company PBI*.

Let's examine the characteristics of these leaders through the way they expressed the mission of the company: "For us, PBI is above all, a company with a soul!" The soul of a company is the reason why the it exists beyond its end function. They continue: "In our lives, the soul reminds us of our mission in this world, and it's this philosophy that we aim to bring to our daily life in the company. We have passion, will, and action, as well as *love,* tenderness, respect for, and dedication to everything we do. Our business is a means to fulfill dreams, and our mission to serve others."

A Brief History of PBI

The company recently celebrated five years of existence and success. It represents the materialization of a dream made possible through friendship, love, admiration, and mutual respect, as well as shared values and a power of vision that unites the partners. "Above all, we are friends; we are brothers," they always affirm when questioned about their relationship.

While they were working together in another information-science company, they dreamed of creating an enterprise different from others—one where people would have recognition and value, participate in the results, enjoy better work conditions, and have much more happiness and dignity.

PBI was officially begun in June 2001 in Porto Alegre. Two of the initial founders invited other partners; they were seven in total. Since then, they went through different phases, some of which were very critical due to conflicts about objectives, focus, and relationships with the initial players.

Another important moment was when the founders realized that their main competence and focus was security and not training or any other activity. At that time, there was an important and significant crisis about the procedures in the company. They discovered they were "acting like capitalists focused on profit," according to the report of one of the partners. And that definitely wasn't what they intended, so they focused again on people and their development.

I can say that there was a realignment of purpose, mission, and values that's still in consideration, as everything is new in this young company. They went back to concentrate on their ultimate objective: people!

I believe that through these declarations and the vision of PBI, the spirit of these young leaders is evident—talented, dedicated, hardworking, evolved, and wise. They're clearly conscious of living in a reality that still favors financial profit above any other value, and that believes in competition instead of cooperation. They're aware of participating and interacting in a reality that has to break paradigms in order to reach the whole, deep, and true vision of the human being, which is holistic and transpersonal and affirms that the humans are *bio-psycho-socio-spiritual* beings.

They know very well that they'll need a lot of work, tolerance, effort, and unity to achieve their dream of building a company with a soul that will survive, grow, and be a reference in the business world and in human relationships. Indigos, the leaders of the future, know very well which values to favor. They have a vision of the world being more peaceful, loving, enlightened, and fair. They believe and know that such a world is possible!

Indigos, the leaders of the future, are convinced that their path is the awakening of consciousness; it's hard work with investment in their own self-knowledge and self-development, both as human beings and leaders. They know that the measure of success isn't increased income, but spiritual development and physical well-being for everybody participating in the company. This is the vision of profit that leaders of the future have: the bottom line is a return of achievement and gratification that can't be threatened, versus a return in dollars, euros, or reals that must always increase.

If we observe new companies, young politicians, and other professionals and leaders, we notice that a transformation is taking place, and quickly. The visionary words of Gary Zukav from ten years ago define the characteristics of a world led by Indigos, leaders of the future:

> When the aim of ultimate contribution is reached, the world of commerce will reflect the values of the soul the same as it

reflects the values of the personality now. As people attempt the task of harmonizing personality with soul, companies will shift from exterior power—competition for market participation and investors—to authentic power or the capacity to confer power to a person and a better life on Earth.

It seems we won't have to wait long to live in such a world! [8]

●●

From Isabel Leal, Ph.D.

PORTUGAL

This submission comes in the form of a short letter to Jan and me (edited slightly for clarity).

●●

Isabel Leal has a Ph.D. in management and has worked for 20 years in several national and multinational companies in Portugal. When she was employed by British Airways, she traveled all around the world and discovered much about herself and the reality of alternative therapies. She works with children now and has some insights for all of us.

●●

Dear Lee and Jan:

In the beginning, personal purposes and personal development led me to start to understand the human condition with "other eyes." As long as I was going deeper in my studies, I started to feel more open, as I did when I was a child. My clairvoyance was back, and I was able to sense my surroundings and the people in my life with more light and reality.

I started to help children with school issues. All of my family members are teachers, and my grandmother had a school in

Lisbon. With this involvement, I discovered my love of working with children. This work gave me a new awareness about life and about the improvement in humanitarian attributes that have been present in the children's eyes since the 1980s.

I organize seminars all over my country with the intention of bringing this knowledge to every person involved with children. Psychologists, doctors, parents, kindergarten teachers, and high-school students are my audience.

My studies were designed for my own improvement and health at first; but after a while, I started to help others on a regular basis. At the same time, I started to give classes for children, and a whole new world was open to me. My interest in children—how to moti-vate them, how to apply energy exercises to help them improve their school results, and how to solve family problems—provided the motivation I needed to create some research.

As I started to read about the colors seen around certain people [by Nancy Tappe] and their accompanying influence on human behavior and conscious awareness, I discovered the Indigo con-cept and later the Crystal and Rainbow Children, too.

I started to work specifically with children and their families. I was invited to do some TV shows, and this exposure led to my being contacted by many parents for family counseling. My goal is to help children on their real spiritual paths and assist the parents to develop their own paths. Parents became aware of the need to study, to elevate their energy to create a better environment at home, providing an equal level of energy and consciousness as their children.

In time, your first book came to Portugal, and people became more interested in this subject. I wrote two books in Portuguese: *Children of a New World—the Indigos,* and *Children of a New World—Crystals.* These books explained the concept to Portuguese people with real cases I had daily in the clinic where I work. Since I believe this is a global concept, I also started to make contact with some families all around the world. All of then were used as testimonies within my book.

I believe you would like to have some Portuguese examples so . . . once I received a couple with a ten-year-old child. They live in the south of Portugal. Both parents commonly participated in meditation conventions and usually studied to attain as much awareness as possible. This child came to me because he was able to leave his body during the day's activities. With perfect consciousness of it, he spoke with dead souls that usually showed up and asked for help. He described the companionship of an elder that had passed away and become a spiritual guide.

Another case involved a seven-year-old who refused to continue to go to school, as he didn't like the teacher. When his mother decided to talk to him, she discovered that the child was right. His teacher was a mother with two girls, and she was going through a divorce. She wasn't caring at home or in school, so he didn't want to be educated by her!

The mother of a four-year-old boy from Brazil contacted me for some help. Ever since he was a little child, this boy reported that he spoke frequently with a being who was three meters (almost ten feet) tall and from another planet. Seven years on that world are like 17 on ours. The other planet doesn't have pollution, and it rains only when every inhabitant wishes it to. This boy also has premonitory dreams, so before he goes to school, he often tells his mother what's going to happen.

A nine-year-old boy who lives in Portugal came to me with his mother. He was having problems with concentration in school, and since he's very smart and always got good grades, something was going wrong. In fact, he had a seven-year-old child always with him. This child had died and was looking for his parents, so he was following my nine-year-old client everywhere. As the younger boy was helped with light, he eventually could go on his way and the nine-year-old could move on as usual. In this process, my young client was the one who gave us the clues to solve this situation. He knew what was going on and served as the guide for the seven-year-old.

I also met a humanitarian girl, and she just wouldn't stop singing or talking. She was obviously very intelligent. One day on the bus while she was coming home from school, she jumped into the lap of a very poor man. According to her mother, this man hadn't taken a bath for a very long time, but she didn't seem to care. She kissed him on the face and said, "If you would bathe yourself more, kids and grown-ups would kiss you more!" And the old man cried.

Loving these children and accepting them as they are is the key. Learning with them, listening to them, and trying to give them all the support to live in this world without changing them will help develop the environment they need to be happy. One day, every single person on this planet will understand, as these children do, that we're all *one*.

• • • • •

Chapter Four

From Health Workers

In the last two years, the highest response to our worldwide call for articles has probably come from health-care professionals. They're often the ones who are called first when there are behavioral issues with children.

In the health-minded holistic world, the last thing parents want is to use drugs as a solution. So, many find psychologists, child-development specialists, energy workers, essence healers, and others who are having good responses in helping both children and adults cope with this new paradigm.

Honestly, we've come to see this group as the first line of defense. The parents understand the "Indigo experience" first. Then come the health-care workers, then the teachers, and finally (gasp) the employers. So really, those involved with health get to see the rawness of the changes that are taking place. Also note that this is an international group.

Again, we had far more submissions from very qualified individuals than we could present here, and we thank all those writers for their interest in what we're doing. We also got our fair share of poetry and beautiful sentiments. Here's a poem from **Hazel Trudeau:**

Child

Beautiful being travels to Earth,
Full of deep love and infinite worth,

A wondrous gift to bring in more light,
A love for our planet, a purpose so bright,

Travels from heaven, on Angel wings ride,
Compassion and knowledge lay deep inside,

Eyes bright with wonder, so much to share,
Gentle and kind, for all others care,

Uniting the Heavens in joyous elation,
Here to teach truths of growth and creation,

A child is born, to grow and unfold,
But world is too harsh, too sharp and too cold,

"You're silly, you're bad,"
"You make me so mad,"
"That's stupid, that's dumb,"
"You've made me feel glum,"
"That's nasty, you're mean,"
"Shut up and keep clean,"
"Look at your mess,"
"You cause me such stress . . ."

A truck full of baggage, "I'm bad and I'm mean,"
So much to carry—and barely a teen.

Mission from heaven almost forgotten,
Seeks numb from world that's painful and rotten,

Colors are fading, spirit is dying,
Draining of life, giving up trying,

Guarding of words, too scared to speak,
Grey, timid, anxious, fearful and weak,

Safety in numbers, be grateful, don't moan,
Work hard, prove worthy, spend more, be a clone,

Follow the crowd, too frightened to think,
Writing a story with watered-down ink,

A cog in a clock, daily existing,
Spirit is crying, yelling, resisting,

Inner-pain, turmoil, growing conflict,
Desperate for peace, self-harm inflict,

Lost and alone, mind seeks solution,
Food, drama, drugs, inner-pollution,

Violence and crime, death and disease,
Mental health problems, lumps of unease,

Enough, stop, enough, too much to take,
Barrel is full, something must break,

Illness sets in but drugs won't resolve,
Patient tries hard but pain won't dissolve,

Symptoms won't patch with medics and pills,
Problems immense, 'mystery' ills,

Crying for help as life-end creeps near,
Thank God an Angel does bravely appear . . .

Love and support, begin to unpack,
Releasing of past, finding way back,

Freer and freer, lighter and lighter,
Visions of purpose, world seeming brighter,

Discovering self, trust guidance inside,
Permission to shine, light spans far and wide,

Forgiving and healing, new day, new birth,
Once again bringing . . . pure Heaven to Earth.

© Hazel Trudeau, February 2006

We wish to be very fair here. We're not bashing the traditional medical community for making fun of this whole theory of an evolving human; rather, we're often frustrated by their lack of desire to even look at the idea. But when we find something that's current and has a bearing on the whole ADD/ADHD issue, we love to present it. These diagnoses are Indigo issues, and the labeling of our children is the subject here.

What follows are excerpts from a very fine *Time* magazine article of November 29, 2007, entitled, "The Next Attention Deficit Disorder?" There's often a fine line these days between a diagnosis of autism and ADD. Many laypeople and medical professionals alike are in the dark when it comes to what might really be causing "off the wall" behavior from a child. Labels are flying, and meanwhile, answers are often difficult to find. We believe that the following information could be a real help for parents reading this book.

●●

The Next Attention Deficit Disorder?

Time magazine, Nov. 29, 2007
by Claudia Wallis

With a teacher for a mom and a physician's assistant for a dad, Matthew North had two experts on the case from birth, but his problems baffled them both. "Everything was hard for Matthew," says Theresa North, of Highland Ranch, Colo. He didn't speak until he was three. In school, he'd hide under a desk to escape noise and activity. He couldn't coordinate his limbs well enough to catch a big beach ball.

Matthew, now ten, was evaluated for autism and attention deficit hyper-activity disorder, but the labels didn't fit. "We filled out those ADHD questionnaires a million times, and he always came out negative," Theresa recalls. "When we found this place, I cried. It was the first time someone said they could help."

This place is the Sensory Therapies and Research (STAR) Center, just south of Denver, which treats about 50 children a week for a curious mix of problems. Some can't seem to get their motors in gear: they have low muscle tone and a tendency to respond only minimally to conversation and invitations to play. Others are revved too high: they annoy other children by crashing into them or hugging too hard. Many can't handle common noises or the feel of clothing on their skin. A number just seem clumsy. Adults can remember kids like these from their own childhood. They were the ones called losers, loners, klutzes and troublemakers. At STAR Center they wear a more benign label: children with sensory processing disorder (SPD).

Never heard of it? You're in good company. Neither have many pediatricians, neurologists, psychologists and teachers. But in the parallel universe of occupational therapy, which focuses on the more primal "occupations" of life—dressing, eating, working, playing—SPD is commonly treated. Last month, at a conference on SPD in New York City, 350 occupational therapists (OTs) and others gathered to hear about the latest research and therapies.

OTs have been treating SPD, also known as sensory integration dysfunction, since 1972, when A. Jean Ayres, a University of Southern California (USC) psychologist and occupational therapist, published the first book on the condition. As defined by Ayres and others, SPD is a mixed bag of syndromes, but all involve difficulty handling information that comes in through the senses—not merely hearing, sight, smell, taste and touch, but also the proprioceptive and vestibular senses, which tell us where our arms and legs are in relation to the rest of us and how our body is oriented toward gravity. Some kids treated for SPD can't maintain an upright position at a desk; some are so sensitive to touch that they shriek when their fingernails are trimmed or if they get oatmeal on their face. Sounds and smells can be overwhelming. When lawn mowers roar outside the home of Lizzie Cave, four, a STAR child, she's been known to vomit.

Families that find their way to the STAR Center and other groups that treat SPD typically have traveled a long road to get there. Their common refrains: My doctor doesn't believe in SPD; teachers can't handle it; insurance won't pay for therapy. There's good reason for that. SPD is not listed in medical texts or in the Diagnostic Statistical Manual (DSM), the bible of psychiatric disorders. Doctors acknowledge sensory issues as a common feature of autism and a frequent feature of ADHD but not as a stand-alone disorder. Lucy Jane Miller, a former protégé of Ayres and head of the STAR Center, is spearheading a campaign to change that. She has organized a national effort to have SPD added to the next edition of the DSM, the fifth, due out in 2012. Earning a spot in the DSM V would make it easier for researchers to win grants, kids to get accommodations at school and families to be reimbursed for a course of treatment, which, at the STAR Center, often costs $4,000.

To receive recognition, advocates must provide persuasive evidence that "this is not just part of autism or ADHD, that it's a better definition of what these kids are experiencing," says Dr. Darrel Regier, director of research for the American Psychiatric Association and vice chair of the DSM V task force. What's needed, says Regier, is a body of peer-reviewed studies that defines "a core set of symptoms, a typical clinical course" and, if possible, good treatment data.

SPD research so far is provocative but limited. "It's hard to get grants for a disorder that doesn't exist," laments Miller, whose recent book, *Sensational Kids,* offers a guide to both research and treatment. Many studies are flawed by vague criteria for identifying the condition, samples that include kids with other disorders, and an utter lack of standardized treatment.

Other experiments at the University of Colorado have found that kids with sensory problems have atypical brain activity when simultaneously exposed to sound and touch. And a 2006 study of twins at the University of Wisconsin gave evidence that hypersensitivity to noise and touch have a strong genetic component.

No one can say with certainty how many kids are severely affected by sensory problems, though preliminary work by Miller suggests it may be 1 in 20. A critical question is where to draw the line between what's normal and what's pathological. Studies conducted by Alice Carter, professor of psychology at the University of Massachusetts, Boston, suggest that 40 percent of children ages seven to ten are so sensitive to touch that tags in clothing annoy them, and 11 percent overreact to sirens. But no one would claim that all these kids have a sensory disorder. Carter thinks SPD is too vaguely defined for prime time in the DSM. Instead, she favors adding it to a section at the back of the manual on disorders that warrant further study. Granting it such provisional status would open the door to more research funds. Then, if validated, SPD could have a shot at being included in the DSM VI—due out somewhere around 2025.

But parents of children who are struggling today are not inclined to wait 18 years, so they spring for therapy that has only anecdotal validation. Treatment is highly individualized, but much of it involves guiding the kids to do more of the things they don't do easily and respond less to the things they can't abide. Lizzie Cave works on noise sensitivity by listening to a calibrated series of audiotapes. Jacob Turner, 3, improves his tolerance for food textures by playing with gooey concoctions and allowing a therapist to put them ever nearer his mouth.

Families get instructions on how to adjust their children's "sensory diets" to help them function better at home and in school. Christopher Medema, seven, now puts a weighted blanket on his lap when he's doing seatwork at school. The steady pressure meets some of his need for tactile input and helps him focus. His family has learned to accommodate his craving for motion. "He likes doing math flash cards standing on his head," says his dad, Steven.

As for Matthew North? He still looks a little limp while dangling from gym equipment, and the blue eyes peering above a sprinkling of freckles gaze warily at people he doesn't know. But the boy who couldn't catch a beach ball last summer is now learning Tae Kwon Do and even soccer. "I saved a couple of goals," he admits, with a little prompting from Mom. That sounds an awful lot like recovery—from whatever it is that ails him.

The original version of this article misidentified occupational therapist A. Jean Ayres as having been on the faculty of UCLA. In fact, Ayres taught and did her groundbreaking research on Sensory Processing Disorder at the University of Southern California (USC).

•●

Lee: The final comment that Jan and I would like to make before we present the healers concerns another *Time* magazine article from Thursday, November 15, 2007, that shouts that it has at last solved the puzzle of ADD and ADHD. The title is "ADHD Riddle Solved." This got me going, since it dismissed the whole range of issues as a growth disorder and suggests that kids eventually outgrow it.

It reports: "The findings, published online this month in Proceedings of the National Academy of Sciences, may help explain why many children diagnosed with ADHD eventually grow out of it, as their brains slowly become more similar to those of their peers."

If this is what parents and teachers were seeing, it might fly, but it isn't. In addition, I'd argue this: even if they're correct, no children are ever going to "catch up to their peers" if they were among the many who got drugged for a few years during their "growth experience." If you don't believe me, just ask them how it felt to be on Ritalin. Many young adults are now weighing in on this, and they've reported that those times were "the lost years." Is it worth it?

••

The Indigo and the Guilt Factor

by Barbra Dillenger, Ph.D.

This article is written by an original contributor to the Indigo series of books. She's a friend of Jan's and mine, and also of Nancy Tappe's. We went to her long ago to help validate the Indigo experience, based on her very profound counseling work with adults over the years. She presents core psychological truths that aren't what you normally see as the traits of Indigos, and she always seems to be ahead of the pack with her wisdom and insight.

••

Barbra Dillenger is a transpersonal development counselor and teacher who has worked in the psychological and metaphysical arena since 1968. She was trained in both of these fields by some of the more outstanding leaders of our time.

Barbra has a doctorate in metaphysical sciences. She holds a B.A. and an M.A. in educational psychology, and she's past educational director of the Unitarian Universalist Fellowship of San Dieguito, guest lecturer and teacher at the University of California–San Diego, and presenter at Escalon Institute in Northern California. At the Kairos Institute in San Diego county, she was director of transpersonal and interpersonal development. She's also a certified herbologist.

Barbra is greatly appreciated for her nonjudgmental approach and accurate, heartfelt guidance in all areas of counseling with both adults and children. Among her peers, she's known as a professional's professional. She has published numerous articles and is a contributing writer for a number of books, especially those dealing with the Indigo children. She's in private practice in Del Mar, California.

Personally, Barbra prides herself on being able to continually learn something of value from all of her encounters and experiences.

••

One of the known hypotheses about the Indigo personality is that these individuals don't come into this lifetime to be hindered by guilt. They feel that we, as an older generation, make guilt-based emotional decisions that aren't in our best interests. For example, we wonder, *How would someone else feel if we did what spoke to our hearts?* With a mission of making changes in existing systems, with a goal of showing us the future—whether we like it or not—and with a desire to be direct in communication, guilt is a deterrent. The Indigos will tell you what they think, even if there's a backlash of emotion that can sometimes hurt them. They're willing to take responsibility if it's their truth. Thus, they're able to uncover hidden secrets in many areas. This leaves them with very little denial. It also makes them appear self-centered and, at times, uncaring and lacking compassion.

On the other hand, those of us who have Indigos in our families and in our counseling practices see another side. While Indigos seem to be self-centered, they can also be caring, compassionate, and supportive of others. They believe in the good of the whole, and they're fair. So how does this work in a society without guilt? To answer that question, let me share a conversation I had recently with the grandmother of a 22-year-old male I'll call "Tom."

It was Easter, and Tom's family had decided to go to the country club for a sumptuous brunch. When the time came, Tom announced that he wasn't going. This was annoying to his aunt, who was planning the event. She wanted him to enjoy the club, which he hadn't experienced before, and she also enjoyed his company. So she asked his grandmother to step in, knowing that Grandma understood the Indigo personality.

When Grandma asked Tom why he didn't want to go, he answered: "I don't care for country clubs."

She replied, "Just think of it as going to a family dinner, one that's going to be at a nice restaurant."

"Well," said Tom, "it's a nice restaurant that not everyone can go to. You have to belong to the club."

Grandma couldn't argue with that, so she tried another tactic. "I know that I can't make you feel guilty, so what can I do that will make you want to go?"

Tom thought for a moment and then said, "You're right, I never do anything out of guilt. I'll do things out of duty."

Then she remembered that there had been several family occasions he'd attended where she thought guilt was a factor. She realized that it must have been duty instead.

After listening to her story, I came to understand that guilt comes from the head and contains fear. Duty, for Tom, is different and comes from the heart. Therefore, for him, duty becomes a true desire based on compassion and love. He really wanted to attend these other functions, even if he didn't like the circumstances. And by the way, Tom didn't attend the Easter brunch.

I find this story exciting and interesting. What an emotionally mature way of behaving! What a lesson for all of us. Can we make decisions without guilt? Can we separate what makes our hearts leap with joy, like a child, versus thinking, *I think I have to, or I should do this . . .* ? If we can, we'll be in touch with that divine guidance that comes from our heart, not the illusion of our negative thinking. We'll certainly have a much clearer sense of direction from self and not from the outside world, more confidence and self-identity, less anger and resentment.

I've always felt that creating a more humanitarian world must start with self and in our own homes. If we could understand which of our own decisions are guilt-ridden and which are heartfelt duty, that could be a start. Possibly we'd be less defensive, and maybe we could find ourselves living in a world community that has love as its core, not ego—a community where there's compassion for all life, everywhere.

Like Tom, who's 22, some Indigos who are now 40 are in the workplace. We're meeting them. They're our doctors, lawyers, politicians, teachers, fathers, mothers, artists, musicians, and so on. They have had the most difficulty adjusting to our current systems that aren't based in truth. They'll show us the new way. We'll be forced to make changes whether we like it or not, because soon we'll be in the minority. I think it's important to listen to their truth without guilt. It will be quite a journey.

●●

Conscious Parenting for a New Paradigm

by Barbra Gilman

Barbra Gilman is the author of The Unofficial Guide for Living Successfully on Planet Earth and a contributing author to Jan and Lee's second Indigo book, An Indigo Celebration. She's the CEO of Success Strategies For Life, a firm assisting families, couples, companies, and individuals in developing their full potential.

Barbra was the director of family education for Neale Donald Walsch's HeartLight School and has more than 25 years' experience as a therapist/coach. She's a certified trainer and parent educator with the International Network for Children and Families, teaching "Conscious Parenting for a New Paradigm."

Barbra served as the director of the center for spiritual awareness and has hosted her own radio show, Conscious Choices. She's also a motivational/inspirational speaker who has taught hundreds of workshops on personal and spiritual development and success through awareness.

••

When Jan and Lee asked me to write this article for their new Indigo book, I was delighted. Spreading the word about our wonderful "new" children and what I believe their needs are has been my passion and vision for many years now. Through my work, I have the opportunity to keep my finger on the pulse of the evolving world of parenting, and I believe I'm able to clearly see the direction parenting must take in order to improve the lives of today's children.

Before I could even ask Jan what I should write about, she said, "It's been ten years since the first book, and I'd like to know what differences you see out there now." As her words came through the phone line, first reaching my ears and then my heart, I could feel a rising sense of sadness and frustration, because what I believed *would have* happened in these last seven years has yet to even begin.

I thought that by now, every parent of an Indigo (whether they knew what an Indigo was or not) would be out there actively searching for a definition of their "job description," as well as looking for the parenting skills to carry it out. Today, I think the average person has no clue as to what an Indigo is or that there even is such a thing as a new and improved version of human beings on the planet—so it's actually easy to understand. If parents don't recognize that today's offspring really are different, they certainly can't imagine a reason to learn new parenting skills to serve the needs of these evolved children!

Oh yes, *Indigo* has become a buzzword within the spiritual community, and it's been talked about on CNN and *Good Morning America*. There's even one famous Hollywood mom walking around wearing an "Indigo Mom" T-shirt. However, this represents only a tiny percentage of our population—and what usually happens within the spiritual community is that we teach, preach to, and heal *each other,* leaving the rest of the world to carry on just as it always has; only now we seem to be living in total chaos!

Please don't get me wrong. I understand that our world is in transition, and the infrastructure of our society is shifting as we raise our consciousness. There's much to be excited about. This is the information age; every day there are new discoveries that can change our world. However, we have to be *receptive* to these new possibilities. We have to allow ourselves to let go of our fear, which keeps us anchored to the past. We must embrace our freedom and reclaim our power.

Here's an example of what I mean by this. A client of mine grew up in a second-generation Italian family. Her mother repeatedly admonished the teenage daughter: "Don't be too smart. The boys won't like you." That age-old fear around gaining security through a man was so deep that this woman's parenting perpetuated the worry, actually serving to stunt her daughter's personal and intellectual growth, even as she believed that She was *protecting* the daughter. How could this teenager embrace her own power when hundreds of years of fear were being passed down to her, disguised as "loving parenting"? This is just one example of how fear anchors us in the past and keeps us from seeing the present as a fresh new opportunity for growth.

Luckily, there are people who are beginning to wake up and see that there are truths to be discovered beyond our "emperor's new clothes" version of reality. We now have films like Aaron Russo's *America: Freedom to Fascism* and Dylan Avery's *Loose Change*—talk about a wake-up call! This is the time we either change ourselves in order to change our world, or we shift into high-speed reverse. And, of course, it's the Indigos who are bringing in this grand new world.

So the real question remains: How do we spread this information so that it reaches the mainstream? How do we get parents and teachers who believe Ritalin is a viable answer to their problem—a quick "fix" for their kids—to be awake and aware that these children have intellectual *gifts*, not deficits.

Even within the spiritual arena, parents are still looking for the most esoteric therapies, modalities, information, and remedies for our Indigos. However, being in the trenches for the last several years, I've seen the many disappointments that these parents face: stories of mainstream individuals who are totally caught off guard by their children and succumb to the pressure to take the "path of least resistance." The use of drugs to make these kids easier to handle is insane. The problem is that most parents are totally unaware that alternatives exist, so in their desperation, they turn to others who are equally in the dark. It's the blind leading the blind.

I'm sad to say that I receive letters from parents needing to share their grief after their child has committed suicide from that so-called path of least resistance! And they all say the same thing:

"If I'd only understood the concept of Indigos, my child would be alive today."

The thing we need to remember is that our Indigos *are* quite different; however, let's not forget that they're still *children*. The point that I feel most people are missing at this time is that we're all basically dysfunctional. We're simply babies in the realms of consciousness. That's okay because one way or another, we're all on our own journey—the journey of waking up, of consciousness, of allowing ourselves to be who we really are, which is love.

But right now who we are is children raising children. Most parents today are grown-ups who have the *consciousness* of kids (average ones, not Indigos) raising youngsters who have the consciousness of adults. And as I said earlier, while parents have one of the most important jobs on the planet, they've had absolutely no training, and they don't seem to be seeking it out! Parenting is one of those critical areas that has simply never really been examined—and even today there's a large percentage of moms and dads who don't believe that they need to take parenting classes. As bizarre as this may seem, it's quite true. There seems to be a pervasive belief that this is something that comes naturally by osmosis as soon as one has a child. This outlook desperately needs to be changed. I can tell you as a therapist and coach that every person I've ever worked with would be in a different place today if they'd had parents who were conscious and aware of their needs.

Parenting: An Evolving Process

What's the difference between the way you parent and the way your parent raised you? Hmm? Now, some of you who were brought up with an autocratic system in place within your home probably said, "Oh no, I'm not going there—I'll never be so strict with my children." So you went 180 degrees over into the land of permissive parenting, which, by the way, is what we see a lot of in today's families. But this only serves to create very self-centered children who believe they're the center of the universe. That might work within their home and their grandparents' home, but when they get out into the real world, it can be a rude awakening for the child and very ugly for everyone else.

Before I raised the question in the last paragraph, had you ever thought of how your parenting strategies compare with the ones your parents used with you? Oh yes, I know that when you were younger, you said you'd never do what they did. However, as we get older, our words come back to haunt us as we start to see how much we really are like our earliest role models. How many of the strategies you find yourself using now no longer work with this current generation? And the more important question is: did they ever work?

Even though most folks believe that parenting is a skill that everyone is expected to know instinctively, many people are beginning to look deeper. And it's often the Indigos who are forcing that reexamination; because with Indigos, parents feel their instincts falling short as the levels of stress keep mounting! And no matter where they look—whether it's into their past to examine their own parents' strategies or right here in the present where they discover that their neighbors are in the same situation—there doesn't seem to be help anywhere in sight.

Do we want our children growing up with our behavioral "programs," continuing to create the same mess that we're all in now? Or do we want to empower them to be conscious and flexible enough to choose the most effective way to be, so the concept of a peaceful and joyful world is achievable?

Our new children are absolutely incredible; they're the peacemakers who *will* change our world, and they'll do a much quicker job if we get out of their way! We're the ones who are missing some strategic pieces to the jigsaw puzzle of parenting. We have trouble understanding who they are and who we are!

So let's look at some of these missing pieces that will answer a question Jan asked me: "What do you believe would help these parents the most right now?" And my answer is very simple: conscious parenting skills!

Conscious Parenting . . . a New Place to Be!

When I speak about conscious parenting, the focus is on the word *conscious*—being aware, paying attention, being in present time. And the question I always receive is: *What would that look like in our families?* When I created the "Conscious Parenting for a New Paradigm" course, I wanted to provide a framework and support system for parenting: a way for moms and dads to learn to relate with their children so that they can navigate intuitively toward their destinies, feeling safe enough to experience closeness and intimacy with others. The goal is for children to claim authorship of their lives and to become motivated from *within,* rather than rely upon external circumstances or events, which is the way most of us live our lives. And quite clearly, we see that it doesn't work!

The secret is to accept children for the unique individuals they are, rather than trying to control or manipulate their behavior or "fix" them. Remember, there's *nothing* wrong with these children; it's our behavior and understanding that needs to evolve. We need to learn how to honor, respect, and understand our kids as we teach cooperation, responsibility, negotiation, and decision-making skills. Furthermore, as we learn how to keep in touch with our adventurous, creative, and fun-loving inner children, we'll find new pathways to success that we haven't yet tapped into.

Universal Principles for Manifesting Stress-Free Parenting

No matter whom I coach—whether it's a corporation, an individual, a relationship, or a parent—the first thing I do is teach universal principles. Learning how this world works and how we, as self-aware individuals, can shape our environments to create our desired outcomes, is the key to a successful life. The bizarre thing is that more than 90 percent of the population doesn't have this information. As I like to say, "We're playing Monopoly with Parcheesi rules . . . no wonder we can't win the game!"

With that said, let's look at some of the basics of these principles so that you can manifest *stress-free parenting.* The most important place to look is within yourself. Always remember that these children have come as our teachers, as strange as that might seem. And irrespective of whether you believe this or not, you *will* find that when you examine the behavior that's driving you crazy, the root of it lies within yourself. They're mirrors—their behavior is the reflection of others' inner wounds. So when you're stressing out about a specific part of their behavior, ask yourself, *What feeling is this bringing up for me?* Then look within yourself and see where *you* feel or have felt that way in your life. Not only will you find the origin of their behavior, but you'll also begin your healing.

At one of the Montessori schools where I was presenting my course, a father and faculty member shared that his son's very needy behavior was driving him crazy. Although he'd tried everything that he could think of, his son was still relentless in his need for attention and love. The father heard my theory of Indigos being our teachers, but he simply wasn't ready to go there. After the fourth week of our class, however, he approached me like a person who had just walked through the desert for three weeks. He stated, "I'm ready to try anything. What do I need to do?"

I asked that father to delve into his own life and see where his son's feelings were a reflection of his own. A week later, he reported back with the story of *his* father abandoning his mother when he was three. Clearly, he'd found his wound and the solution to his son's behavior! I gave him a copy of my book and told him to do some inner child–healing work. A few weeks after that, he showed up at another one of my classes to share his triumph: after three weeks of healing his inner child, his son's behavior simply ceased!

Here are some questions and techniques you might want to work with:

- Which of your child's behaviors would you like to change?

- What feelings are representative of your child's behavior?

- What's your child trying to teach you in present time?

- Is there a period in this lifetime when you experienced these feelings?

If the answer to that last question is yes, do some inner-child work to heal that part of you. (There are lots of ways to do this, including changing your history, which I wrote about in my book. However, I believe the quickest is Randall Oppitz's method, called "THP" (**TheHealProcess.com**) Here's the nutshell version: Randall's THP work is based in physics and its law that states energy can't be created or destroyed. All thoughts, feelings, and emotions are energy that need to be transferred. Learning how to do this is the key to healing. A simple THP exercise to aid that goal is to give yourself permission to let go of any thought, feeling, or emotion while holding the intention to forgive. Breathe deeply through the mouth, inhaling high into your upper chest while filling your heart with love. Then go directly into the feeling while exhaling through the mouth and letting go of the energy.

Work with these questions and suggestions:

- What can you do to change your perspective on the situation?

- What can you do to allow peace to be your dominant feeling?

- Bring your child into your meditation and communicate with him there.

- Send your higher self to your child's higher self to help work it out.

- Surround your child with white light and release him to his highest good.

Here's another way to look at it: when Indigos are behaving in ways that make you want to pull your hair out, you can try changing yourself, rather than changing them. When you have people in your life whose behavior, to you, is like hearing the sound of fingernails scratching on a blackboard, and you continually think of their negative behavior, you're literally holding their vibration (and their behavior) in place with your energy. You're thinking, *That's the way they are!* And guess what? You're right. That *is* the way they are, as long as you hold them that way! It's sort of like putting children in Halloween costumes and then sewing, gluing, stapling, and cementing the outfits in place—they're on and aren't going anywhere else too soon!

What you need to do is think about them the way you want them to be. Your feelings will go along with your new perception. In doing so, you're creating a space for them to change, along with the energy to help them. This is what I call holding the vibration or frequency of what you want—as opposed to what you don't want.

When my daughter Heather was a teenager, she went through a stage where she simply didn't want to have a mom who was different from all the other moms. Who, me? Yes, clearly, I was, well, maybe a little unlike the others. I was a "metaphysical mom" who didn't yell, who tried to teach about consciousness and spirituality, and who wanted to be a friend as well as a mother to my daughter. Well, that was simply too strange. I had doors slammed in my face as my heart was pulled apart by the sound of those piercing words *Why can't you be a normal mom?* anytime I used terms that sounded "weird" to her!

At the time, I felt like such a victim. It just didn't make sense to me. I used to tell Heather, "If I had a mom like me, I'd be flying through the sky right now!" But all my efforts were in vain. My arguments fell on deaf ears. I found myself telling my victim story (how my precious Heather turned into a witch) to my girlfriends, and getting answers such as: "Well, that's just how kids are, isn't it?"

One day I was speaking to a client who had a child who was treating her in a similar way. I heard myself giving her the advice I should have been giving myself: "The solution is easy. Just don't keep holding him in that frequency!"

Wow! It hit me the moment I said it. There it was, the answer to my victim story. As the saying goes, we teach best what we need to learn most. Being the good student that I am, I listened to my own words. I began to create the story that I wanted to live and started telling it to my friends. Within the month, Heather's behavior began changing. I was still known as the weird mom, but I was able to go to sleep at night with a smile and a heart filled with gratitude. As I always say, life is very simple. It may not be easy; but if we understand universal principles, we can get what we desire!

The following sections outline what I did.

Step 1: Know What You Want

As crazy as it may seem, most people don't take the time to really focus on and feel what they want. They're too busy concentrating on what they don't want without even realizing it. To my surprise, I was doing just that. I was haunted by the sight of Heather slamming her bedroom door and screaming her favorite phrase—the one she knew would get me right where she wanted me: with tears running down my cheeks and a hole in the middle of my heart.

Luckily, knowing exactly what you *don't* want in your life helps you create a new story. This time you can make it one you *desire* (as if you're an artist painting a picture that's in your mind and in your heart). As it evolves, you'll feel as if it's coming from your soul, which is exactly where the heart's desires come from.

And of course in my case, I knew exactly what I wanted: a peaceful, loving, and joyful relationship between Heather and me . . . just as it had been before she put on her witch costume!

Step 2: Live, Eat, Breathe, and
Most of All *Be* What You Want

Carry the vibration of the way you see and feel yourself being (in your visualization) with you in every moment of your day. Let it be as if you were running across the playing field of your life, trying to win the Academy Award for the specific role you've just created. Do this as often as you can. And if you forget, start over the minute you remember. This is where the concept of being "present in the moment" comes into play.

I began to visualize life the way it was before. I saw Heather and me having fun, spending time together without my having to feel as though I was walking on eggshells and not wondering if I'd say something that would send her off into her anger and me into my tears. By envisioning this desired outcome, I began to realize that my vibration was changing. Not only did I feel happier, I actually started to let go of some of the resentment that I had for my daughter, which allowed me to once again feel that a joyful relationship was an option.

Step 3: Don't Go into the Land of "What Is"

You might not see what you want instantaneously, but keep going in that direction. Stay focused in present time—being patient, excited, and hopeful. Far too many people give up too quickly out of disappointment. When a farmer plants a carrot seed, he doesn't go out into the field every few days, digging up the ground because he doesn't see the carrot. He knows that there *will* be a carrot! Most people get lost when it comes to manifesting their desires by focusing on "what is" in their life—in other words, what presently exists (which isn't what they want). However, they don't realize that their focus (vibration) on what they don't want is what got them to this point. The thing is that the universe is always giving you what you want, which is equal to the vibration you're holding. Now, rewind and go back and read the last sentence, because this is one of the secrets of living a joyful life!

There were a couple of times during the first week that I got caught in the "what is." However, even with a door slamming right in my face, I visualized my outcome, felt the happiness of it, and forged ahead!

Step 4: Feel Gratitude

As soon as you see or feel that the change you desire is occurring, then rev up your motors, intensify your feeling of joy, and go excitedly into the next segment of your desire. Gratitude is a very powerful energy, and the more that you acknowledge it, the more you'll see those wonderful things flowing into your life.

Slowly but surely, I began to see a transformation occurring in Heather. The sheer excitement of that made me want to get down on my knees and give thanks—and I did!

Is Discipline Your Top Priority?

Why is it that almost everyone who attends a parenting class has discipline as their top priority? It's the most important topic of *their* class agenda, and they're quietly praying that their challenge will be answered and answered quickly. I can feel them anxiously waiting with bated breath for that glorious moment when they'll be set free . . . free from a life of screaming, nagging, arguing, punishing, cajoling, and whining. No more confusion, stress, chaos, guilt, or power struggles. . . . Need I go on? Yes, parents are waiting (as everyone is) for the state of peace and harmony—a world of open communication, cooperation, responsibility, accountability, positive problem solving, self-control, and self-motivation—and yes, even some fun!

Have you ever witnessed a parent/child confrontation at Wal-Mart or your local supermarket? I'm sure you're quite familiar with that feeling—you know, the one where the parents want to dig a hole so deep they can jump right in and hide from the fear of such embarrassment. Why is that? Well, you see, in this world, we have it wired that a misbehaving child is a bad child, and standing right next to that bad *child* would, of course, have to be a bad *parent*. And no one wants to look like a bad parent. Because of that fear, we believe that our job description is to mold, control, manipulate, and discipline (punish) our children—or in other words, fix them—so that they'll be good children. Then by association, we'll be good parents, or at least look like we are.

Now, please don't get me wrong; I'm not blaming or throwing rocks at anyone. The thing is, as long as we live in a world of perpetual chaos marked by fear, hatred, judgment, moral corruption, and weakness, we can't expect our children to miraculously show up demonstrating truth, compassion, respect, moral strength, character, confidence, self-esteem, unconditional love, and trust. I think you get my point here.

Human beings are the microcosm, and our world is the macrocosm. If you're interested in seeing how we humans are evolving, all you need to do is pick up your local newspaper or listen to the news. The stories you see out there are *our stories,* the energetic reflection of what's going on within us. Every thought, feeling, and choice we make is leading us down a path. The good news is that each one of us is creating our own path . . . we simply have to be aware of that!

Once we realize that there's nothing *wrong* with our children and that they don't need to be fixed, we can then come to realize that there are no *bad* children. There are only discouraged children, and we're the ones who are discouraging them. They're actually quite magnificent beings and, in fact, are more conscious than we are.

I'm certainly not implying that discouraging children is our intention or goal. However, due to our lack of understanding of who these children are—or because our lives are so stressful—we either believe that when it comes to parenting we've got it handled, or we simply don't have the time or inclination to learn more. I find it quite amazing that whenever I speak to an audience, a good percentage is made up of grandparents who feel that their grandchildren aren't getting what they need at home. And they don't know how to get that across to *their* children without it seeming like they're butting in. Oh, it makes for such an interesting story, doesn't it? Well, the good news is that we're also the ones who can encourage our children, and it's never too late to learn!

It's time to wake up and smell the lies that we believe, live with, and hand down to our children. I'm not blaming our society for the stories that we *believe*—clearly, that would only be adding more judgment to this already chaotic and overwhelmed world. However, I do feel that the change we're seeking can be created from within us by focusing on healing ourselves first, waking up and living and parenting consciously.

Let's examine some strategies that will work as long as you have those basics down.

Dissolving Power Struggles

In all my interactions with parents over the last few years, the biggest topic under the heading of discipline is power struggles. It's not very surprising because if you look around at our world, that's mostly what you'll see. Whether we're examining politics, finances, relationships, medicine, or another field, everyone seems to want it their way—as if there were only one way! Life gets very sticky when the ego runs rampant, and our evolution of consciousness is mostly stuck in ego. So where does that bring us?

Well, I speak about power struggles in a variety of forums, from the parenting community to corporate settings. (Actually, power struggles are a pretty big topic in the corporate world, simply because even though our adults are dressed up in designer clothing and drive expensive cars, most still react from their inner five-year-olds.) When I'm training on this subject, the first thing that I say is: "Take your sail out of their wind." In other words, if no one shows up for a fight, there simply can't be one! However, once that's said, it's important to go a few levels deeper and see where the conflict is actually coming from.

If you were in a power struggle with someone and I asked you, "What's the first thing you'd do in this situation if you were being honest?" I'm sure your honest answer would probably have something to do with trying to find a way to take *more* power *from* the other person. Now, those might not be your exact words; however, if you paid attention to your feelings, you'd find that was exactly where you were going. That's simply because we were all programmed that way—it falls under the "eye for an eye" theory, or what you do to get even when you're five years old.

You might be asking: *What would a more conscious person do?* And the answer is: find ways to make the other person feel more powerful! You see, anyone who needs to create a power struggle feels powerless in their life. It's as easy as that. And being a conscious person understanding this, you'd want to help your "opponent" feel mightier and more valuable in his or her world.

So for all you parents out there who are finding your households consumed by power struggles, here are some practical things you can do:

1. Allow your child to help you in ways that you choose together. Possibilities include grocery shopping, watering plants, writing checks, being in charge of family outings, washing dishes, washing clothes, making a meal for the family—all age appropriate, of course. That said, most people have a different idea of what age appropriate is. My belief is that when your children are tall enough to reach the dryer, they can start helping you fold clothes; and when they're old enough to reach the buttons of the washing machine, they can start washing their own clothes. This makes it very easy when it's "blue-shirt day" at school. Instead of asking you where their blue shirts are, the situation is their responsibility!

Here's another example: There was once a man who had lost his wife and was raising his son by himself. The son was depressed and had slowly let go of his life . . . friends, school projects, sports. When the father got to this section in my class, he decided that helping his son feel more powerful sounded like it would really work. He simply needed to think of how to do it. It just so happened that the father owned a store, so he decided to ask his son if he would be willing to help out every Saturday. His son agreed. Then the father had to decide what task would be the most appropriate to help create a feeling of power and value for his son. He thought and thought, and came up with paying the store's bills. The father commented that when he told his son what he'd like the child to do, his son's face lit up in astonishment, realizing the power that his father had just bestowed upon him.

(*Note:* To be more specific, the father gathered together the store's bills and told his son that he should choose which were the most important ones to be paid. Of course, he was going to end up paying them all anyway; this simply added a little more power to the task. Once his son had made out all the checks, the father came and signed them, and then his son addressed the envelopes and mailed them!)

A few weeks had gone by when the father met one of his son's friends while he was out jogging. He was very pleased to hear that his son had been telling his friends that the store couldn't get along without him! Shortly after that, friends, activities, and sports were all part of the boy's life again.

2. Share your feelings with your children and allow them to be there for you. If you were feeling a little out of sorts one day—sort of moping around—and your child came in and said, "Mom (or Dad), what's wrong?" what would the average parent say? I've presented this question to hundreds of classes, and the answer has always been *"Nothing!"* Once again, our programs are intact. This is one of those things that seems to be passed by osmosis from generation to generation.

The first reason that this isn't the appropriate answer is that it once again encourages our negative programming to be passed from one generation to the next. In this case, what we're really saying is that feelings are dangerous, and we don't want to go there, so just stuff yours! As a therapist, I can tell you that one of the biggest ongoing problems we all have is the fact that most of us run on *numb* because somewhere in our lives, someone modeled or taught us this lie.

Another reason not to give that answer is that most Indigo Children have come into this lifetime with an absolutely brilliant gift of really being able to tune in and feel what others are feeling —in some cases actually knowing what others are thinking. As out there as that may seem for some, it's still true. So once again, what we'd be telling these children is that their brilliant gift, which will help change our world, isn't working, is wrong, or isn't real. Either way we'd be doing them the greatest disservice—that is, of course, next to putting them on any types of drugs. (I believe that ADD can stand for Adults Demanding Drugs to make their lives easier!)

Now, does that mean that when you have a fight with your husband, and your child asks, "What's wrong?" you have to say, "Your father is an idiot"? No! However, you can say, "Dad and I agreed to disagree, and I'm processing my feelings." It serves your children and anyone else in your life to always come from your truth. You know what they say: "The truth shall set you free." Yes, I realize that only conscious people would be able to say that; however, isn't that why you're reading this book?

3. Allow your child to teach you something—anything at all will work. Here's an example: When I bought my computer years ago to write my book, knowing absolutely nothing about technology, I went to my daughter for classes. Even though she lived far away from me on the West Coast, we had two sessions a week over the telephone. When I spoke to one of her friends, I heard: "Heather is so excited because she's actually teaching you!" Do you think that made her feel powerful and valuable?

4. Ask your children for their advice. You could ask, "What do you think I should wear to work today?" Or you might say, "I have a conflict with my friend at work. What do you think I could do about it?"

The amazing thing is that these children will have answers that will absolutely surprise and delight you . . . if you're only willing to listen and realize that sometimes our teachers come in pint-size packages!

Before you put down this chapter and walk away, I suggest that you take a blank piece of paper and write down five ways in which you'll allow and encourage your children to feel more powerful and valuable this week. Next week, come back and create a weekly to-do list based on the article. Remember, nothing changes until you do!

Pulling It All Together: The Family Meeting

It's clear that the actual concept of *family* is almost nonexistent today. We can't expect to create a peaceful, loving, and harmonious world when our own families are so out of balance. We're running so fast in our daily lives and getting nowhere that makes any sense. We're trying to take care of what we believe are our most important responsibilities; and for most of us living in this postmodern world, it seems to be the almighty dollar! Oh yes, I understand that there's so much to do and so little time to do it and . . . well, let's not get into what comes next (which of course is our stories) right now. What I'd like to share with you, though, is a wonderful way to start evolving your family into a loving, honoring, peaceful, conscious, and fun-loving group of people. Voilà: the family meeting!

When I first thought of a family meeting, I remembered being a child watching TV with my dad (it was probably *Gunsmoke* or another one of his favorite Westerns), and of course there was a town meeting going on. Today, towns still carry on this age-old ritual. The question is *Why?* And the answer is the same as why we'd want to have a *family* meeting: It creates a feeling of being involved, of cooperation, of being accountable to the group, and of feeling supported. It's a forum for everyone to express their opinions in a place of safety. To maintain that security, it's essential that no criticism be allowed during these meetings. It's better to view them as think tanks, where only creative thought is allowed.

Family meetings can be a very successful time for problem solving as well as having *fun*. The fun part is very important, otherwise no one's going to show up! As adults, we start to lose our kids when we forget our own childhood memories—we forget what it was like to be a child or adolescent, to feel all the emotions that were surging through us at those ages when *our* parents were the enemy! Remember? Forgetting sets *you* up in the enemy camp, and that's when you're on your way to compromising your relationship with your children.

Here are some ideas for the format of your family meeting:

— **Who:** Everyone in the family with no exceptions!

— **When and where:** Hold your family meeting on the same day and at the same time each week. This way, everyone knows that the meeting takes priority, and everything else will be scheduled around it. Allow your answering machine to pick up all calls . . . once again stressing the importance of the task at hand. Choose an environment that creates a sense of warmth and safety with a little fun thrown in.

— **What to do:** create a space on the refrigerator or bulletin board that will hold the family meeting agenda. This will include any challenges that come up during the week that can wait till the next family meeting. However, if Johnny is dangling his little sister out the window by her shoelaces, please handle that immediately! All other issues will be dealt with during the meeting, exploring all alternatives that can lead to creative and conscious solutions.

Before you begin the meeting, hold a family intention as to what you want to create, such as having all challenges met in a peaceful, harmonious, and loving way, creating clear-cut solutions and figuring out the necessary steps for their completion.

Each week you'll need to elect a leader and secretary. The leader's job is to help you stay on topic, while the secretary keeps notes about what was discussed and decided. Having it all in print makes it accessible in case anyone should forget or have a different recollection of what happened.

As a group, visualize the end result you desire, envisioning it as a short movie that's run in your mind with the feeling of great excitement. During the week, support the family and have them act as a "mastermind" group, turning on their little mental movie at the same time (possibly at the dinner table) and helping create the manifestation of the desired state.

End the meeting in a fun way. Remember, having fun is the most important part. Without it, no one will want to show up! Go see a movie, bring in pizza, or play some of the family's favorite games.

To Sum Up

If creating a peaceful and fun-loving home is what you desire, it's quite doable—despite how difficult it might seem in those moments when you're ready to pull out your hair. As I've mentioned before, it's simple, but not easy. Learning to become conscious of who you and who your children are is the first step. Understanding how you actually create your reality is the second step. Being in present time is the third step, and allowing the unfolding of the sacred relationship between you and your child creates the miracle!

••

The Indigo Teenager

by Becky Engler Hicks, Ph.D.

***Becky Engler Hicks** is a parenting expert with outstanding creden-tials who offers a unique professional experience and a blend of training. She received her Ph.D. in pre-perinatal psychology from Santa Barbara Graduate Institute after receiving her master's in dance therapy from UCLA and doing undergraduate work in psychology at Mount Holyoke College.*

Becky founded The Mothering Coach and is the director of Baby Bright Infant Learning. She was an adjunct professor in dance therapy at Washington University–St. Louis; and she's been a clinician with infants, children, adolescents, and adults at Barnes-Jewish Hospital. She has worked with more than 400 infants and their families teaching her innovative programs. She has been a parenting educator at Villa Majella of Santa Barbara, California, and she currently works at the Conscious Parenting Center in St. Louis. She's the mother of two grown daughters, stepmother of three, and grandmother of three. All of her children have been her greatest teachers.

••

Indigo teens are bright, talented, sensitive, and caring indi-viduals who need to be deliberately engaged in discovering their personal interests and purpose in relation to caring for individuals in their lives.

It has been my delightful opportunity to work with this group in private practice as a body-centered psychotherapist. These adolescents are referred to me for a creative outlet, psychotherapeutic help for actual depressive disorders, and stress management. Many of them find it supportive to do some creative movement and internal bodily focusing in order to be able to identify where in their body they're feeling certain negative and positive emotions and in order to have a means for identifying and releasing their feelings and personas in a safe, supportive environment. Early on, they become empowered to self-express and discover their strong, enlightened, authentic, and spiritual selves. This information provides motivation for learning and developmental mastery, which in many cases has been missing. They need to explore their personal wisdom and have the opportunity to share their insights.

I've observed that they love to improvise, sing, act, dance, do art, tell stories, and journal, as they're natural nonverbal communicators. Frequently, they voice frustration over not being understood by their parents and teachers, who don't allow them the freedom to do in-depth creative work, the time to explore feelings, and the ability to engage on multiple levels of being. They also need exposure to beauty in nature, art, and music in their home and school environments to enhance their sensitivities. They need to be loved.

Many Indigos who are particularly sensitive to inner and outer conditions have been hurt by a variety of negative situations at home and in school, beginning with harmful early programming in their early years that has produced self-esteem problems. They sometimes missed developmental opportunities for secure attachment and for regulating their nervous systems as their parents were busy in their careers and didn't spend enough time with them at critical periods.

Expressive arts-therapy methods are always well received because they seems interesting and personal. Imagery; breath and dream work; sand-tray activities; and art, dance, and music therapies in the studio are particularly conscious and creative activities that allow them to easily access subconscious material that has been buried in the body, mind, and spirit. This can be very person-ally rewarding to Indigo teens who want to know the real truths about their circumstances and to receive confirmation of their own reality so that there's no need to use addictive substances, which block this awareness. Some of my clients get in touch with very early prenatal, birth, and childhood memories of not being wanted; being in a toxic womb; or not being birthed, bonded to, and/or parented in a conscious, nurturing, and loving way.

When they trust in me as a supportive therapist and facilita-tor, that confidence is transferred to themselves. Then they can naturally and easily move to the oldest sources of their pain. In therapy, early negative imprinting can be cleared with attention and intention. This kind of emotional release needs to be done with awareness and at the individual's own pace. Internal access to traumatic events that occurred when the teens were infants and children becomes a simple process of self-discovery that's reliev-ing, as layers of less optimal patterning are released and identified. It helps repair the self that has been hurt from earlier missteps in development.

The teen years are an optimal time for self-reflection, personal growth, and therapeutic intervention that may help prevent fur-ther emotional problems in young adulthood, which can be actu-ally debilitating and derail the individual at a later period. Sponta-neous nonverbal, imaginative, body-centered work is freeing and serves as a resource for these Indigo teenagers, who are often right-brained and who benefit from flowing and intuitive approaches that allow them to unfold at their own pace, to self-calm, and to receive information directly from Source. It also helps provide energetic clearing for their greater health and wholeness, with the opportunity for somatic integration of feelings.

I am an Indigo. I have two grown Indigo daughters and two Crystal grandchildren, and I grasp the essentials for understand-ing us. My intuition regarding my own personal needs throughout my life has influenced the creative nature of my work. My caring and playful attitude has been well received in my own family and with my clients of all ages, who require sensitive, attuned, and intelligent interactions through openhearted giving and receiving. We all require a means for creative self-exploration and the discovery of our own uniqueness and gifts in relaxed and beautiful ways. May we all walk in beauty. May we all become encouraged at all stages of development to evolve our human capacities!

••

Nutrients That
Are Beneficial for
Indigo Children

by Howard Peiper, N.D.

*Dr. **Howard Peiper** is a nationally recognized expert in the holistic counseling field. His healing, health-care, and natural-professional credentials extend over a 30-year period and include naturopath, author, lecturer, magazine consultant, and radio personality.*

Howard, who was nominated for a Pulitzer Prize, has written numerous works on nutrition and natural health including 12 bestsellers:

The A.D.D. and A.D.H.D. Diet!
Zeolite: Nature's Heavy Metal Detoxifier
"Viral Immunity with Humic Acid"
The Secrets of Staying Young (from the inside out)
Nutritional Leverage For Great Golf
The All-Natural High-Performance Diet
Natural Solutions for Sexual Enhancement
Cancer Disarmed
Super-Nutrition for Dogs n' Cats

*Dr. Peiper is co-host of the award-winning television show Partners in Healing. You can get an even better idea of his prominence on the Website: **www.walkthetalkproductions.com**.*

••

What supplements do we *need?* We should take only what we actually require. Most people need trace minerals, digestive enzymes, polysaccharidepeptides, and essential fatty acids. Beyond these, it's an individual road.

Taking individual vitamins or minerals—magnesium, zinc, or vitamin B$_6$ for example—may be necessary for certain individuals who exhibit symptoms of deficiencies. But to avoid creating an imbalance in our body chemistry through the indiscriminate use of supplements, taking natural whole-food complexes keeps the body in balance (homeostasis).

Polysaccharidepeptides (PSP)

One reason many children and adults suffer from a lack of focusing ability is that they're living with an insufficient supply of necessary nutrients to the brain, nutrients which must make it through the protective envelope known as the blood-brain barrier. The functioning of the brain depends upon specific chemical substances called neurotransmitters that act as electrical switches for information transmission and are ultimately responsible for all the functions of the body. If the brain doesn't have an adequate supply of neurotransmitters, or if nutrients needed to make them aren't present, it begins to develop the biochemical equivalent of a short circuit.

Polysaccharidepeptides (PSP) are a whole-food complex that improve brain function, the cellular-repair process, digestion, metabolism, blood-sugar balance, and overall homeostasis. Preliminary clinical observations carried out by several physicians in Thailand, Malaysia, and the United States indicated significant improvement with children and adults diagnosed as ADD/ADHD.

Trace Minerals

At least 11 trace minerals have been recognized as essential for human development and overall health. These are copper, iron, zinc, cobalt, iodine, molybdenum, manganese, selenium, chromium, and fluorine.

Trace-mineral deficiencies can cause anxiety, limited attention span, and short-term memory problems. Severe depression, which strikes 1 in 48 American teens, has been linked to deficiencies of copper, molybdenum, vanadium, and zinc. A person lacking dietary copper and chromium may have difficulty with their blood-sugar levels at the cellular level. Abnormal blood-sugar fluctuations can produce violent behavior, mood swings, fatigue, and irritability. An adequate supply of minerals, properly balanced, is necessary for health.

Minerals are the building blocks—the basics—and when they're combined in a solution of water, trace minerals create electrolytes, the spark of life.

Enzymes

Enzymes are essential in maintaining internal cleanliness, health, youth, and strength. Proteins can't be utilized without them, nor can vitamins and minerals. Enzymes are destroyed after use and must be constantly replaced. Cooked foods draw from the enzyme reserves, depleting the body's precious "labor force."

Enzymes are produced by the pancreas. When cooked and processed foods use up enzymes at every meal, the pancreas gets tired. This compromises the immune system and may complicate the symptoms of ADD/ADHD. Raw foods contain their own enzymes, but when we cook, we kill them. Therefore, the food isn't processed unless the pancreas supplies the digestive enzymes. Undigested food in the intestinal tract supports bacteria and parasites. In addition, if digestion isn't functioning properly, then protein can't be broken down into free-form amino acids, which then are unable to produce serotonin for the proper functioning of the brain.

Essential Fatty Acids

From all the emphases on low-fat diets and fat-free foods, you'd think that fat is the body's worst enemy, but that really isn't the case. Some often-overlooked fats that are *essential* to life are the omega-3 and omega-6 fats, known as *essential fatty acids* or EFAs. These can't be made by the body, and therefore must be ingested. Many people are deficient in these essential fats because their diets lack the foods that contain these nutrients.

EFAs aid in the transmission of nerve impulses that are needed for normal brain functioning—this is their direct connection to treating people with ADD/ADHD. The brain is about 60 percent fat, and just as the body is 75 percent water and requires a daily supply of it to survive, the brain requires essential fatty acids.

EFAs also support cardiovascular health and energy metabolism, and they help us handle stress. They're good for most skin conditions, visual function, fertility, and many other complex functions of the body.

We all need essential fatty acids, but in the case of those with ADD/ADHD, they're not only recommended, they're *essential*.

Green Foods

Dark green leafy vegetables, chlorophyll, blue-green algae, kelp, spirulina, kamut, wheatgrass, and barley grass can provide us with the tools to fortify the immune system. Used in conjunction with magnesium, calcium, and other trace minerals, green foods support the body's basic nutritional needs.

Sea vegetables such as kelp, spirulina, and blue-green algae provide a high source of micronutrients. Small doses can provide biologically active vitamins, minerals, trace elements, amino acids, simple carbohydrates, enzymes, fatty acids, carotenoids, and chlorophyll. Its protein content is of a type that may be more easily broken down and assimilated by the body than the proteins in meat and vegetables.

Zeolite

Zeolite is an amazing crystalline mineral capable of adsorbing and absorbing many different types of gases, moisture, petrochemicals, heavy metals, and low-level radioactive elements, which all may be contributing factors to ADD/ADHD, autism, cancer, chronic fatigue syndrome, fibromyalgia, and other diseases and disorders.

Studies have shown that zeolite has a high affinity for trapping lead, cadmium, arsenic, mercury, and other potentially harmful metals, all potential contributors to behavioral anomalies found in those diagnosed with ADD/ADHD. Through the process of ion exchange, zeolite can lower overall heavy-metal exposure in individuals. What's very interesting is that the mineral appears to remove toxins in a certain order. It deals with the above-mentioned heavy metals in the first few weeks; then it removes secondary-priority toxins, including pesticides, herbicides, and plastics.

Humic Acid and Viruses

There are more than 42,000 known types of viruses, and new ones are being discovered regularly, but less than 3 percent of identified viruses have been well characterized. Examples of those that have been described include measles, chicken pox, influenza, warts, shingles, the common cold, and bronchitis, which are all common childhood illnesses. The virus can have a negative affect on the body and thus affect the child's ability to cope with other stressors, including ADD/ADHD.

Viral immunity is the ability of the immune system to prevent, defend against, neutralize, and eliminate viruses from the body. There are various ways to achieve this: build a strong immune foundation with lifestyle, diet, and nutritional supplements; boost the immune system with natural immune enhancers; and target viruses with natural antiviral alternatives.

Humic acid, according to many scientists, is the antiviral answer. One of the key reasons for this designation is that it puts a coating around the viruses and prevents them from reproducing or adhering to a healthy cell (the agents for this are called *viral fusion inhibitors*). The viruses then become vulnerable to attack by the immune system. Humic acid also has the amazing ability to alert the immune system to the virus or disease invader and to regulate and strengthen the body's defenses.

Flower Essences

Flower essences are an old form of nutrient/vibrational medicine that were redeveloped back in the early 1930s. They work by reaching into the deeper emotional sections of our minds and bodies, where they directly effect change. In this way, flower essences are often explained as being an emotional medicine, targeting the underlying feelings that affects us from day to day.

There are several flower essences that have had positive results in treating ADD/ADHD. One formula helps flighty children become centered and more focused by grounding their thoughts and helping control the distractions that seem to come from everywhere. There are flower remedies for stress, tension, and forgetfulness.

Summary

I believe that ADD/ADHD drugs are all-too-often used as "skill enhancers" to help children get good scores on tests and receive teacher approval. The drug overload of today's society is a sad testament to the enormous pressure our children are under to perform and produce at any cost, even at the cost of resorting to mind-altering drugs. Nutritional therapy needs to be our primary focus for long-term relief.

●●

What Does Sound Healing Look Like?

by Karyne Richardson-Meads,
SpLT, HA, ON

What's the answer to the challenge of hyper kids? Often, it's to trot them down to the doctor so that they can get labeled and drugged. Is this for the children or for the parents? Are there other ways? Can this behavior be treated, reversed, or helped in some way besides taking a mind-enhancing drug? Many believe so.

In our first Indigo book, Jan and I firmly linked the Indigo experience with the perception that many Indigos are being diagnosed with ADD and ADHD—so many that it seems like an epidemic! We explained why, as did many of our contributors. The overwhelming consensus was that most children didn't have ADD or ADHD at all, but that their symptoms were caused by evolving minds that simply weren't ready to be "dumbed down" to fit into a 100-year-old education system and a parenting paradigm that was authoritative and often without intuitive direction. They were bored; they were obstinate; they were doing everything they could out of frustration and to get attention.

But some children have real ADD and ADHD attributes, with learning challenges that possibly even border on autism. What do we do then? Indigos aren't immune from these disorders, but one of the remarkable findings is that they react to intuitive treatments better than any other generation has. In fact, some of them are redefining "what kids can do" in treatment.

Can children find balance points for themselves? Can they reverse an actual brain disorder? Is this a generation that will bring in a new concept of what "self-help" really is? Read on, for this author has something you've probably never heard of and that you now won't be able to forget. Indigos are intuitive . . . even the ones who are in trouble.

●●

Karyne Richardson-Meads *is the SETI (Sound Entrainment Therapies Institute) clinical director. She was nominated in 2007 for the National Institutes of Health Pioneer Research Grant, which will create cutting-edge programs to be part of the daily fare at the Sky of Dreams Ranch, a place for kids of all ages.*

SETI's revolutionary Sonic Neurotechnology protocol is safe and enjoyable. The special hardware, combined with the software programs, affects the speed of sound delivered to the brain and body. The results are like a brain "defrag" program that promotes deep sleep, alert daytime focus, learning and speech development for children, memory improvement, and behavior and self-awareness changes.

Letters of reference to the NIH come from neurosurgeons and osteopathic medical doctors who recognize the multiple disciplinary fields that Karyne has mastered in order to lead research teams to find answers to reverse ADHD and autism. The puzzle begins to unravel and make sense when stress issues in the body are addressed first. These fields include environmental neurotoxicology, speech pathology, endocrine and autoimmune relationships to neurotransmitter function in the brain during child development, and finally specialized brain nutrition for learning enhancement. The ranch experience will be like nothing else in the world for any child with learning challenges.

●●

In Stillness we can hear the Sound of Love.
That is where all healing begins.

A family waits in the quiet circular reception area for their child's doctor visit. An inviting and sunny playroom is just to the left of this welcoming station. Both father and mother have traveled from the East Coast for this twice-yearly appointment in San Diego, California. An intern on staff has befriended the boy in anticipation of leading him to the doctor's office without the screaming incidents of previous visits.

The intern is successful in helping the child, who has been lovingly dubbed "Ricochet Rabbit," down the corridor to the doctor's private-therapy room. Within moments of studying the child, the intuitive Dr. Viola Frymann, D.O., turns to the Russian classical pianist in her therapy room and instructs her to play a musical piece that matches the boy's own fast-paced rhythm. His response to this soundscape created in the room is an immediate *relaxation response*. His body becomes less tense, his face almost shows a smile, and he willingly climbs up onto the treatment table when invited to do so by Dr. Frymann.

During the treatment, the doctor will invite the pianist to transition into several other pieces that invite the child's body and mind to "entrain," or become similar to, each new melody and rhythm. Slowly and gently, the craniosacral therapy that Dr. Frymann performs on the child's body brings into harmony the internal rhythms of the cardiovascular, breathing, and autonomic nervous systems. Profound healing changes begin from this peaceful foundational therapy. In this very room, it happens many times each day.

The Core Temperament

Addressing children's core body and mind rhythms and bringing them into harmony involves the foundational bone structure, according to Dr. Frymann. Her vitality at 82 years young keeps all the staff hopping. Her English accent and adherence to strict protocol give structure and vibrancy to the 30,000-square-foot facility dedicated to neurodevelopmental healing of children. I was reminded of my childhood British boarding-school headmistress, and I felt right at home.

Healing all the way to the bones is what the Osteopathic Center for Children & Families is all about. If we compare a grand piano's soundboard to the bone structure of the body, some interesting parallels may be seen. When the soundboard is cured and prepared during manufacturing, it becomes the foundation or backbone that resonates and amplifies the tones and harmonics of the strings when they're played. When a piano is first fitted with strings, there's great tension and pressure put on the soundboard, and the strings need to be tuned up repeatedly at first to keep their pitch. To tune up a piano that *stays* in tune requires more than a strong arm to stretch the strings.

Here, the touch of the master's hand is required to "set the temperament" of this particular piano, which involves the center octave of the instrument. The tuner spends deliberate time and focus in order to tune each key in the core octave. Most keys have three separate strings that all have to be in harmonic resonance or entrainment to each other, or the tone sounds "out of tune" when striking that one key. Once the core octave's temperament has been set, its exact pitch and harmonics then serve to tune all the rest of the piano's octaves, fifths, and thirds. A master craftsman's ear listens for the oscillations or beats per minute, not just the tone itself.

"Setting the temperament" of a child's body that's out of tune within itself requires entraining the oscillations of all the body rhythms so that they come into coherent harmony with each other. It begins with the soundboard of the body: the bone structure. This is the nature of osteopathic treatment. With the touch of the master hand, Dr. Viola Frymann brings her lifetime of healing wisdom into her daily practice. As she listens, observes, and feels the temperament of the child, she then invites and entrains the child's body to come into harmony using music combined with osteopathy. This kind of treatment, given early and often in a child's life, serves to correct the rest of the notes (issues) that are out of harmony with health.

Tuning Often

As the daughter of a master piano technician, I remember dinner conversations when I was a child about my father's frustration over beautiful pianos that couldn't hold their pitch very well and needed more tunings per year, simply because they hadn't been tuned during the first years after they were manufactured. Could there be a parallel to a child's health? If any disharmonies within the body are "tuned up" in the first weeks and months after birth, is there a greater possibility for health and vitality? Dr. Frymann's decades of practice indicate this to be true.

My father was also an amazing opera singer. His ears served him well as he transitioned into the technical-piano career that allowed him to be with his family. At 88, he has a calm and vibrant manner and heartbeat. His face and hands invite peaceful conversation and kind service. His voice and hands have guided my life; he's my master teacher. Did he tune up himself each day as he tuned up a piano? Is there a relationship to music and the physical health of the body? My own career as a speech therapist and pathologist rings out joyfully with a resounding *yes*.

Just a few doors away from Dr. Viola Frymann's office is where I work at the Osteopathic Center for Children & Families in San Diego. I use sound-entrainment therapies to restore listening ability and expressive language to children. I'm a speech pathologist and therapist, using musical-technology software and hardware designed to invite the children to listen through their bones. It sets the temperament and the harmony of their breathing. It invites their left- and right-brain hemispheres to entrain and work as a team, and the music programs entice their out-of-sync body systems into coherent synchronous patterns. The process invites their spirit to be at peace within the body.

This therapy invites the child to self-listen because the sounds come through the bones first. To self-listen invites the motivation within a child for a *desire* to learn and dialogue with others. Awakening a child out of autism must begin here, at the still-point core. The autistic child has blocked out the world. Sounds seem too overwhelming to comprehend, so there's physical or psychological shutdown. Awakening the desire to listen can't be forced. It's a gentle invitation to self-listen through whole-body bone conduction. This is known as "precession."

Voyage into Recovery

Inspired Mozart music using precession bone-conduction headphones is the foundation of the Voyage into Recovery therapy that's used at the Institute for Sound Health and Integrative Medicine. Designer sound-engineering programs then layer specialized filters over the Mozart sound tracks. Additionally, gating mechanisms that appear to "audio burst" during the listening session serve to exercise the tiny muscles of the middle ear. When ear muscles aren't strong and toned, they can't filter out background noise and enable a child to focus. When they *are* strong, the tiny muscles can accurately transfer high-frequency tones of speech to the brain so that it can interpret and organize them correctly. This is all part of the combined-therapy approach for children at the Institute for Sound Health. There's a vast library of prescription programs from which to choose, and the Sound Health counselors then program a single iPod that will be used by a particular child during his therapy. This iPod is sent home with the family, together with the special whole-body bone-conduction headphones.

Enhancing and Balancing the Core Structure

Since children visit us from all over the world, we teach parents how to use the iPod technology so that the sound-entrainment therapies can continue at home. Weekly e-mail reports serve to connect the Sound Health counselors at the Institute to each child's progress. The counselors don't rush the process. Maturation and neurological organization of the child comes in phases and stages.

Sound therapists know that the *rests* between the notes are as important as the notes themselves. The pauses help create the rhythm, which is sound you can feel. Movement is sound you can see. Sound protocols developed over decades, originally by Dr. Alfred A. Tomatis, have now been extensively expanded by the sound-engineering team of counselors. Even for the most difficult of cases, gentle progress is made month by month through consistent weekly guided sound-therapy sessions at home.

The bones represent the structure that influences the health of our blood, immune system, and endocrine system. Louise L. Hay suggests that bone marrow represents the deepest beliefs about the self—how we support and care for ourselves. If our core structures are balanced, we can feel safe, loved, and totally supported within ourselves. If that's lacking, it creates a disharmonious mental pressure and tightness. Muscles can't stretch and relax, so out-of-sync and disrhythmic movements and behaviors manifest in the body.

When our core bone structure (our physical soundboard) temperament is in tune, we can literally breathe in life fully. We can relax and trust the flow and process of life. We stay in tune and in health easily. Our voices are an auditory picture of our health. Our ability to express our thoughts and feelings flows easily each day. Our own voices can be the musical instruments through which we express kindness and joy for the miracle of the gift of speech.

Inner Change

What does sound healing look like? Children all over the world are playing quietly during whole-body listening for an hour each day, and the change is internal. Neurological reorganization is being stimulated daily. This leads to mental and emotional maturation. It's the miracle of sound that has been with us all along; like sunlight, it has been all around us. Now a bit of technology can focus us back to the still point at the beginning. In Dr. Frymann's room, and now even in every home, healing and recovery are happening. All possibilities begin in sound stillness.

There is much yet to learn. There is an entire generation of children who have learning challenges, and who cannot hear their own inner voice. Awakening children's potential is the invitation to self-listen and then discover their authentic voices. The voice can produce only what the ear can hear.

Bring back the joyful wonder of learning to your child's world. We invite you to come, join the chorus, and create a symphony with us.

••

It's All about
Learning to Love

by Ann Callaghan, L.C.H., ISHom.

Ann Callaghan graduated from the College of Practical Homeopathy in London. She then established a homeopathic practice in Ireland, specializing in the treatment of children. She also became a teacher of homeopathy, a founding member of the Irish Society of Homeopaths, and a director of the Irish School of Homeopathy. She closed her homeopathic practice in 2000 to concentrate on producing a range of gem essences for children, which she created with the help of her two nephews, Ben and Mica. These are called Indigo Essences and have been designed especially to help address the emotional and energetic needs of the new children and their families.

••

When I was training to be a homeopath, I came across a book claiming that humankind was about to make a giant leap in consciousness and that special children would be born to facilitate this leap. It said that these children would be born enlightened, and their energy would change the world. I was deeply affected by this information and decided that from that moment on, my work would be with children.

I graduated, set up a clinic for children, and sat and waited for the baby Buddhas to show up. I grew more disappointed on a daily basis. The children who were coming to me were nothing like sweet, peaceful Buddhas. They were little dynamos with all sorts of strange behaviors and diagnoses. Slowly, I realized that the children I was seeing were the forerunners of the enlightened ones. These kids were preparing the ground. It's been almost 20 years since I read that book, and I can see that we've made some progress, but there's still a ways to go. What follows are some of the things that I've learned from these children along the way.

Trust Them

I remember the day that Sean (not his real name) came to my homeopathic practice. He was nine years old and wet his bed every night. He'd been to several different therapists and tried lots of remedies, none of which changed the situation. Sean's mother was bright and funny—a good mother, I guessed. She loved her son very much and was desperate for his condition to change, both for herself and because it was impacting Sean's social development.

As Sean came into my consulting room, his expression dulled and a here-we-go-again look came over his face. He gave off an air of polite tolerance. Another consultation to be endured.

I knew that Sean's case wouldn't be straightforward because he'd already been to other therapists. I knew that he wouldn't slot into a standard prescription as I started to ask him questions. Then something happened that's hard to explain. I looked at him, and he looked back at me, and there was a recognition—a flash of energy and a connection. I looked at him again. His expression had changed from boredom to bright enthusiasm. I usually ask children to draw their family for me so that I can get an idea of what's going on for them. But this time I said something different: "I know that you know what you need. Now draw me a picture of what it is."

Again, he smiled brightly. He drew a representation of a homeopathic remedy that I recognized. I showed him a big box holding about 200 remedies, and he ran his hand carefully over the whole box.

"It's not in there," he said.

Then I showed him another box, and he ran his hand back and forth, feeling the energy of the remedies through his palm. He slowed over a particular spot, then reached down and took out a bottle. It was the remedy he'd drawn. He held the bottle in his hand, closed his eyes, and wiggled his body a bit.

"That feels better," he said.

And so it was. He didn't wet the bed that night, and his mother reported some time later that he was still dry at night.

Sean was a wonderful teacher for me. He showed me that children can choose their own medicine if we allow them to. He taught me about trust. I had to let go of my notions that only I, the homeopath, could know what this child needed. My job as a practitioner changed from being a prescriber to being a partner in the healing process. All I needed to do was create the space for children to use their own intuition, present them with a few choices, and trust the process.

We know that these very bright children respond well when offered choices in other areas, such as activities and food, so why not extend that choice to the area of health? I believe that if we allow children to stay connected to their true desires, they'll always know what they need to heal themselves. Most of my generation were forced to swallow medicine we didn't want, so we became completely disconnected from our intuition about what could help us and what couldn't. With these very sensitive children, we have a chance to change that. We have a chance to rear a whole generation of people who can heal themselves.

After my consultation with Sean, I looked for this connection with children in every appointment. Repeatedly, I found children responding to this recognition with heartwarming affection. It was like opening a door or turning on a light. Suddenly, our spirits were connecting in the consultation. Child after child came and showed me more of who they were and how we could help them. I liken the experience of the Indigo Child in this world to that of being in a country where you don't speak the language. Your body is present, but your spirit drifts off. You don't listen to the conversation very closely until someone turns to address you in your own language.

Now more and more people know, largely thanks to the information gathered and promoted by people like Jan Tober and Lee Carroll, that these children have a job on the planet. They aren't just "behaving badly" or developing new syndromes for the heck of it. All the symptoms and behaviors these children are exhibiting have a purpose.

Love Them

In my homeopathic practice, I began to see more and more children with behavioral problems and autistic-spectrum diagnoses. Often, they were very difficult to deal with. While I waited for the baby Buddhas to show up, I asked an enlightened being what the children are trying to teach us with these behaviors.

The reply was: "Unconditional love, Beloved, for you have never experienced it before."

"So all the symptoms and behaviors these children are exhibiting are designed to bring us, the adult population, closer to a state of unconditional love?"

"Yes, love without conditions. Imagine that, Beloved. To be loved whether or not you achieve in school, whether or not you're bright and academic, whether or not you fit into the social norm, whether or not you become what your parents want you to become! Imagine that, Beloved."

"But how are they going to teach us?"

"Through your fear. They'll bring up every fear you have and some you don't even know about. Every fear that you let go of will bring you closer to a state of love, closer to the state of the child. When you can live in this state of love and acceptance, then these baby Buddhas, as you call them, can come in."

"Aaahhh . . ."

That information helped me see more clearly that I wasn't just dealing with a set of symptoms in isolation, but with behaviors that were designed to bring about a change in the whole family and society in general.

For example, I saw a three-year-old boy, whom I'll call Patrick, with a diagnosis of ADHD. His parents told me that they'd been advised that Patrick would be prescribed Ritalin when he started school at age four. They wanted to see if there was any alternative.

Patrick bounced into the consultation room and ran around, pulled a few leaves off a plant, and climbed up and over me on my chair. I looked at his parents. Both were sitting rigid in their chairs. His father, leaned forward slightly, sending "you'd better behave or you're in for it later" vibes every couple of seconds. This seemed to fuel the boy, and he'd run faster every time he got another dose of this energy.

The dad was a teacher, and his son was pushing all his buttons. His worst fears were about to come true. He'd seen children like this before, and they were never good in school. The father thought, *He'll fail all his exams. He'll be a social outcast and end up living on the street.* Patrick's mom was a nurse. Her worst fears were also about to be lived out. Her lovely child would be drugged and probably have to take Prozac during the school holidays. *He'll always be different; he'll never fit in and be normal,* she worried.

I sat and watched this drama for a while. Then something clicked, and I spoke directly to Patrick: "Do you know that your mother really loves you, and do you know that your father really loves you?"

Well, it was like putting a pin in a balloon. Both parents flopped back in their chairs. The child looked at me, then lay down on the floor and went to sleep.

Very often, when a child develops a behavioral problem, the parents get so stressed and tired that they loose perspective and become immersed in their fears. Children respond to this energy of dread and judgment by behaving even worse, and a vicious circle is set up. This is what I observed with Patrick and his parents. You can break that cycle by reminding yourself that you love your children at a deep level, even if you don't love their behavior.

Children need to hear on a daily basis that they're loved, they'll always be safe, and they'll always be looked after.

As the enlightened being said, we don't know much about unconditional love, but we do need to learn. Some people mistakenly believe that this means allowing your children to rule your life, to do exactly what they want, when they want, without boundaries or respect for anyone. Not so. Children need parenting. These kids have a great need for well-defined boundaries and consistent and fair discipline.

Unconditional love means that you love your children freely for who they are, without placing conditions and expectations on that love. I sometimes liken parenting Indigos to sowing a packet of mixed seeds. You don't know what kind of plant you're growing. There are no instructions; you've just got to do what seems to help the plant best. In Patrick's case, lots of love and homeopathic remedies worked wonders over a couple of months, and he started school well and Ritalin free.

Family

So Sean taught me to trust, and Patrick taught me the importance of love. The next thing the children taught me was the importance of healing the family.

By the time I realized this, I'd made, with the help of my nephews, a series of gem essences for children. In my practice, I continued to ask children to choose the essences they wanted themselves. I love this way of working, and the kids love it, too. They become active participants in their own healing. Often, children with a diagnosis have attended many different therapists and, like Sean, have learned to tune out during consultations. Once they're recognized and included, they become very enthusiastic healers.

I found that after children chose essences for themselves, they'd often pick out ones for their parents and siblings. In some cases, the children would say that *they* didn't want an essence but that their mom or dad needed one instead. Parents need lots of reassurance when this happens. As adults, we often believe that we're okay; it's the child who has the problem. These new kids won't allow us to keep deluding ourselves. If we continue to ignore and hide our own fears, the children will continue to create havoc until we take some responsibility and engage in the healing process with them. After all, they have a job to do, and it's getting urgent.

One of the easiest and most effective ways of including the whole family in the healing process is to ask everyone to sit down and choose an essence for themselves. That way, everyone is taking responsibility for their parts in the energetic mishmash that makes up a family unit. The pressure is lifted from the "designated" patient, and usually, even at that early point, stress starts to dissipate. The essences can then be mixed together in a big bowl of water and will act like an energetic air conditioner in the house.

Home

Once when I was teaching this method in a workshop, a parent said that there was no time when her whole family was gathered together, ever! They never sat down together to eat; they all had TVs in their bedrooms; they all came and went at different times of the day. Several others said that it was the same for them, most particularly the ones with teenage children. Most of these parents said there was no adult in the house during the day, no adult at home when the children came back from school. How sad. Children need a warm, fuzzy, safe place where they can retreat, heal, hang out, tell stories, and ground themselves. As more and more teenagers opt out of this world by committing suicide, we must as a society examine the world we're asking them to inhabit.

My experience is that by their behaviors, these children are prompting adults to heal their own inner children, which in turn make the adults sensitive to the needs of every child. When enough adults have regained this sensitivity, we'll be able to look at the world through the eyes of the children and change it. We'll feel the pain that we're inflicting on children. We'll realize how we stifle and constrain them, and we'll feel the fears that we impress upon them. We'll know their needs and provide for them. We'll listen to their wisdom, laugh with them, and love with them. We'll become free like they are. Roll on, baby Buddhas . . . we're nearly ready.

•••••

Chapter Five

From the Parents and Indigos

As you might imagine, Jan and I had more submissions from this group than any other. The subject is a very popular one, and two years ago when we asked for contributions, the floodgates opened and in came dozens—no, *lots* of dozens—of articles from parents and Indigos. We've selected a few to round out this book for you.

Since this is the parents' section, and the last one of this book, we wish to give you a different perspective on where you think the youth of this planet is going. Heard the news lately? Seen the violence in schools? Concerned about what's going to happen to our young people?

It's good that you're concerned, but perhaps you should also hear the facts. Perhaps it's time for all of us to examine the "horror machine" that the mass media has turned into, where only news that's dramatic and horrific gets attention.

The Mainstream Is Starting to Notice, Too

What follows is a portion of a small *Time* magazine article written by John Cloud. He writes a column called "The Contrarian," so you know that he's going to give you a view that's contrary to public perception. Well, his subject just happens to be exactly what we've been showing you! In fact, take a look at the subheading of the article: *"There's Strong Evidence That Adolescents Are Getting Smarter. Could the Teen Brain Be Evolving?"*

There it is for all to see—the conjecture that we've been presenting all along. Take a look at some of these facts and what this *Time* writer has to say in a very mainstream venue.

●●

Parents: Relax
There's Strong Evidence
That Adolescents Are
Getting Smarter. Could
the Teen Brain Be Evolving?

Time magazine, April 9, 2007
by John Cloud

Probably since the second generation of humanity, it has been a widely accepted bit of folk wisdom that kids are worse off than their forebears. Our ancestors surely thought the kids just didn't rip the hides from big game with the same skill as Grandpa. Now we think teens are wastrels who get high on OxyContin and rouse themselves only to shoot up a school or update their MySpace profiles. But there's strong evidence that U.S. adolescents are actually getting smarter—or at least making better decisions.

Could the Teen Brain Be Evolving?

Consider: teens are less violent and more sober than they have been in years. Despite those rare school shootings reporters cover with such lip-licking zeal, the rate of school violence fell from 48 crimes per 1,000 students in 1992 to 22 per 1,000 in 2004, according to the Department of Education. In raw terms, the number of student crimes (including theft) shrank from 3.4 million to 1.4 million in that period, even as the U.S. teen population grew by 5.4 million kids. Post-Columbine security explains some of the decline, but the school crime rate started to drop in the mid-'90s. And the rate at which 12- to 17-year-olds committed murder (at school or elsewhere) plummeted an astonishing 68 percent from 1993 to 2003.

Fewer teens take drugs now than a decade ago. In 1995, according to the National Institute on Drug Abuse, 19 percent of surveyed school kids said they had used an illegal drug in the past month; in 2005, 16 percent did. That's a small dip, but kids' smoking tumbled 40 percent during the same period. And teens' use of alcohol is also down, despite stories you may have seen about parents' letting their high schoolers drink. Nearly 40 percent of teens reported drinking in the past month in 1995; less than a third did in 2005. Plus, the teen pregnancy rate is the lowest since 1976, and the teen suicide rate is lower today than in 1980.

All this good news about teens raises an old question: should we now be prepared to reward them with more rights? A new book by a prominent psychologist says we should. In fact, Robert Epstein, Harvard Ph.D., former editor in chief of *Psychology Today* and host of Sirius' *Psyched!* program, argues that we should abolish the very concept of adolescence.

He's not alone: in 2004, Oxford University Press published *The End of Adolescence,* by psychiatrist Philip Graham, who argued that British teens deserved more respect and less condescension from adults. But Epstein's book, *The Case Against Adolescence: Rediscovering the Adult in Every Teen,* goes even further: it says that once they can prove themselves competent, kids should have all the rights of adults. "Just about everything we do tells [teens] they're incompetent," Epstein writes. "We protect them from danger (driving, cigarettes, alcohol); we don't trust them to work or own property . . . We don't allow them to make basic decisions about their health, education or religion." Epstein's proposal? Allow any kid—of any age—who can "pass one or more relevant competency tests" not only to do constructive things like sign contracts and vote but also to do essentially anything he or she wants: have sex with people of any age, drink, smoke, drive, get a tattoo. "If they can pass an appropriate test of maturity," Epstein writes in a passage that left me a bit queasy, "young people of any age should have access to pornographic materials commensurate with adult access."

Epstein's central psychobiological contention—that teens have the brain potential to make adult-level judgments—also doesn't hold up. True, teens have better reaction times and memories than adults, and most have adult-like moral-reasoning skills by adolescence. But a 2000 paper in *Behavioral Sciences and the Law* confirms common sense: adolescents score significantly worse than adults on assessments of their psychosocial maturity. Teens may know how to make good decisions, but they don't actually make good decisions as often as adults. Epstein points out that some teens do score higher than some adults, and he says most teens score worse because we infantilize them. That may be true, and it's a good idea to consider, say, civics tests that precocious teens could take in order to vote. Kids who start businesses should also be able to own them outright. But kids have been making better decisions in the past 20 years—drinking and drugging less and, as studies have shown, studying more. It would be perverse to reward them by saying that we now don't care if they get drunk and watch porn instead.

●●

Joshua Joseph

by Cathy Jacobs

*In 2005, **Cathy Jacobs**, with the assistance of several others, started the Children's Indigo Support Society of Alberta, in Calgary, Alberta, Canada. The society is a new support system for finding alternatives to helping in the healing of children and ourselves. She's truly blessed to have an Indigo son, whom she calls: "My son, my friend, and my teacher, Joshua."*

●●

In 1990, my third child, Joshua Joseph, was born. From the first moment I locked eyes with my newborn, I knew there was something unique about him. I believed that this had to be one of the oldest souls that had ever come to Earth. He pushed his way in early, six weeks as a matter of fact, eager to make a difference, I suppose. Josh was born into a very volatile parental relationship that ended in his third year. He was such an extremely sensitive child—always needing me to hold him when I needed to have my space the most. He had such a calming effect on me whenever I held him, despite my desires.

At a very young age, Josh started to tell me stories that caused me great distress because I was afraid of what people would think of my son. He saw things from both the past (before this lifetime) and the future, and I never knew where he was going with the stories. He always had so much emotion when he told me stuff, and I had to reassure him that everything would be all right, that he could control his future. I wasn't even convinced that this was the truth as I heard the words spill from my mouth.

One such incident happened when my children and I were driving in from outside Calgary after visiting a friend in the town of Okotoks. Josh was five years old at the time. As we passed a very well-known hill (Signal Hill) Josh noticed the large numbers made of small painted rocks, indicating longitude and latitude, that were left over from wartime.

He turned to me and asked, "Mom, do you know what it's like to kill another person?" I looked at him and realized that this was going somewhere. I asked, "Why Josh? What are your thoughts on this?" I learned a long time ago not to answer my children's questions but to offer them back. I was in awe as Joshua went into a very long explanation of the journey that two souls take as they meet again in a time of war and are faced with having to kill each other. The knowledge that they *are* someone—son, father, brother, friend, or grandson—was very distressing as the decision to kill happened. He spoke so deeply about it and in words that I'd never heard him use before that I was shaken for the rest of the day. Josh also explained about the afterlife of the two souls and a contract. It was too much for this mom at the time, as I was just beginning to understand some of the spiritual journey.

By the time Josh turned seven, our life was feeling like it was way out of control. He had temper tantrums that got so out of hand that there was no reasoning with him. If he was physically hurt by mistake in any way, he lashed out until someone else felt what he did. We could do very little to support him and his perspective of what was happening to him. One day when Josh had his sandal broken while roughhousing with my brothers, he lost control so badly that I decided to walk down the street with him, holding his hand tightly so that he couldn't do any further damage to others or himself.

While we were walking, Josh ripped his hand from mine and ran into traffic. It happened so fast that I didn't have time to react.

The next thing I knew, he was sitting down on the sidewalk beside me, rather dazed. I thought that the passing vehicle had hit him. I rushed him to the hospital, where he was checked over. The medical staff found nothing wrong. Now he was calm.

The children's hospital had Josh assessed by their psychiatrists. When the dreaded time came for me to meet with them, I feared that they'd tell me that my son was crazy. I didn't get the response I'd expected. Instead, the head doctor shared with me what Josh told him about the day I thought he was hit by a car, but according to Josh, someone pulled his "life cord" and helped him out of harm's way. The time for change was near.

I couldn't believe what I was hearing. I looked into the doctor's eyes to get a reading on what he was thinking. This doctor reassured me that Josh was more than okay and that he was connected to something we normal folks don't quite understand. He believed that my son would be fine, and if we had further concerns that he wanted to be the one to work with Josh. He was fascinated with the things he'd been told during their visit.

From that day on, things *did* change, and Josh never again spoke about anything from the past or future. He never was normal and still doesn't fit into the regular system, but he helps those around him who love him to expand their spiritual understanding. We're growing with him as we sometimes struggle to help him make his way in life. We don't know what's in store for Josh, but we're remaining tuned in as best we can.

I love him to the core of that which we are.

••

Guns at Schools and Indigo Kids

by Jasmine LoveLsTzy

Jasmine LoveLsTzy is an Indigo and sent in many submissions. This one was the shortest, and best. Oh, by the way, that's her name, but perhaps not the one she was born with. Indigos do that.

● ●

One of the main characteristics of the warrior personalities of the Indigo Children is that they express their anger and frustration outwardly rather than inwardly. When the feelings of anger and frustration are judged and have no channel to be communicated either in the school system, a workplace, shopping centers, or the home, they become a charged energy that can explode and be expressed through yelling, swearing, stealing, breaking things, or even killing another living being.

The solution is to create a place at home and at every single public location on the entire planet for nonduality—a place where plus and minus, male and female, good and bad, yin and yang aren't judged, but become one and transcend right through the heart center. So in addition to love, laughter, education, songs, music, and celebration being expressed there, it should also be a safe place with no discrimination, where a killing gun is replaced with open and clear communication with nothing held back. The charged energy of anger, frustration, yelling, and swearing can be expressed and cleared to open the space for co-creation and for joining hands together to make this world a better place for all.

May the force of pure love essence be with every breath we take.

Wisdom from Kristine

by Kristine McDonald

Kristine McDonald is an older Indigo. She's one of those who recognized the attributes within her and has gone on to try to help the younger Indigos as an educator. There are many people like her, and Jan and I celebrate that fact! Without this, help would be difficult to find. Indigos understand Indigos.

● ●

I wrote the following letter a few months ago, and since then I've enrolled several new students at my school. One of them will always stand out in my mind. He came in with his mother, who teared up as she talked about the struggles her son had faced. I knew by the way she was talking that he was an Indigo Child, and I went out on a limb to ask her if she'd ever read your [Lee and Jan's] book. (This was terrifying, by the way, because I work in a public school, and I have to be ever so careful about the risks I take!)

Anyway, the look on her face was indescribable. It's that look you get when you finally find someone who can relate to what you're saying, who doesn't think you're crazy, and who doesn't judge you. You think, *Wow! Someone actually gets what I'm saying! Someone hears me! My feelings are valid.*

To be able to give her this gift was amazing. I couldn't have made this connection with her had I not read your book. And that's what I'm about—making connections, helping people feel a little less alone in this crazy world. So thank you for that. I couldn't have done it without you!

Kristine's Letter

Dear Mr. Carroll and Ms. Tober,

I'm so happy to have read your first book, *The Indigo Children*. I can't wait to read *An Indigo Celebration* next! I've felt different from other people for as long as I can remember, and your book really resonated with me. I've never met anyone who feels the way I do, but some of the people in your book may have come close. I have so many emotions that I have trouble sorting through them all. Fortunately, I've always been really good at detaching myself from them, and I'm sure that's how I've avoided the pitfalls of drug addiction and alcoholism.

The closest I can come to describing myself is that I although I'm human, I don't feel completely human. I don't feel completely connected to this earth or this body. I know that this isn't my home, that I'm only here temporarily, and that I'm here to guide and serve others and help get/keep them on their paths. I also know I'm not crazy. I'm not an alien or an angel. I can't see spirits or talk to them or even feel their presence, really, although I know that they're there. I'm not psychic, per se, although I know we *all* are to an extent, and I do have pretty good intuition usually. I may not even be an Indigo, but I can relate to a lot of the things you described in your book, which makes me feel less like an outcast, so for that I thank you!

I'm a high-school counselor, and I'm thrilled to have another resource to use with my kids. I work in a small, conservative Texas town, so sadly I know that many parents aren't going to be open to these ideas yet, but at least I'll have more insight into helping their children.

I don't know whether you'll be interested in my story for your book, since I was born in 1971, but here it is anyway:

I never felt like I fit in and still don't really, although I don't feel alone anymore at all. I believe in God again so much, and I'm so excited about the future! I've always been fascinated with anything modern and futuristic—never cared about the past, except for wondering who I was in my past lives.

I feel very much like I belong here, that I'm here for a reason, that maybe I'm even supposed to do something great. I feel very confident and have always believed in myself, so I don't need validation from others, but I still want it. I want to be understood. Some people think I'm cold, which hurts. I feel things very intensely; I just don't let my emotions control me. I can love deeply, but I can let go when need be. I know that Earth is just our school, a learning ground, and not our home. Our loved ones are always going to exist, whether it's here or elsewhere. I think I've always known this on some level, although not consciously until the past year or so.

I was never really a kid; I've been a grown-up for as long as I remember, and my son is the same way. Yet I'm very quick to know what I want, and I constantly fight the urge to be impulsive. I think this makes me seem childlike to others (that or the fact that I look young), and I've sometimes had people tell me to grow up, which makes me want to smack them. I want to scream at them: "I've been a grown-up my whole life! Don't you know that?!"

I also have never really seen any boundaries between myself and others. My grandfather always said that I'd argue with Jesus Christ if he were here; he was right, I'm sure. I think of everyone as my equal, regardless of their title or age. Those things have always been superficial and unimportant to me. Fortunately, I've finally learned to be respectful to those who have authority over me, but it took a long time and a lot of conflict with my "superiors" to get here.

Sometimes I worry that maybe everyone feels this way, and that I'm really not any different from anyone else. You'd think that would make me happy, because all I've ever wanted was to fit in. But the truth is that I like being different. I want very much to believe that I might be able to change the world a little bit. I'm quiet in most settings, but secretly I'm very competitive. I feel like

I know more than others, not trivialities, but intuitive stuff—the stuff that matters.

I'm very balanced, and I don't really need help from anyone when it comes to solving my own problems, nor do I want it. That's not to say that I don't make mistakes. But really, I feel like I have a better handle on life than most people. I want to shake others most of the time when they're complaining about their lives and say, "Don't you get it? It's so easy! The answer is right in front of you!" Which is kind of stupid because, as I said, I've certainly made my share of mistakes. I wish that others could see what I see. I wish I could jump into their bodies and fix their lives for them, give them part of the happiness that I have now. But instinctively, I know that isn't my role. My role here is not to be in the limelight—at least not yet. Right now, I'm here to lead others, but to do it quietly and behind the scenes.

People are usually surprised when they get to know me and know my background. The family I grew up with is mostly deceased, and when they were alive, they were pretty dysfunctional. I was raised in a small town, and all of my friends' families were normal, or what was normal back then—biological parents, married for years, family vacations, the whole perfect package. I was as angry as any other kid in this situation; I felt cheated out of a happy childhood. I was depressed and even suicidal at about age 16, yet I never turned to drugs or alcohol. I loved school and made excellent grades. I was in lots of clubs and activities and had lots of friends. Yet I still felt so alone.

Maybe I wouldn't have done so well in this generation—there are so many more distractions and temptations nowadays, and our kids have so much more to contend with than we did. They have to fight harder to survive. But they have more resources, too, and I like to think I would have utilized them.

I feel like I'm always struggling with opposing feelings on any given subject. I feel uncomfortable being the center of attention, yet I desire it. I want to fit in, but I like being different. The human side of me feels fear and self-consciousness, but my spirit knows better. My spirit knows that everything in my life has happened for a reason and has happened just the way it was supposed to. It always has, and that has kept me grounded these past 30-plus years. I'm very proud of myself, and I consider myself lucky because I didn't have any of the support or resources I have now, yet I managed to stay on track. I've accomplished a lot, and I've done it all pretty much by myself with very little guidance.

I spend my time working with teens now, and I hope I'm making a difference in their lives. I treat them the way I wanted to be treated. I don't talk down to them. I treat them as my equals. I value them and pray for them, that they'll realize they actually do have control over their lives and aren't trapped the way they feel they are, the way I felt that I was as a kid. I hope that I can help them feel less alone, and I can't wait to see what amazing things are in store for us in the next few decades!

● ●

The Importance of Teachers in the Life of an Indigo

by Carolyn L'Hommedieu Davies, O.M.C.

Carolyn L'Hommedieu Davies is also an older Indigo. This is her story about teachers in school. Read between the lines: what is it that really made a difference to her? Listen to the way she talks about somehow "knowing she was different," and what happened when a teacher "saw" it. This is what Jan and I teach: that the Indigos have the innate knowledge that they represent some kind of advancement within humanity. But with a society trying to drug them instead, they keep it to themselves until teachers and others notice. It made a difference in Carolyn's life!

••

When I was in school all those years ago, they used an ability-tracking system that was certainly a blow to most young students' egos. But it also taught us to understand where we were with different subjects. You might think that school is just starting to be ineffective lately, but I remember that it wasn't so effective way back then either! As imperfect as the school system was, I did manage to learn. But I also have the bravery to say that it was due to some motivated teachers who had a real passion for teaching and loved their subject matter.

Those teachers were few and far between. Now throw an Indigo into the mix, and it gets confusing. According to the system, I was in track one (the highest) for English, track two for social studies and science, and track three for math. I never did pass my beloved algebra, so I simply gave up on math at that time. However, I've since figured out my own ways of getting the answers I need. Any Indigo will do that—if there's a will, there's an empathic way! Once my curiosity for a certain interesting subject was ignited, I'd spend hours reading about it, needing to know every last detail. The public library was my home away from home.

The Synchronicity of Intuitive Teachers

The things I did learn in school, and more from my parents, were the commonsense things such as: do unto others as you would have them do unto you and be kind to everyone you meet, even if you don't really like them . . . you never know what burdens they're carrying. Now that we understand a little more about the fact that Indigos and Crystals exist, we also understand that they're often born into a tough set of life circumstances, whether it be a dysfunctional home life or a personal disability of some kind.

I was lucky enough to meet several kind teachers through my years who could read between the lines and sense that I was something different. They got me through school, taking a moment to look into students' eyes and really get down to the soul level of children. These were the teachers who didn't have to follow the crowd in order to be popular. They showed the human side of who they were and allowed us to see them, warts and all. I was lucky enough to have had a few of them, and they saved me from going crazy in school—because I felt as though I *were* crazy.

It seemed like the timing of such teachers was right on target, because every year I had at least one such saving moment with a teacher, which taught me that I was really intelligent and worth teaching, and that I should keep on learning.

In third grade, we had an exchange teacher from Denmark named Miss Peterson. She was the first teacher to truly understand my worth. My kindergarten teacher yelled at me for eating too slowly, my first-grade teacher told us there was no Santa Claus, and then my wonderful second-grade teacher allowed me to babysit the classroom rats on summer break (because I loved them so much). Miss Peterson, however, was the one who looked into my eyes and really got to understand me, heart and soul.

As I looked back on my third-grade school year, I realized that it was a turning point for me because I learned a lot and understood for the first time that even though I was "different," I was worthy of a place in the classroom to excel and run with the "intelligent" kids. Until that year, I felt that I was so different that I was unworthy of learning, let alone even being in the classroom. I felt this even though I had an inner knowing that in some ways, I understood life more than my teachers, as well-meaning as they were. To most educators, I was invisible and nonexistent because I chose to "hide my light under a bushel." I felt so different that I didn't want to draw attention to myself. I had no real friends back then except the other resident oddball, Dorothy.

As I climbed up the ladder of grade school and inconsequential learning, I became somewhat of a prankster with a new friend, Billy, drawing comics and making up little stories. Billy was a bona fide genius, and I bet he was also an Indigo like me. But his gifts were more apparent, in that he could pass math, whereas I struggled. I was a creative Indigo. I learned how to play the clarinet, and my genetic makeup included an abundance of musical talents on both sides of the family, which meant that I was a natural musician. I was good; I always excelled at playing the clarinet. It came easily, and I had the good fortune to have a wonderful teacher who recognized this and gently nudged me along with a smile on his face and patience in his heart. Playing the instrument and being involved in music was my saving grace all through the junior-high and high-school years . . . some awfully tough times.

Not All the Teachers Were "Gems"

I had some other teachers, further up the education ladder into high school, who were interesting to learn from—and I also had some real stinkers, too. A few were way past their prime and shouldn't have been teaching anymore. They had no patience left. With my 11th-grade social-studies teacher, all we had to do was mention Ann-Margret or President Nixon, and off he'd go into a tirade. The kids who were really shrewd and never did their homework brought up these topics quite often! This was a "regents year," another antiquated idea. For what is a regents (state-standardized) test but mostly a regurgitation of facts that one doesn't need to know to exist in this world?

When this particular man didn't feel like teaching, he sent us to lunch. I often wonder how many of us in that class would have passed the regents test if they hadn't been stolen that year? I see that the 11th grade was another awakening year for me. To me, it was the real beginning of understanding that I was directly responsible for learning the subject matter at hand, even if the adult in charge was incapable of teaching it. It was my *coming of age* regarding learning; it was the year I became an insatiable reader and a musician. The failure of that teacher to pay attention to us students somehow spurred me on to teach myself, and it has been a wonderful journey since then.

About ten years after I graduated, I bumped into my high-school music teacher at a concert where I was singing. His chorus was performing at the same event. He said, "It's so nice to see you still in music. So few of you students actually continue into adulthood." I thanked him for being one of the teachers who believed in me—one of the few. He smiled, and that was the last time I saw him before he passed years later (still way too young), but I'll never forget him. In a world of teachers, he was one of the gifted and compassionate ones who looked into my soul and understood who I was, why I was there, and what his role was regarding me. I would say that he was an Indigo, and since like attracts like, he attracted me to be his student. He was without a doubt the most wonderful, insightful teacher I ever had.

Teachers play an important role in the Indigo world because they have to recognize that not all children/students are on the same emotional and vibrational level. I feel, and it has been my experience, that Indigos are often pushed to the side because they're either introverted and don't excel, or, as my daughter demonstrated in school, they demand explanations for why things are done in a certain manner. These kids are consequently labeled as having behavioral problems.

Indigos: Baloney Sniffers!

Indigos recognize nonsense. They have the uncanny ability to sniff out "baloney." They understand that when teachers are smiling at them, at that same moment, the teachers may be insecure because they don't know what in the world to do with the students who are so different. These kids are round pegs who can't fit into square holes, and there are many more of them arriving at this crucial time. Unless we have teachers who can read into the souls of these children, we'll have more and more of them labeled ADD, ADHD, and so on—and then pushed aside.

I feel that the solution lies in the generation that's coming of age now. They're more capable of understanding the children coming into the school system. The problem is that many of these kids can't excel enough at college to qualify to be teachers the way they're currently being certified. The solution? Partnering; homeschooling; opening schools committed to the needs of these children; "cyber" schools, where Indigos can team up, teaching and encouraging each other to grow scholastically; taking apart the current public-school system piece by piece and funneling that funding toward more efficient learning methods, where the children become mostly self-taught.

We know that we're our own best teachers, and most of us also know that we'd be wonderful teachers for others like us. Indigo Children understand the value of learning; they're born with the hunger to excel and have knowledge of many of life's mysteries.

For the most part, these children know that they're being pushed through the public schools, only capable of working the most menial tasks to become part of "the system."

That is what happened to me, a very smart and talented Indigo. If it can happen to me, it can happen to anyone. Most of what I learned in life, I discovered after I left school, and I owe that to a few very good teachers. Since that time, I've grown more into the role of Indigo advocacy and have also become a minister, helping many people understand and believe in their true value as humans on this planet and assisting them through life's transitions.

I believe in these children. It's time we changed the qualifications of being able to teach others and allow those young adults with an affinity or talent for teaching to instruct those younger than themselves. Look at the Internet: this is already taking place in chat rooms and on Indigo message boards and blogs. The time for that change is now. It's in the hands of the young-adult Indigos who are coming of age to partner with the Indigo elders, who are now walking forward to greet and teach them.

••

Advice from an Indigo

by Jorge Valentin

---

*Here's an article by **Jorge Valentin**. He's 16 and has advice for dealing with Indigos.*

∙ ∙

I realize that I was never much help to my parents when I was younger; it was in my nature to be incredibly difficult, if you will. Nonetheless, they never regarded it as anything out of the ordinary. Even I didn't realize that all the dreams and vibes I received on a constant basis were actually messages from God. Being young and naïve, I just found them to be interesting coincidences.

As I got into my early teens, I started to make the connections for myself. I realized that I was seeing things I'd envisioned before within my dreams; this scared me at times. I remember one instance not too long ago when my ride home from school made my mind quite idle. My grandmother was lecturing me about something that I paid no attention to, and I suddenly encountered a really bad vibe. I vividly and unintentionally pictured a bright yellow school bus.

I arrived home after this little event and started eating an early dinner when I overheard the news, which was playing in the background. Apparently, a school bus had overturned on the highway. After this, I was afraid to "feel" anything like what I'd experienced earlier, for fear that I might cause another accident. This was just one of many such instances.

I didn't know anything about Indigos until one of my best friends told me about them. I have an incredible connection with her; she's honestly the only person I feel like I really belong with, which is quite an accomplishment, seeing as I find it hard to even connect with my family. Put simply, I've never felt like I fit in with anyone besides her. With a little investigating, I realized that I had the common attributes of an Indigo and highly suspect that it's a major part of who I am.

I realize this is mainly a compilation for adult readers looking for advice as well as experiences relating to Indigo Children, but I felt as though I might be able to shed some light on the subject. One thing I truly believe is that Indigos will be more comfortable in their skin if we have the support of the ones we love. My family would probably think I was crazy if I told them any of this, but there's no other explanation. Also, we're bound to do a little rebelling in school. Try to understand where we're coming from. We honestly have problems with a good amount of the school system's attributes nowadays, so be as understanding as humanly possible with your children.

Above all, love your children with every inch of your heart. Nothing will make them feel more at home than to hear their loved ones let them know just how much they care. Don't get me wrong—I'm not telling you to lay it on thick because that might come off a little strong, but it doesn't hurt to hear "I love you" every now and then.

Creativity is also a large part of Indigos' lives. Some act; some write; some have an incredible connection to music. Whatever it may be, be sure to encourage them to follow their hearts. As for the gifts that they harness, they may be scared or confused. Answer any questions they have. Just let it all unfold naturally. Fate has its plans for everyone, including us Indigos.

●●

Why Would a Young Indigo Child Drink Upward of 40 Units of Alcohol a Week, and Smoke More Than 20 Cigarettes a Day?

by Katharine Dever

Katharine Dever is a 24-year-old Indigo. She knows it, and she has a message not only for adults, but especially for those who are younger and who have been like her. Perhaps these words will be found by someone who needs to see them? Take a look at her Website: www .butterfly-mastery.com. She also has a new book, called BetterMorphosis, and is on her way to becoming a passionate self-help speaker.

• •

At the age of 24, I'm just beginning to understand myself and discover that I'm one of what many call the Indigo Children. How do I know? What makes me see this?

I've spent the last two years on an inward journey of self-discovery. After battling addictions and unhealthy lifestyle patterns and compulsions since the age of 12 or 13, I finally broke free from the cigarettes, alcohol, and even occasional drug use that I'd previously relied upon to help numb me to my feelings. I used them to avoid facing up to the pain I saw around me and the fear and confusion I felt deep inside.

Always a rebel, I found myself drawn to the most exciting, experimental, dangerous, and sometimes crazy situations and people. I grew up finding ways to break the rules and get away with it. Unfortunately, this got out of hand in my early 20s, and

I was drinking so heavily that I became dependent on alcohol. It was the main focus in my life.

I didn't know how to balance myself and couldn't understand why people didn't see life the way I did. I felt so much joy and absolutely loved people, but I was incredibly upset by the damage and destruction I perceived around me. I felt alone, angry, and frustrated; and deep down I was very afraid, especially of feeling "blamed" or being somehow "wrong."

As soon as I stopped smoking and drinking alcohol, I found myself being drawn to only natural foods and drinks. I became fascinated with the body, and the life-giving power of the foods of God's earth. I was amazed by creation. Suddenly, the wool dropped from my eyes. Everything seemed clear. I resolved to live healthily and began exercising, practicing yoga, and using my hands to heal people through the power of the universal life force or energy.

I began to see meaning and purpose for everything in the world—even the chaos seemed to fill me with a sense of peace and an overriding sense of safety. I began to trust the process and understand the cycles and rhythms of life and of my self and body. I remembered lots of transcendent experiences I had regularly as a child, and I began praying and meditating a lot more.

I'm not saying I'm perfect now. I'm still learning and finding my way through our amazing world, still making mistakes, still having bad days; that's just the way it goes. The big difference now is that I have a new perspective that's so healing. Would you be interested in knowing what this is?

It's simply that I am me. Not ADD, ADHD, bipolar, or any other label or box. To some extent this includes the term *Indigo*, I guess, although I don't feel condemned by it. We're all just human beings, doing the best that we can at any level of consciousness. I'm doing my best to shine my light in spite of my fears, my doubts, and my own ego telling me that this is all mumbo jumbo. Deep down, I know that these sensitivities and the perception that has sometimes caused me so much pain is really my blessing and not a curse.

The development of my gifts and reaching to achieve my potential to serve all life on this planet now preoccupies my mind. My new question is more along the lines of "How can I serve?" rather than "How can I stop the pain?" Join me at **www.butter fly-mastery.com**.

••

A Message from Indigo Children to Adults Across the World

by Kaisheen Wong

*On November 18, 2007, **Kaisheen Wong** passed away at the age of 20. She was very ready to let us know what it was like to be Indigo and what we might do to help. She wished to represent the Indigo population (a very Indigo thing). There was frustration here, or at least past frustration. And the source? It's what the educators have all told you: recognition.*

●●

I've submitted this written text because I think it's highly relevant to your book: setting the record straight on Indigos. I think that I have something valuable to offer because many individuals, even the ones working with us, are still misunderstanding what I, an Indigo Child, am experiencing . . . what I really feel and what I really want.

Here's a message from Indigo Children to adults across the world:

The best way that you can help us, truly, is to fully find your own spirituality, love yourself, discover the joy that's in your life, and uncover the peace in the center of your being that you know is always there and has never left you. Until you've found your spiritual roots, your own center of love for yourself, and your mature and steady calmness, you can't help us, nor can you guide us to our missions.

We're not here to learn your lessons for you, but to bring a piece of Earth's heaven. We hope that it may set fire to your hearts and confirm so much of what you've believed but have been afraid to assert in complete confidence. This will happen when you see us for who we are and feel our love. We're here already with you on this gorgeous earth! We're waiting for you with much love and patience. Some of us have chosen to experiment with meeting you halfway: that is, to set down our missions for the time being and embark on a journey of becoming one of you, so that as you move toward us, we move toward you at the same time. We know you try to help. We love you for this reason, and many others! Please, listen to us first—not to our words, which reflect back to you what you're supposing—but to our efforts, and to our intent.

— *The Indigo Children*

I'm a 19-year-old Indigo Child. I've avidly devoured *The Indigo Children* by Lee Carroll and Jan Tober and have also given it to my parents. It has had no effect whatsoever besides scaring them and making them feel as though I've gone off the edge and lost my ability to concentrate on my future. I've also recommended the book to my counselors. Their reaction is to refuse to read it. They insist that I'm suffering from depression and that it's the depression that's making me seek reasons for why I'm the way I am. This is unbearably frustrating, but I do have compassion for them. I know it's difficult to understand these things and find acceptance since they've never heard of the ideas before. I also have compassion for the people I meet on the Internet who are on spiritual quests and who think they understand me but aren't there yet. It's very, very difficult, I'm sure.

I'm aware that I know things that other people don't know. However, it's tough to share because people don't understand. I'm also so frustrated that there's so much information available on how to *care* for Indigos—tips for the parents and teachers of Indigos—and so little information for the Indigos themselves. I want information that actually speaks directly *to* the children and teenagers about their spiritual purpose, their well-being, and what they can do to help society. I'm upset that so little of what's written speaks directly to me about what I'm here to do. I'm so tired of suffering and of people telling me what I should be doing—for example, not suffering! They haven't got a clue. They need to see who and what I am, then they wouldn't dare treat me like this. And I'm so irritated when people accuse me of always thinking others misunderstand me because people don't misunderstand me; they both understand and misunderstand me at the same time. Where's the guidance?

I've been spending a lot of time with spiritual adults, trying to get them to see that part of what they're here for is to do what's really in their hearts, to offer to us new children the guidance that's in God's heart to give. This isn't because we need to be guided, but because it's an expression of God's greatest love; and since we're all made from God, we can all participate in this. I hate it that I'm so smothered that I can barely feel my essence anymore, and I hate that I know others who are also feeling so terrible. I *hate* it when people say, "Take care of yourself; put yourself first ahead of all else. That way you won't have to suffer the way you are. Don't let yourself be smothered. There are methods you can use . . ." and on and on. Yes, I know that! I *am* taking care of myself, but they can't see it. They think I don't know what I'm doing, and then they try to cram their smothering advice on me. Oh, my God. Where is the relief from this horrible experience?

In summary, I'm feeling extremely suffocated by humanity because most of it can't "see" me and seems to be trying to give me advice all the time. I dislike this because I already know what they're telling me. In fact, I can already predict what they say before it occurs to them!

Thus, I don't need people to tell me what to do. What would I like? I'd like to be able to breathe. That's what I'd like the most. In addition, I'd like spiritual adults who are capable of understanding "far out" things to stop suppressing me and to listen to me. I know that's what they want to do, but somehow they aren't doing it yet.

Perhaps they aren't even aware of the level of suppression they're exerting on me. It's such gross inhumanity that I'm suffering due to this situation and have *no one* to hear or understand!

I'd like these adults to see me. They can do so by quieting down and listening to my voice. If they're occupied in projecting their own difficulties onto my situation, they won't be able to hear me, and consequently, they won't see me. Therefore, the two things I want right now the most are: (1) to experience a decent and healthy feeling of breathing, and (2) to feel the human warmth that comes with human contact. This second is really a bare minimum, and I long for it so very much. I do suspect that maybe the other Indigos I've talked to are feeling similar to me for these same reasons.

I'm sure some people would like to know what Indigos are dreaming of these days, too. As a young human being of the 21st century, I do dream of great things, including many of the common ideals people have dreamed of forever and ever. Why? Because it's human to desire them! For example, I have the dream of a peaceful planet; of nations loving and accepting each other; of no more racism; of a clean environment in harmony with nature; of helping those suffering with self-misery, self-hatred, and depression; of resolving conflicts in human thought, philosophy, and behavior.

People don't need to ask me what I want; they only have to ask themselves, and they'll know. My dream is your dream, and yours is also mine. We're dreaming the eternal dream of God.

••

Becoming a Play Activist

by Jenny Ward

Play is next to our hearts, and Jan Tober, especially, has told parents and teachers so many times that it is often the key to communication. It might seem counterintuitive to be able to change serious things with play, but not to an Indigo.

●●

*Jenny Ward calls herself a "Play Activist." Her company, Playward, was created to start a play revolution in the world. She's excited about educating the world and loves to share her knowledge and enthusiasm. Check out her work, books, and all other important stuff at her Website: **www.playward.com.***

●●

This is an article I wrote recently for *Vision* magazine. I'm an Indigo Child and recently had my first daughter, Leela, who's rocking my world! Needless to say, this subject is close to my heart.

I've always had a playful spirit. I remember wanting to run around naked singing any Debbie Boone song I could muster as a child. Expression was important to me, and I loved to express myself through the arts. Looking back on my life thus far, I feel grateful for the gift of remembering who *I am not*. My parents put me in my first dance class when I turned three. I'll never forget the excitement of making lots of noise in tap class and twirling around in ballet. I had endless energy and a passion to move my body. Not only did I enjoy dance, I was also gifted in it. No matter what the form was, I could pick up steps quite easily and loved to perform in front of many people.

Being the best didn't really matter to me, but it did to my teachers. I was put into a competition group and all of a sudden stepped into a box that began years of limitations. I always knew that my love for dance and singing surpassed the need to be the best, but as time went on, I became very confused about the ideals of the world.

I began realizing that I was "different" when I hit my teens. Things that were important to others didn't really mean that much to me. I yearned for a connection with my parents and friends and *never* understood the educational system.

I got by in school because of my charming personality. I loved to make people happy, and that was way more important than memorizing dates for history. Looking back, I don't know how I graduated. School was last on my priority list. My junior year, I was asked what college I was going to apply to, and I'd never really given it that much thought. That was when I realized how undervalued the arts were, not only by my teachers and guidance counselors, but by the world. That's when the beginning of my denial truly began. I wasn't like all of my friends. I felt isolated and stupid. My parents were telling me that it was time to be "responsible," yet I noticed that along with responsibility, there was sadness. The inner rebel in me decided to go as far away as possible for school and major in dance. Even though my heart didn't want to go to college, I felt the need to belong in some way.

For most of my young adulthood, I was always caught up in the turmoil of what I wanted to do and what the world expected me to do. *Responsibility* was a word I loathed, yet I felt as though I had to achieve it. I went to college and graduate school, yet still felt that what I majored in was "useless" in getting a *real* job. I got married, taught full-time (a "good" job), and still felt as though I was living someone else's life. And I was.

This is the dance for most Indigos. How can we coexist in a structure that doesn't serve anyone? How can we take our teachers seriously when we know that they're devalued in our society?
We all choose our paths, no doubt. I chose parents who didn't (and don't) get who I am fully. I know that this was an essential part of my path, for it has given me the courage to stand in front of many people who don't *get* me and *still be me.*

When I turned 28, my life changed. Years of trying to be like everyone else had led me down the road to "perceived perfection." I had everything that I was supposed to have by my age, yet I was still not a size two. After receiving liposuction and spending thousands of dollars to achieve *no* difference, I finally surrendered. I began to accept that I wasn't happy living for the ideals our society has deemed important. In fact, I noticed that not a lot of people were happy living up to what was expected of them.

This began my quest for inner knowledge. *Why am I here? What brings me joy? How can I do that and pay my bills? Is it a bad thing that I'm not like others? How can I let go of pleasing my parents and begin to embrace that I'm a free being who's in charge of her life?*

I quit my full-time position and all other "jobs" and moved out of New York City to Portland, Oregon. Why? Because it was different, and I could find my stillness there. I began to write about my journey through eating disorders, self-neglect, fitting in, the educational system, marriage, and jobs and found myself overwhelmed by the gifts in life. I knew about that lack of creativity and growth in the educational paradigm because *I was in it.* I knew that marriage was based on old paradigms of ownership and sacrifice, written lifetimes ago, because I was *in it.* I lived most of my life understanding how this world "operated" so that I could fully comprehend it.

All of what I'd been writing eventually became a book. I moved from Oregon to California, not knowing where or how, but I knew the *why.* It was there that I met angels who helped publish my book and support my mission.

The word *playward* came to me in a dream. I had a vision of myself dancing all in white and making people around me giggle. I loved the feeling of playing in the dream and heard my company's name (Playward) being repeated over and over. Playward started from an idea. It began with me completely being open to who I truly was: a play activist. As such, I empower all people to remember who they truly are, to bring back the *joy* that society has chosen to forget, and to live life from the heart, not from to-do lists.

I began to remember more and more that the limitations I set upon myself were inherited, and that *life is truly a playground*. More and more, angels appeared to support my purpose. Now, after two years of its creation, Playward is working with major corporations in the hopes to completely re-create the paradigm of "work" and life.

Having a child recently has also inspired me to continue paving the road for her. I see my responsibility in re-creating motherhood and giving her permission to be exactly who she is. This is a responsibility that I'd *love* to take on!

••

From Daniel Roth

Daniel Roth is another Indigo. He has a Website called Indigo Energy: *www.indigoenergy.ca*. It has a spiritual basis and was developed from his experience as an Indigo. This is his mission statement: "Our intention is to begin the process of re-educating the population to live a more spiritual, healthy existence in order to ease the transition to the next paradigm."

••

It wasn't until I was in college at the age of 21 that I learned about Indigo Children. I discovered the information through the guidance of a Reiki practitioner I decided to see. She recommended a few books, and it was at that time that I found out why I felt different from other people my age. Considering that I was born in 1980, a number of people classify me as an "older" Indigo. I've been through high school and university. Looking back, my experience in the academic world was unique, especially for an Indigo Child. I now have a theory that the "older" Indigos were allowed to remember more about their purpose and how to deal with different types of energy in order to help prepare the following generation.

When I was six years old, I sat in my first-grade classroom, being totally aware of everything going on around me. I could hear everything at the same time—the clock ticking, others whispering, the birds outside, the sound a pencil makes against the paper when someone is writing, people walking in the hallway . . . everything.

I was also highly intuitive. I always knew where the teacher was going with the lessons, being incredibly bored as a result, and I'm clairsentient (I feel energy). If someone was feeling sick, I could feel their sickness. If someone was upset and crying, I could feel their emotions. Multiply that by 25 other students and a teacher, and add to it the constant noise around me. That would overload the untrained mind, but I was able to consciously separate and control everything. I just knew how to do it.

What's unique about my situation is that I didn't act out. I was shy and didn't like to be around groups of other children. I preferred the company of adults.

I think that things started to change as more and more Indigo Children entered the school system. When this started to happen, higher-frequency energy would come with them, which made things tough to deal with. As a result, kids now act out because they can't handle or process the tremendous energy.

The easiest solution is to pump them full of drugs and think they'll be fine. Drugs may numb the pain of the constant bombardment of energetic and physical stimulation. But aside from the physical problems that can develop after years of taking a suppressant-style medication, the only thing that these intuitive children are learning is that it's okay to take drugs for problems.

It would be to everyone's advantage to teach self-control. The brain can process extraordinary amounts of information if we let it. Over the years, I've learned to hone my skills. I studied Reiki and have become a Reiki master teacher and trainer. This is an excellent practice for me since Reiki is the channeling of higher-frequency energy to bring balance to the situation or people around me. That skill, combined with self-control, results in my being able to do really cool things. I still hear and feel everything at the same time, but through meditation and visualization I've learned to use this to my advantage.

I can sit in a bustling restaurant surrounded by people and servers and listen to 8, 10, or 13 conversations simultaneously. In addition to that, I'm intuitively picking up the physical attributes and emotions of my fellow diners. That's followed by psychic flashes of what's going on in the lives of all these people. And to the average person sitting near me, it merely looks as though I'm quietly perusing the menu or daydreaming. I can talk while doing this, but it slows down the process significantly.

After I finished my formal education, I decided that I couldn't work in a cubicle or for anyone, so I decided to start my own business. I developed an alternative-thinking company called Indigo Energy. I specialize in practicing holistic therapies that teach clients to manifest their dreams. This is done through one-on-one life-coaching sessions. Services offered include: Law of Attraction assistance, Reiki therapy, intuitive consultations, and meditation coaching. Individual, group, or corporate sessions are available. The intention is to reintroduce the ancient practice of energy work into everyday life. The immediate focus of the company is to work with individuals or groups of people and help them to realize their soul potential on a personal level.

⏺ ⏺ ⏺ ⏺ ⏺

Afterword:

Final Words from the Authors

Jan and I wish to thank you for your interest in the new children of this planet. It's a controversial concept that perhaps we're witnessing human evolution, but within these pages you've seen it echoed over and over by the very educators who must teach the teachers. As you saw, even *Time* magazine used the words *human evolvement* in an editorial about our young people.

Could it be that the children are far better off than we thought, and that it's we who must now change to facilitate a new kind of thinking? Could it be that these new-consciousness kids are far more receptive to early wisdom than we have been?

Your Part in All This

The next time you hear people talking about Indigos on mainstream TV or radio, listen closely. Are they having fun with a notion that is way off base from the truth? Then let them know! Eventually, they may get the idea that there's substance to the Indigo name and concept. Finally, we have very credible educators, psychologists, and industry professionals who are beginning to notice and "buck the system" themselves as champions of this human-evolution notion.

Don't buy into a popular movement of "Indigoism." It's easy to use the name and tell others that your children or your grandchildren are Indigos, thinking that you're saying that you have some kind of very special kids. Well, you might, but they'll be special in ways that may challenge you to the core.

Ten years after Jan and I wrote the first Indigo book, introducing the concept that Nancy Tappe had seen and developed, we stand amazed by how many books and other media venues have swept in to take advantage of the subject. Some are really good, helping parents and children, and some are there just to make a buck. It's time for you to discern which is which. Do the books, films, and programs help all the kids; or is it information for just a spiritual niche of society? Is there valuable, credible information from those who deal with kids or young people every day? Are educators and children's workers involved? Look for credentials or experience! Jan and I would never think of putting out this kind of information without the backing of those who are on the front lines of education and children's issues. It's time for some integrity regarding the very use of the Indigo name.

Are good facts and solutions represented, or just the sensational stuff . . . a display of psychic kids or the supergifted that lifts up the special interests of the producers to get you to buy tickets? Does "Indigo" appear in the title just to get you sucked into being interested, but then the program has nothing to do with Indigo Children or helping them? If so, make a stand. Let them know you noticed!

Why does it matter? Because the time has arrived when these children are becoming young adults, and they're having their own children. If we don't buckle down and take this seriously, we'll wake up some day and be "out of the loop." We need informed adults to help guide our educational systems using common sense and forward thinking: grandparents who know what's really going on and parents who can begin to communicate with their kids on a quality level.

Let your actions and your voice be a catalyst for change on this planet, and let it start with acceptance that maybe, just maybe, we don't know everything about everything.

— **Lee Carroll** and **Jan Tober**

• • • • •

Endnotes:

Contributor's Notes

1. Interview with Nancy Tappe. Jan and I believe that Nancy is speaking about a "pure" Indigo color here. In previous conversations, she has indicated that many have come in with an "Indigo overlay" which she has seen as a mixture of the traits of an Indigo in much older individuals. These have been very strong overlays, but not a pure color, so many who are actually in their 50s and 60s may have this attribute and feel very Indigo. This was also mentioned in the second Indigo book.

2. References and sources—Jill Porter

Bartholomew. *"I Come As A Brother": A Remembrance of Illusions*. High Mesa Press, 1986.

Clash, Kevin. *My Life as a Furry Red Monster: What Being Elmo Has Taught Me About Life, Love, and Laughing Out Loud*. Broadway Books, N.Y. 2006.

Lacey, A. R. *A Dictionary of Philosophy*. Third Revised Edition, Barnes & Noble Books, N.Y. 1999.

Sartre, Jean-Paul. *Existentialism and Human Emotions*. Citadel Press, Inc., Secaucus, N.J., 1957, 1985

Emoto, Masaru. *The Hidden Messages in Water*. Hillsboro, OR, Beyond Worlds Publishing, 2004.

Websites and sources for further information
Dan Millman: **http://danmillman.com/**

Recommended reading for children:
Secret of the Peaceful Warrior. Appropriate age range: first through fifth grade.
Quest for the Crystal Castle. Appropriate age range: elementary school.
The ToDo Institute: **http://www.todoinstitute.com/dreams.html/** Offers wonderful books to help guide parents and Indigos in the life process.

Recommended reading for parents:
Little Dreams Come True: A Practical Guide to Spiritual Parenting by Linda Anderson Krech.

Websites and sources to assist educators with lesson plans and strategies:
http://math.com/teachers.html: good math link, especially for practical and didactic math strategies in real-world situations

Peace Education: Cyberschoolbus, **http://www.un.org/cyberschoolbus/ peace/home.asp**

Global SchoolNet: **http://www.globalschoolnet.org/index.cfm**

Practice Random Acts of Kindness: **http://www.actsofkindness.org/ classroom/** This is an awesome Website that can send you a *ton* of free things. It also has wonderful ideas.

Oasis of Peace: **http://oasisofpeace.org/** This site gives free curricula for high-school teachers to integrate in their lessons (especially good for stereotype and bias discussions).

Tolerance.org: **www.tolerance.org/teach/resources/posters.jsp** This is an awesome Website that can send you a *ton* of free things. It also has wonderful ideas.

3. References and sources—Jennifer Townsley

R. Plutnick, "A Language for the Emotions," *Psychology Today* 14 (February 1980): 68–78.

M. Emoto, *The Hidden Messages in Water,* (Hillsboro, OR: Beyond Worlds Publishing, 2004).

4. References and sources—Sue Haynes

1. Parker Palmer quote cited in: Glazer, Steven, ed. 1999. *The Heart of Learning: Spirituality in Education.* From the chapter "The Grace of Great Things: Reclaiming the Sacred in Knowing, Teaching, and Learning" by Parker J. Palmer, p.15. New York: Jeremy P. Tarcher/Putnam.

2. Armstrong, T. 1997. *Myth of the A.D.D. Child: 50 Ways to Improve Your Child's Behavior and Attention Span Without Drugs, Labels, or Coercion.* New York: Plume.

Clark, E.T. 1991. "The Search for a New Educational Paradigm: The Implications About New Assumptions About Thinking and Learning," in *New Directions in Education: Selections from Holistic Education Review,* edited by Ron Miller. Brandon, VT: Holistic Education Press.

5. References and sources—Carol Crestetto

— Specific Learning Disability, Nonverbal Learning Disability, Attention Deficit/Hyperactivity Disorder, Asperger's Syndrome.

— His name has been changed and any identifying details disguised to protect privacy.

— From Wikipedia, online free encyclopedia.

— There are other reasons for such feelings, like the idea of forerunners or scouts. I expect to devote a chapter of my book to providing more information on this subject.

6. References and sources—Gates McKibbin
From *The Aliens Have Landed* by Eric Chester at **www.generationwhy.com**.

7. References and sources—Karin Roten
Gut and Psychology Syndrome: Natural treatment for Dyspraxia, Autism, A.D.D., Dyslexia, A.D.H.D, Depression, Schizophrenia, Dr. Natasha Campbell-McBride, M.D., MMedSci (neurology), MMedSci (nutrition), Medinform

8. References and sources—Ingrid Cañete

Carroll, Lee, and Tober, Jan, *The Indigo Children: The New Kids Have Arrived.* Hay House, CA, 1999.

Cañete, Ingrid. *Crianças Indigo e a Evolução do Ser Humano.* (Indigo Children and the Evolution of the Human Being). Independent Edition, 2005, Porto Alegre, Brazil

Galeano, Eduardo. *O Livro dos Abraços* (The Book of Hugs). Editora LPM. 1989, São Paulo, Brazil.

Maslow, Abraham. *Maslow no Gerenciamento* (Maslow in Management), Editora Qualitymark, 2001, Rio de Janeiro, Brazil.

Rinzler, Alan, and Michael Ray. *O Novo Paradigma nos Negócios* (The New Paradigm in Business). Editora Cultrix-Amana, 1993, São Paulo, Brazil.

Roddick, Anita. *Meu Jeito de Fazer Negócios* (My Way of Doing Business). Editora Campus, 2002, Rio de Janeiro, Brazil.

Vianna, Marco Aurélio Ferreira. *O Líder Cidadão* (The Citizen Leader). Editora Quality Mark, 2003, Rio de Janeiro, Brazil.

●●●●●

References:

Contributors' Contact Information

Sandie Sedgbeer
Web: www.childrenofthenewearth.com
E-mail: Info@childrenofthenewearth.com

Nancy Tappe
P. O. Box 278
Carlsbad, CA 92009

Chapter One: The Educators Speak

Jill Porter, Ed.D.
E-mail: jillsporter@hotmail.com

Jennifer M. Townsley, Ed.D.
E-mail: jtownsley3@cox.net

Charlotte Reznick, Ph.D.
Web: www.ImageryForKids.com
E-mail: DrReznick@ImageryForKids.com

Carolyn Hadcock, ECE, C
E-mail: misscarolyn@sympatico.ca

Pat Childers, M.S. Ed.
Web: www.patchilders.com
E-mail: ajipat@cland.net

Sue Haynes, M.S.ed., M.ed
Web: www.creativemavericks.com
E-mail: sue@creativemavericks.com

Quinn Avery, Ph.D.
E-mail: quinn.avery@hawaiiantel.net

Julie B. Rosenshein, LICSW
Web: www.indigochildcoach.com

Carol Crestetto, Ph.D
E-mail: newchildrennow@yahoo.com

Jan Hunt, M.Sc.
Web: www.naturalchild.org/jan_hunt/
E-mail: jan@naturalchild.org

Chapter Two: Indigos at Work

Bruce I. Doyle, III, Ph.D.
Web: www.indigoexecutive.com
E-mail: IndigoExecutive@aol.com

Gates McKibbin, Ph.D.
Web: www.gatesmckibbin.com
E-mail: gates@gatesmckibbin.com

Kimberly Kassner
Web: www.empowermind.com
E-mail: kimberly@empowermind.com

Chapter Three: Other Lands

Mariella Norambuena, Chile
Web: www.ninosindigochile.cl
Email: info@ninosindigochile.cl

Karin Roten, Switzerland
Web: www.thefreechild.com
E-mail: karin.roten@bluewin.ch

Ingrid Cañete, Brazil
Web: www.ingridcanete.com
E-mail canete@terra.com.br

Isabel Leal, Portugal
Web: www.planetaisabel.no.sapo.pt
E-mail: criancasde1novomundo@yahoo.com

Chapter Four: From Health Workers

Hazel Trudeau
Web: www.hazeltrudeau.com
E-mail: hazel@hazeltrudeau.com

Barbra Dillenger, Ph.D.
E-mail: micbar@pacbell.net

Barbra Gilman
Web: www.barbragilman.com
E-mail: barbraspks@aol.com

Becky Engler Hicks, Ph.D.
Web: www.motheringcoach.com
E-mail: becky@motheringcoach.com

Howard Peiper, N.D.
E-mail: hpeiper@yahoo.com

Karyne Richardson-Meads, SpLT, HA, ON
Web: www.SoundLegacy.org
E-mail: info@soundlegacy.org

Ann Callaghan, L.C.H., ISHom
Web: www.indigoessences.com
E-mail: ann@indigoessences.com

Chapter Five: From the Parents and Indigos

Cathy Jacobs
Web: www.pathwayangels.ca
E-mail: pathwayangels@shaw.ca

Jasmine LoveLsTzy
E-mail: jlovelstzy@yahoo.com

Kristine McDonald
E-mail: wmcdonald1012@sbcglobal.net

Carolyn L'Hommedieu Davies, O.M.C.
Web: www.pathwaysoflight.org, www.theministryoftransition.com
E-mail: carolheals@aol.com

Jorge Valentin
E-mail: j.a.valentin@hotmail.com

Katharine Dever
Web: www.butterfly-mastery.com
E-mail: indigo@butterfly-mastery.com

Kaisheen Wong
(deceased)

Jenny Ward
E-mail: jenny@playward.com

Daniel Roth
Web: www.indigoenergy.ca
E-mail: info@indigoenergy.ca

Authors

Jan Tober
Web: www.indigochild.com
E-mail: jantober@jantober.com

Lee Carroll
Web: www.indigochild.com
E-mail: info@indigochild.com

●●●●●

About the Authors

From a very early age **Jan Tober** was using her voice to enthrall others. Not quite out of high school, she was noticed by some very big names in music and asked to share her talents on the national American jazz stage. She toured with jazz greats like Benny Goodman, Si Zentner, Les Elgart, and Stan Kenton. Then Fred Astaire called her to help represent his new jazz label! After many exhausting years, and finally tiring of traveling, she settled in Del Mar, California, and continued her work in music. In the San Diego area, she was featured daily on *The Bob Dale Show* on local Channel 8, performing with a popular local musical group. She would leave the studio, run home, and get ready for her regular evening performances in a local jazz club.

Slowly, Jan got tired of daily TV and the constant grind of live performing, and she became interested in doing something with her voice that would forever change her and others. Her profound interest in metaphysics led to her using her voice in a meditative way, releasing many albums over the years to help others heal and find their "sweet spot," using her music and meditative processes.

She joined Lee Carroll in the late '80s and started traveling, singing to thousands in many countries as the two of them gave their esoteric and self-help messages around the globe. Today, she continues her quest to touch as many as she can with her inspiring and uplifting vocals, creating Indigo books with Lee in between all that . . . and yes, still in beautiful San Diego.

Jan's personal Website is **www.jantober.com**.

●●

Lee Carroll is an audio engineer. His interest in sound engineering in particular led him to open the first multitrack recording studio in San Diego, which he developed into a nationally known facility and managed for almost 30 years. At the time he sold it, he'd personally accumulated more than 39 Clio nominations, done almost 4,000 commercials and film scores, and was ready to move on to something . . . ah . . . not so loud!

He was unprepared for what came next: his first esoteric book, *Kryon—The End Times,* led to exposure that eventually propelled him into an international spotlight in metaphysics. In 1995, he was invited to the United Nations in New York City to speak at the Society for Enlightenment and Transformation, a UN cultural club. The response was so great that he has been asked to return five more times over the years, speaking to many about hope for a planet that's experiencing a great shift. He continues speaking there almost every other year.

At the time of the publication of this book, Lee is still traveling the world with more and more meetings in places he never thought he'd go. He's now featured yearly in Moscow, speaking to crowds of thousands, and he's developing a following in the Baltic areas as well. Western Europe is also a popular place for Lee, as are the many countries in South America. He now has 14 books translated into 24 languages, creating more than 175 individual books worldwide. The Indigo subject is at the top of his list, and he's passionate about continuing his efforts to let the earth know that human beings are evolving!

Want to see some of his meetings? Go to **www.kryon.com/ countries**.

• • • • •

Notes

Notes

Notes

Notes

Notes

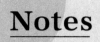

Notes

Notes

Notes

Notes

Notes

Notes

We hope you enjoyed this Hay House book. If you'd like to receive
a free catalog featuring additional Hay House books and products, or
if you'd like information about the Hay Foundation, please contact:

Hay House, Inc.
P.O. Box 5100
Carlsbad, CA 92018-5100

(760) 431-7695 or (800) 654-5126
(760) 431-6948 (fax) or (800) 650-5115 (fax)
www.hayhouse.com® • www.hayfoundation.org

Published and distributed in Australia by: Hay House Australia Pty. Ltd.,
18/36 Ralph St., Alexandria NSW 2015 • *Phone:* 612-9669-4299
Fax: 612-9669-4144 • www.hayhouse.com.au

Published and distributed in the United Kingdom by: Hay House UK, Ltd.,
292B Kensal Rd., London W10 5BE • *Phone:* 44-20-8962-1230
Fax: 44-20-8962-1239 • www.hayhouse.co.uk

Published and distributed in the Republic of South Africa by: Hay House SA
(Pty), Ltd., P.O. Box 990, Witkoppen 2068 • *Phone/Fax:* 27-11-467-8904
orders@psdprom.co.za • www.hayhouse.co.za

Published in India by: Hay House Publishers India, Muskaan Complex,
Plot No. 3, B-2, Vasant Kunj, New Delhi 110 070 • *Phone:* 91-11-4176-1620
Fax: 91-11-4176-1630 • www.hayhouse.co.in

Distributed in Canada by: Raincoast, 9050 Shaughnessy St., Vancouver, B.C.
V6P 6E5 • *Phone:* (604) 323-7100 • *Fax:* (604) 323-2600 • www.raincoast.com

Tune in to **HayHouseRadio.com**® for the best in inspirational
talk radio featuring top Hay House authors! And, sign up via the
Hay House USA Website to receive the Hay House online newsletter
and stay informed about what's going on with your favorite authors.
You'll receive bimonthly announcements about Discounts and Offers,
Special Events, Product Highlights, Free Excerpts, Giveaways, and more!
www.hayhouse.com®